Newspapers and Nationalism

NEWSPAPERS AND NATIONALISM

The Irish Provincial Press, 1850–1892

Marie-Louise Legg

FOUR COURTS PRESS

Set in 10.5 on 12.5 point Ehrhardt for
FOUR COURTS PRESS LTD
Fumbally Lane, Dublin 8, Ireland
e-mail: info@four-courts-press.ie
and in North America for
FOUR COURTS PRESS
c/o ISBS, 5804 N.E. Hassalo Street, Portland, OR 97213.

A catalogue record for this title
is available from the British Library.

ISBN 1-85182-341-7

Printed in Great Britain by
MPG Books, Bodmin, Cornwall

For Tom

Contents

List of Tables

Preface

I am grateful to Roy Foster for encouraging me for over five years and for suggesting themes and ideas which have proved of great value to me in enlarging the scope of the subject of this book. Any errors of fact and interpretation are entirely mine. Vincent Comerford encouraged me from the start to tackle what proved to be an elusive subject and introduced me to T.C. Luby's letters to John O'Leary, National Library of Ireland Ms 331–3, a manuscript which deserves publication in its own right.

In particular I am grateful for the help and advice of Brian Donnelly, Surveyor of Business Records in the National Archives of Ireland, Brian Walker, Sheridan Gilley, John A. Claffey of Tuam, Paul Bew and Theo Hoppen. I should especially like to thank Declan Macauley of the Kilkenny County Library for drawing my attention to the Kilkenny Circulating Library Society archive and John McTernan, of the Sligo County Library. Ms Una Sheridan of the Provincial Newspapers Association of Ireland took great trouble in putting me in touch with a number of provincial newspaper editors, in particular David Burke of the *Tuam Herald*, T.E. Crosbie of the *Cork Examiner* and the editors of the *Midland Tribune*, the *Sligo Champion*, and the *Nationalist and Leinster Times* were helpful with information about the past history of their papers. Also librarians in the Public Record Office of Northern Ireland, the Bodleian Library, Oxford, the National Library of Ireland, the British Library, the University of London Library, the London Library, Birkbeck College, Gloucestershire County Council, Public Record Office, National Register of Archives, St Bride Printing Library, Cambridge University Library, Galway County Library, the Trustees of the Chatsworth Settlement, Tipperary County Library and the librarians of the King's Inns and Trinity College, Dublin.

The Scouloudi Foundation and the Isobel Thornley Bequest Fund made grants to support the publication of this book. I am grateful to them both.

Birkbeck College
March 1998

Introduction

'The word spoken was a word for millions, and for millions
who themselves cannot speak' W.E. Gladstone.[1]

Of all the sources for historians, the press is in one sense pre-eminent; as Arnold
Bennett said of Darius Clayhanger's printing business, it was 'a channel through
which the whole life of the town had somehow to pass'.[2] The historian of nineteenth-
century Ireland needs to stand back from its newspapers and the vast mass of material they contain, and put them into context.

In 1855, the Librarian of Trinity College, Dublin, wrote to the Commissioners
of Inland Revenue asking that provincial newspapers over two years old be sent to
the Library for reference, as they would be 'useful for historical, as well as for statis-
tical purposes in time to come', and the Commissioners were disposed to agreed to
this request.[3] Historians have increasingly relied on the provincial press to confirm
local tendencies and reactions. But it is notable that newspapers are so lightly regarded, that they are used as sources with so little care for the veracity or validity of
their statements, that they seem not to be tested as other archives are tested and
compared. Newspapers are believed to be not entirely 'serious' and, as a result,
assessment of this source obscures its intrinsic importance. This rather casual use
of newspapers as easy copy, and its low valuation has also infected studies of the
press. As Stephen Koss has said, 'too many studies of the press ... have been more
assembled than written'.[4] The besetting sins of studies of the press are, on the one
hand the obsessive logging of titles and variations between editions and on the other,
the anecdotal accretion of random notes on particular papers without either proper
citations or any understanding of the society from which the press sprang.

In the prologue to his major work on the nineteenth-century British political
press, Koss summarises why it is central to studies of the period: the impact of
increased literacy, the advance of technological changes in communications with
development of the railway system and the electric telegraph, the impact of elec-
toral reforms which brought new constituencies and new relationships between

---

1 H.C.G. Matthew (ed.), *The Gladstone Diaries*, 14 vols (Oxford, 1868–1994), entry for 28 December
1879. 2 Arnold Bennett, *Clayhanger* (1910; Penguin edition, London, 1954), p. 103. 3 Librarian,
Trinity College Dublin to Inland Revenue, 11 August 1855: PRO IR56/26. 4 Stephen Koss, *The Rise
and Fall of the Political Press in Britain*, i, *The Nineteenth Century* (London, 1980), p. vii.

politicians and journalists and a realignment of politicians according to party. Partisanship by the press became not just a right but a duty, and the need to preach to the converted was a service that should not be underestimated in the move towards political solidarity; it fortified the resolve of political organisations. Koss deliberately excluded the Irish press from his work on Britain, but if Ireland is included what he says is even more true. If the movement towards political solidarity in the formation of parties was important in Britain, how much more so in Ireland, where different social classes were finding their feet in the wake of the Famine and, from the 1860s onwards, against the gradual decline in the influence of the Anglo-Irish landlords. New men were buying estates and running the Boards of Guardians; those on the make found an arena in which to shine. How much more important was the local press in this world where people were moving geographically, socially and economically; families were emigrating abroad and coming into towns from remote rural communities, and there were shifts and changes in occupations.

The response of the press to the rise of literacy, and the politics and motives of newspaper proprietors is an important field for research. While newspapers are quoted extensively by political and social historians, until recently with the work of Niall Ó Ciosáin,[5] the part that newspapers played in society is absent from studies of popular culture. Mary Casteleyn's work on the development of literacy[6] has no references to the press and to the holdings of newspapers in literary institutes. In Mary Helen Thuente's study of the influence on Yeats of Gaelic legends and history,[7] she traces the interests of antiquarians during the eighteenth and nineteenth centuries but passes over the role of the press played in the growth of Gaelic nationalism from the early nineteenth-century antiquarians to the founding of the Gaelic League. Until recently, historians using the provincial press have tended not to examine the motives of those who ran the newspapers from which they quote so liberally. Vincent Comerford[8] has paved the way for the emergence of studies of the Irish press in their own right, and the role the press played in the creation of Parnellism after 1879 has been explored by James Loughlin.[9] This book aims to extend knowledge of the structure of the provincial press and to set such specialized studies into context. Newspapers exerted an increasing influence on their readers: there is ample evidence that reading newspapers in newsrooms and elsewhere was influential as an essential part of Father Mathew's temperance crusade, in the Repeal movement and in the Land League, who all recognised the place of the press in provincial

5 Niall Ó Ciosáin, *Print and Popular Culture in Ireland, 1750–1850* (London, 1997).   6 Mary Casteleyn, *A History of Literacy and Libraries in Ireland* (Dublin, 1984).   7 Mary Helen Thuente, *W.B. Yeats and Irish Folklore* (Dublin, 1980).   8 R.V. Comerford, *The Fenians in Context* (Dublin, 1985) pp 36 and 94–5 and his material on the place of the press and journalists in mid-century Irish politics in *A New History of Ireland* (Oxford, 1989), *Ireland 1850-1870: post-famine and mid-Victorian*, pp 376 and 429–30.   9 James Loughlin, 'Constructing the political spectacle: Parnell, the press and national leadership, 1879–86' in D. George Boyce and Alan O'Day (eds), *Parnell in Perspective* (London, 1991).

society. London and Dublin Castle anxiously watched its growth. The abolition of the taxes on the press after 1855 has been generally agreed to have been crucial for the growth of the newspaper industry on both sides of the Irish sea. But in Ireland the availability of a cheaper press coincided with the growth of nationalism.

Yet so much work on the press has tended to be dull and pedestrian. Human life is missing and the mentality of those who ran the press is absent. Who were they? How were they educated, what did they read? Why did they run newspapers at all? The nature of the nineteenth-century press encourages the obsessive because of the difficulty both of classifying newspapers and of discovering any information about those who ran them. Newspapers were seemingly founded and run by anonymous people – almost all of them men. Most newspapers are born and die out of and into a void. One day they are there; the next they have gone, and gone without explanation or obituary. To compound these difficulties, the archives of newspaper owners and proprietors are sparse; they lived for each day's edition and were, then as now, secretive about their correspondents and their sources.

We know the press through the holdings of back numbers in copyright libraries, but no complete run of journalists' correspondence, and almost no extensive runs of newspaper business letters and accounts, exists in archives in Ireland and England. With a couple of exceptions, the present day survivors of the nineteenth-century provincial press have been unable to help. To construct this book, the letters of journalists have been disinterred from the correspondence of others and newspapers have been approached by examining the phenomena of provincial life, through reading rooms and libraries and the observations of travellers.

However, the apparent problem of simultaneous feast and famine in the quantity of material available has actually proved an advantage in writing this study. Because of its size, as Koss points out[10] it would be impossible (and probably pointless) to read every copy of each newspaper in detail and at length. A device had to be found to 'know' newspapers by other means, and an attempt has been made here to eschew the anecdotal and to turn the mass of detail to account. The Irish provincial press has been examined through the ideas of provincial newspapermen, using their own memoirs and the memoirs and correspondence of the landed gentry, academics, politicians and the government.

The size of the feast in terms of material is demonstrated by the sheer bulk of Irish newsprint available between 1850 and 1892, when about 218 provincial papers appear to have been in print. It is impossible to be entirely accurate about numbers of newspapers published at any moment. Some were in print before the period started and are still in print today. The *Belfast News-Letter*, founded in 1737, is the oldest daily newspaper proper in the British Isles and is still in print. Others lasted a very short time; the *Belfast Times* for only six months in 1872. Newspapers printed sepa-

10 Op. cit., p. 27.

rate editions for particular areas carrying slightly altered titles which may lead one
to believe they were different papers altogether. The annual volumes of the *Newspaper Press Directory* have here been used to assess the Irish provincial press, but these
do not indicate (except by the absence of a title) whether a newspaper had gone out
of print. Some newspapers never bothered to have any entry in the *Directory* at all;
they may not have lasted long enough to do so. The *Newsplan* project is valuable in
giving information on the dates of particular newspapers and their location in holdings in the British Isles and Ireland, but some titles which do not appear in *Newsplan*
appear in the *Newspaper Press Directory* volumes, and vice-versa.[11] This study is
based on entries in the *Newspaper Press Directory* over the period. These entries,
with their prices, circulation areas, their proprietors and politics appears as an appendix at the end. This exercise has proved useful in charting the changing nature
of the press; the rise of the cheap newspaper and the evolution of the nationalist
press are here gradually revealed. Even more valuable, the *Newspaper Press Directory* volumes have rendered up the names of the proprietors, most of them probably
also the anonymous editors, of the press. This makes it possible to attempt to chart
their careers.

The years 1850–1892 which mark the boundaries of this study exclude the Famine period, and end after the split in the Irish Parliamentary Party following the
death of C.S. Parnell. These 42 years have been broken down here into three periods
which are identified by the tone of the press of the time. The first, 'The Moral
Nation', covers the period from 1850 to 1865, and reflects the desire for atonement
in the wake of the Famine and the need to remodel Ireland to a new image. 1865–
1879, 'The Emergent Nation', details the press during the rise of Fenianism and the
Home Rule movement. Last, the section on 1879–1890, 'The Militant Nation', be-
gins with the Land War and exposes the use of coercion which was brought increasingly to bear upon the provincial press. Criteria needed to be drawn up to decide
which newspapers merited particular attention at any one moment within the period. Content analysis has not been attempted: rather than study newspapers from
the inside out, they have been examined by looking at their role in local and national
affairs, through documents and literature and by their marking of particular events.
Only after incidents and ideas were identified were particular newspapers read for
their reactions and for their part in provincial society. This was another reason for
the chronological approach rather than by dealing separately with ownership and
circulation. Thus circulation is looked at within each period, and not in a single
chapter from 1850 through to 1892. A chronological approach made it possible to
reflect the development of the press as a whole, and especially its place in the consciousness of nationality.

By studying within particular dates which newspapers started publication and
which failed, trends of ideas and allegiances and variations in local reaction have

11 James O'Toole, *Newsplan: report of the Newsplan project in Ireland* (London, 1992).

been identified and examined. By reading the prospectuses of papers founded within certain dates (prospectuses were printed in their first edition and for some time thereafter, and extracts from prospectuses appear in entries in the *Newspaper Press Directory*) clear themes could be discerned.

The physical growth of the provincial newspaper industry is charted through the numbers of newspapers published during the period and the possible causes of change. There are clear geographical and political links between these statistics which change between the decades, again underlining the utility of a chronological approach. The absence of accurate and verifiable sales and circulation figures, except in the first decade with some information on the sale of newspaper stamps, is a well-known problem in the study of the nineteenth-century British press. The lack of reliable circulation figures between their abolition and the introduction of certified circulation figures long after 1890, means that the historian has to cite claims made by newspapers themselves for sale and advertisement purposes, always an uncertain source. However, as will be seen, Dublin Castle archives provided some figures which carry a ring of authenticity.

Levels of literacy and illiteracy in both English and Irish are taken from the decennial census figures and can be broken down into provinces and counties, but these figures are bare without some idea of who read what and where. Travellers in Ireland noted the importance of newsrooms. Although some previous work has been done on the founding of newsrooms and reading rooms,[12] their use of the provincial press and their part in provincial society has needed further examination. The archives of the Kilkenny Circulating-Library Society between 1820 and 1910 contain detailed information about the titles taken by their newsroom which give an idea of the evolution of political allegiances in one provincial town. There has been little work on the reading of the middle-classes later in the century, and the accounts of Wynne's, the newsagents in Castlebar, give a new insight into what both the professional classes and the priests read during the Land War.

Census statistics also provide information about the numbers of journalists and newspaper proprietors in business between 1851 and 1891. In the 1850s and 1860s, newspapers were still run as sidelines in small town shops. John Hackett of Clonmel, Co. Tipperary, was in business as a grocer, patent medicine vendor, bookseller and stationer when he ran the *Tipperary Free Press* in 1851. In 1882 the paper was taken over by the Fishers who were successful newspaper proprietors, pure and simple. The *Kerry Sentinel* was started by Timothy Harrington in 1878, who used it as a platform in Land League agitation. When he was elected to Parliament in 1880 it was continued by his brother, Edward. What may have begun in the 1850s as an extension to a small printing business, and as an adjunct to the selling of patent

12 Kieran Byrne, 'The Mechanics Institutes in Ireland before 1855', Master's thesis, University College, Cork, 1976; Breda Gilligan, 'The Conolly Circulating Library, Galway' Diploma in Librarianship thesis, University College, Dublin, 1987.

medicines and insurance, ended in the 1890s with men founding newspapers as a major part of their bid for a place in the larger political scene in Ireland and at Westminster. Similarly the stated political affiliations of newspapers became more sophisticated and distinct; papers which started as independent or neutral increasingly adopted political parties and movements.

As one historian of the press has pointed out, there is an urgent need for a 'Dictionary of Victorian Journalists' with analytical biographies of editors, proprietors, reporters and columnists.[13] The Crime Branch Special Histories of Suspects in the National Archives and the Register of Suspects in the Public Record Office, London are particularly helpful on newspapermen involved, or believed to have been involved, in agitation.

Within each period, particular newspapers have been studied in depth. William Johnston of Ballykilbeg is best known for his prosecution under the Party Processions Act in 1867. However, his newspaper, the *Downshire Protestant*, published between 1855 and 1862, is a revealing example of Protestant proselytism within a local newspaper. Johnston founded the paper not only to give himself a platform on which to speak, but also to meet a particular need of the moment – to counter what was seen as the weakness of government in the face of the menace of resurgent papal aggression. Martin Andrew O'Brennan's *Connaught Patriot* (1859–69) was one of a number of papers that continued a tradition of antiquarian scholarship through popular literature. The *Connaught Patriot*, published in Tuam, was certainly allied to the Catholic church. St Jarlath's College, Tuam educated O'Brennan and many Fenians, and the newspaper's accounts of Gaelic history and the Gaelic language, Irish products and national ideals are an important aspect of what Comerford has described[14] as the 'largest political fact of Irish life in the mid-nineteenth century', the development of a nationalist Catholic identity. Douglas Hyde is credited with the popularising of Gaelic history and language in the 1890s, but the role of some mid-century newspapers in publishing simple tales of past heroes and battles, and in urging the importance of preserving the Irish language, has until now been ignored. The alliance of the same newspapers with Fenianism in the 1860s was not particularly welcomed by the Fenian movement at the time, but with hindsight the links between accounts of Irish pre-history and the nationalist movement is not now surprising. In the 1880s, in different ways, newspapers such as James Daly's *Connaught Telegraph* and Timothy Harrington's *Kerry Sentinel* played a part in spreading the National League across Ireland, and part of the provincial press was essential to the dissemination of knowledge of the activities of National League branches in campaigns of intimidation.

13 Joel H. Wiener, 'Sources for the Study of Newspapers' in *Investigating Victorian Journalism* ed., Laurel Brake, Aled Jones and Lionel Madden (London, 1990), p. 163. The biographies of a substantial number of nineteenth-century Irish journalists will appear in the *New Dictionary of National Biography* (Oxford, forthcoming).   14 *The Fenians in Context*, p. 31.

Some work has already been done on the Irish nineteenth-century press before 1850. Niall Ó Ciosáin's recent work has already been cited. Brian Inglis's work on the freedom of the press in the first half of the century stops at 1848, and Aspinall's *Politics and the Press* ends in 1850.[15] Inglis's work centres in the main on Dublin, and Aspinall deals mainly with the British, not the Irish press. Their research is now over forty years old. Two historians attempted work on the press but never published their findings. R.R. Madden, the historian of the United Irishmen, never completed the volume dealing with the nineteenth-century for his *History of Irish Periodical Literature* (1867). Madden's research notes in Dublin City Library were helpful in providing the names of proprietors and journalists. Inglis says that Francis O'Kelley did extensive research in the 1940s on Irish newspapers without being able to commit himself to writing a book.[16] A collection of essays on the Victorian press in Britain contains useful chapters on subjects common to studies of newspapers as a whole, on technology, distribution and the problems of research, and Joel Wiener's article cited above suggests some valuable practical lines to follow. Lucy Brown's *Victorian News and Newspapers* (1985) has some material on news agencies and the finances of the press, but this is very much centred on the metropolitan press in England. A.J. Lee helps to set the provincial press in context, but again his work concentrates on its rise in England, particularly in the industrial north, and its association with the Liberal party.[17] L.M. Cullen's history of Easons, the newsagents, is centred almost wholly on Dublin.[18] The Irish provincial press and its peculiar and localised problems has not been touched.

Two recently published books on the Irish press illustrate the tendency of some historians simply to assemble information; one obsessively indexes and the other paints with a very broad brush. The need for a good modern reference book on nineteenth-century Irish newspapers and periodicals is great, and should have been met by the *Waterloo Directory*.[19] Unfortunately the *Directory* suffers from errors both major and minor, and has to be used with great care. The political allegiance of papers such as the *Sligo Champion* are described as 'Independent and neutral', when in fact during their existence they have radically changed their political allegiance. Hugh Oram's wide-ranging study of the Irish press,[20] tends to the anecdotal and, unfortunately, his failure to provide proper citations of sources renders it difficult for others to follow up his interesting leads.

Five types of archive have been studied. First, government papers and the papers of politicians in the National Archives, in the Public Record Office in London and the British Library. These focus on the concern of government about the influ-

15 Brian Inglis, *The Freedom of the Press in Ireland 1784–1841* (London, 1954); A. Aspinall, *Politics and the Press*, (London, 1949). 16 Brian Inglis, *Downstart* (London, 1990), p. 70. 17 A.J. Lee, *The Origins of the Popular Press 1855–1914* (London, 1976). 18 L.M. Cullen, *Eason & Son: A History* (Dublin, 1989). 19 John S. North (ed.), *The Waterloo Directory of Irish Newspapers and Periodicals*, Phase II, (Waterloo, Ontario, 1986). 20 Hugh Oram, *The Newspaper Book 1649–1983* (Dublin, 1983).

ence of the provincial press on its readers, and they also provide information about the taxation and control of the press through the enforcement of bonds and by Post Office regulations. However, government archives and parliamentary papers tend to concentrate on the nationalist press, particularly in the later part of the period. This in turn produces an observable geographical skew towards to the west and south west of Ireland, due to government's perception of the involvement of newspapers with extreme nationalism. Second, there are a very limited number of business records. The Public Record Office of Northern Ireland has the financial papers of one printing business, the Ulster Printing Co. Ltd, publishers of the *Belfast Mercury*. Third, the correspondence of journalists and of national figures like T.C. Luby, John O'Leary, James Stephens and Timothy Harrington, which are mainly in the National Library of Ireland. Fourth, the published writing of journalists has been traced in the British Library and the National Library of Ireland. Finally, contemporary observers' references to newspapers in the journals of travellers in Ireland have proved to be a fruitful source.

The press is, of course, an essential source for local studies. The names of newspapers alone testify to their commitment to a locality, especially in the early part of the period. The early papers use the names of towns: *Drogheda Conservative* (1837), *Cork Constitution* (1822), *Dundalk Democrat, Castlebar Telegraph* (1830). They changed to counties when their circulation widened: the *Castlebar Telegraph* became the *Connaught Telegraph* in 1877; the *Skibbereen and West Carbery Eagle* (1858) was the *West Cork and Carbery Eagle* by 1868 and in 1891 became the *Eagle and County Cork Advertiser*.

But the names of newspapers were also statements of their stance. The essential ingredient of the liberal and nationalist press after 1850 – its inheritance of the mantle of the past – was claimed by newspapers who took their title from Gavan Duffy's *Belfast Vindicator* (1839), the first Young Ireland newspaper. Galway, Tipperary, Kerry and Donegal all had their *Vindicators*. Freedom of the press to survive without government subvention, and to speak in the face of government repression is asserted in many titles of liberal newspapers. Thus after 1850, 'Independent' newspapers were published in Wexford, Sligo, Tipperary, Longford, Leinster, Clare, Down, and Kerry. Speed in delivering the news, first by mail coaches and then following the mid-century introduction of the electric telegraph, was promised through the 'Express', the 'Courier', the 'Mercury', the 'Mail' and the 'Telegraph'. Both in and outside Ulster, the increasingly isolated conservative press counselled the need to watch and warn, with words like 'Argus', 'Guardian', 'Watchman' and 'Sentinel'.[21] Other papers advertised their commitment to the existing constitutional arrangements. Those which include the word 'Constitution' in their title were almost all published in Ulster. The demotic titles of papers later in the century

---

21 James Grant said of the *Carlow Sentinel*: 'It is, as the name imports, on the Tory side of politics ... conducted with no small ability': *Impressions of Ireland and the Irish* (London, 1844), p. 69.

asserted local support for nationhood: the *Tipperary People* (1865), *Wicklow People* (1882), *Connaught People* (1883), *Western People* (1883). The mottoes of newspapers conveyed none-too-subtle messages: 'Venite sans peur' (*Ballymena Observer*, 1855); 'The Noblest Motive is the Public Good' (*Cashel Gazette*, 1864); 'We believe in the intelligence of the age and progress of the human race' (*Kingstown and Bray Observer*, 1870), 'Vox Populi Vox Dei' (*Clare Independent*, 1875); 'Live and let Live' (*North Down Herald*, 1880).

The great political issue that was central to the development of newspapers in both England and Ireland throughout the nineteenth century was the freedom of the press in a society both literate and pressing for the extension of the franchise. In the early part of the century the European revolutions had heavily influenced the attitude of government towards the press. Its relationship with newspapers in Ireland between 1798 and the 1840s has been covered by Brian Inglis in his examination of the corruption of journalists and the repression of newspapers. The twin weapons of curbs on freedom to publish and the granting of subsidies to compliant newspapers were both employed. In England, which watched the control of the European press (particularly under Napoleon III) with anxiety, interference of this kind gradually became unacceptable and was eventually abandoned. In Ireland, however, government was less willing to tolerate such complete freedom.

Nineteenth-century British public opinion of the Irish people was contradictory. While the Irish were expected to behave as if they were English, self-improving, deferential and, in the main, law abiding, they were treated as though they were an alien race. 'This, then is the country of the aliens,' said Thackeray when he returned to Ireland in 1842.[22] He and Thomas Carlyle looked on the country as essentially foreign, and Carlyle describes Ireland as a savage, primitive world.[23] Cartoons of the Irishman as an ape, common in the mid-century, underline the image held by the English politicians, that the Irish were not ready for full membership of a modern state.

Contradictory opinions were held of Irish intellectual capabilities. They were thought to be extremely stupid and illiterate, and at the same time highly intelligent, devious and therefore dangerous. The Irish could read but they only read inflammatory material, and having read it would at once take violent action against their landlords and the state. To English politicians, the press in Ireland was thought to be one-sided and unreliable, and with no balancing reading matter the people could easily be persuaded into insurrection. However, this popular image of the Irish press was ill-founded. The majority of Irish newspapers were moderate in tone and insignificant in circulation. By the end of the 1880s, out of a total of 144 provincial newspapers in print, about 45 of them declared themselves as nationalist and most of those were published in the west and south-west of the country. But

22 W.M. Thackeray, *The Irish Sketchbook* in *Works*, vii, (1885), p. 63. 23 Thomas Carlyle, *Reminiscences of my Irish Journey in 1849* (London, 1882).

because of the alliance of some newspapers with movements for reform, successive governments took steps through coercive legislation to control the press. Between 1848 and 1890, the Irish executive ordered the closing of newsrooms, the breaking up of type and machines, the seizing of newspapers and the arrest of proprietors for printing intimidatory and illegal material.

The fear of politicians in Dublin and Westminster was that their own ability to interpret and lead public opinion, an important element of successful government, was lessening. Power was slipping out of their hands and into the hands of those over whom they had no control. This fear was recognised in the 1880s by W.T. Stead, who described the impotence of Westminster and the increased ability of the cheap modern newspaper to mould the opinions of its readers.[24] Stead argued that because the mandate of the press was renewed daily, the press was closer to the feelings and wishes of its readers than politicians at Westminster. If English politicians could be out of touch and losing influence at home, it followed that they were even less able to influence the Irish.

Between 1850 and 1890, the press became an increasingly important element in the movement of political opinion in Ireland. The place and influence of the provincial press and those who ran the local newspapers should be given greater weight when historians interpret nineteenth-century Ireland.

24 W.T. Stead, 'Government by Journalism', *Contemporary Review* 49 (1886), pp 653–74.

I

The moral nation, 1850–64

'To re-model the young mind of Ireland ... to elevate the social and moral condition of this island – to aid her in redeeming her lost character, and to restore both her and her natives to some noble position in the scale of nations and of society' Prospectus of the *Waterford Chronicle*, 3 August 1850.

The seeds planted in the decade after the Famine brought changes which influenced Ireland for the next forty years. In political debate, the need to modernise the nation took a higher place than considerations of constitutional reform, and many provincial newspapers put ideas on religion, education, and communications foremost. The experience of the Famine profoundly affected previously held beliefs, and changed the structure of society. During the Famine, people living in remote communities were attracted into the towns seeking food, and census figures suggest that they tended to remain there. Although the population as a whole declined after 1850, the numbers of people living in towns grew,[1] and the construction of railways and the spread of a reliable postal system reinforced the towns' links with the outside world.[2] Newspapers are essentially urban phenomena, and the growth of the provincial press in Ireland was just one of the processes of change that informed the 1850s; founding a newspaper was part of the modernisation of the country. Anthony Trollope wrote in 1847 of Mohill, Co. Leitrim: 'The idea that would strike one on entering it was chiefly this: "Why was it a town at all? – why were there, on that spot, so many houses congregated, called Mohill? – what was the inducement to people to come and live there? ..." Mohill is by no means the only town in the west of Ireland, that strikes one as being there without a cause'.[3] A decade later, Mohill had its own paper, the *Leitrim Gazette*, which advertised 'General news of markets, proceedings of local institutions, railway and other public boards, reviews of new books'.[4] The numbers of newspapers and the size of their circulation began to grow, and

1 Population of towns as a percentage of the whole population of Ireland, 1841–91: 1841: 13.89; 1851: 17.03; 1861: 19.36; 1871: 22.20; 1881: 24.07; 1891: 26.44. These figures include Dublin. The figures for 1851 and 1861 exclude those living in public institutions which would include workhouses. Source: W.E.Vaughan and A.J. Fitzpatrick (eds), *Irish Historical Statistics* (Dublin, 1978). 2 In 1850, 400 miles of railways were open; by 1870 39m. letters were delivered; by 1870 this had increased to 65m., equal to 12 letters per head of the population and twice the level in 1855: Comerford, 'Ireland 1850–70 ...', pp 374–6. 3 Anthony Trollope, *The Macdermots of Ballycloran* (1847; Oxford, 1989), pp 124–5. 4 Entry in the *Newspaper Press Directory* for 1857.

grew sharply after the abolition of taxes on newspapers in 1855 and 1861. With the increased numbers of newspapers came an increase in newsrooms to cater for the demands of an increasingly skilled workforce.

Before 1850, it had been generally agreed that the Irish press was of poor quality, and this judgement was not confined to observers outside Ireland. Thackeray's intimate knowledge and understanding of the press, and in particular the Irish press, he used to great effect in *Pendennis*.[5] Although the press there is centred on Fleet Street, the journalists Mr Hoolan and Mr Doolan are Irish and their papers, the *Dawn* and the *Day* are unmistakeably products of Ireland. As Thackeray said, 'Many of our journals are officered by Irish gentlemen, and their gallant brigade does the penning among us, as their ancestors used to transact the fighting in Europe ...'[6] The leading article quoted from the *Dawn* is a fair sample of the prose of some mid-century Irish provincial papers. Thackeray was observant also on the way newspapers plundered their rivals by using each others' material to fill up space. The Fleet Street sub-editor, Jack Finucane, was used by the *Pall Mall Gazette* as a scissors and paste man, mainly working in a public house. Here, 'from the most recondite provincial prints, and distant Scotch and Irish newspapers, he fished out astonishing paragraphs and intelligence regarding the upper classes of society ... Errors of description, it is true, occasionally slipped from his pen; but the *Ballinafad Sentinel*, of which he was own correspondent, suffered by these, not the *Pall Mall Gazette* ...'[7] The practice was (and is) common; but in 1850 the journalists described are Irish.

Giving evidence to the Select Committee on Newspaper Stamps in 1851, Michael Whitty, the editor of the *Liverpool Journal*, said that although the Irish newspapers of twenty years before had been 'very degraded', Ireland now had the best conducted press in the world. He attributed this to the 'fact of a great number of well educated men editing the papers'.[8] A mid-century historian of British journalism echoed Whitty's poor opinion of the Irish press at a time when it had 'neither inducements nor power to elevate itself. Even its outward appearance indicated poverty, helplessness and sloth. The sheet ... was usually much smaller than the English or Scotch journals – the paper thinner the type larger and coarser – the ink browner – the typographical errors infinitely more frequent and more glaring. Internally it betrayed evidence of starvation; the subjects of discussion chosen without judgement, and treated without talent – the style bad – the reasoning false – the language by turns coarse or feeble ... The very news was stale and meagre; the advertisements few, for who would address in print a population which could not read?'[9] James

5 J.C. Mangan wrote a piece for the *Belfast Vindicator* set in the office of a Dublin newspaper, where the Man in the Cloak (Mangan) reads a doggerel poem he has contributed to the *Far-Away-Down-in the-South Gazette*, 'my safety valve when I am desirous of letting out my redundant political steam ...': Royal Irish Academy Ms 3.c.6. n.d.   6 W.M. Thackeray, *The History of Pendennis* (1848–50; London 1987), p. 381.   7 *Pendennis*, p. 375.   8 Select Committee on Newspaper Stamps, HC 1851 (558), Q 1054, QQ 670–1.   9 A. Andrews, *The History of British Journalism*, 2 vols (London, 1859), p. 144.

Grant, a Protestant journalist travelling in Ireland in the 1840s, observed that even by then the provincial press had undergone great improvements in content and appearance which he attributed to improvements in the country itself. He believed that the newspapers were trying to conduct themselves properly, and he was torn between allowing the newspapers the credit of having, 'a due regard to the decencies of life', and worried about the 'violent writing' in the editorial columns. However, even that was only party squabbling, not the vilification of individual people.[10] The more thoughtful newspapers of the post-Famine years went further in their determination to use their position to influence the country for the good and to shake off their past.

At the same time as the quality and quantity of newspapers improved, the levels of illiteracy dropped, and dropped faster in the west and south-west of the country.[11] Sidney Godolphin Osborne had noted in 1850 that, while a large proportion of peasants in the west of Ireland could speak only Irish, publications in Irish were rare, and some of those were published only for polemical purposes.[12] The newspapers did not print articles in the Irish language, though some journals addressed to a specialist audience did include short pieces in Gaelic. Dr Robert Cane's monthly Kilkenny periodical, *The Celt* – part antiquarian, part nationalist – had poems accompanied by a translation into English. English was the language of progress and opportunity and the opening to jobs at home and abroad. To be literate in English provided the means to transform one's condition.

Young Ireland and the Repeal movement were of importance as a nursery of talent for journalists. Those writers who survived the events of the 1840s, and who remained in Ireland, looked for opportunities to aid their country in moderate policies which would not compromise their own careers. For aspiring nationalist politicians, journalism was a respectable profession unconnected with the problems of land ownership and the governing powers. For newspaper editors who became active in the movement for tenant right in the 1850s, it was the start of a political engagement that prefigured the involvement of journalists and their newspapers in the Land League in the 1880s. With some exceptions, after 1850 for about fifteen years there was general acceptance that rule from Westminster would continue. The exceptions were some papers founded before 1850 and run by those who had been at the centre of agitation in the 1830s and 1840s. The *Kilkenny Journal* (1767), the *Cork Examiner* (1841), and the *Limerick Reporter and Tipperary Vindicator* (1844) were major papers edited by men who had been strongly influenced by, and involved, in Repeal politics. Cornelius Maxwell of the *Kilkenny Journal* was close to Dr Cane of *The Celt*, who had had strong links with Young Ireland, and whose

10 Grant, pp 289–93.   11 Percentage levels of illiteracy in Ireland, 1851 and 1861: Ulster 35/30%; Leinster 39/31 %; Munster 56/46%; Connaught 66/57%; Ireland 47/39%. Source: Vaughan and Fitzpatrick, *Irish Historical Statistics*.   12 Sidney Godolphin Osborne, *Gleanings in the West of Ireland* (London, 1850), p. 193.

influence stretched forward to the Fenianism of the 1860s. In common with other political writings in the 1850s, *The Celt* had rejected physical force, and it looked for the 'restoration of Ireland's rights by moral and constitutional means ...' Its early use of the phrase 'Home Rule' has been noted by Roy Foster.[13] Until 1867, Cornelius Maxwell's paper continued to speak of 'Ireland for the Irish' and the need for a national legislature. Maurice Lenihan of the *Limerick Reporter and Tipperary Vindicator* was a protegé of O'Connell and mixed cautiously with Young Ireland. In 1851, his paper continued to advocate an independent parliament for Ireland, but began also to speak of the need for the legal recognition of tenant right.

After 1855, there were sporadic attempts to rekindle the nationalist flame: William Kenealy's *Tipperary Leader* was first published in the wake of John Sadleir's disgrace in 1855. Its masthead is wreathed in shamrock and its 'Poet's Corner' celebrates the battle of Thurles, where Strongbow was defeated by Roderick O'Connor and Donal O'Brien, the king of Thomond. In his first editorial Kenealy wrote of the want of political honesty in Ireland and advocated political education as the 'grand lever' to bring Ireland to the level of other nations.[14] But, as will be seen, the time was not yet ripe for a sustained programme of overt nationalism.

The press of this period confirms that 'the mythic march of the nation' image of Irish history is indeed a distortion.[15] Far from being militant, many provincial newspapers demonstrated that the majority of people in Ireland wanted to be credited with a good character, and their foremost wish was to be free from the dependence on others that had been forced on them by the Famine. The ideas that created the Fenianism of the 1860s should thus not be imposed too early; far from rebellion or revolution, the press of this period demonstrates (with only isolated exceptions) a wish for an accommodation with Westminster. The place of the Irish language in the formation of an independent nation, and the importance of a knowledge of Irish history, which had been discussed by Thomas Davis in *The Nation* in the 1840s, and would be again in newspapers like *Connaught Patriot* in the 1860s, were in general put aside. In the newspapers of the 1850s, parts of Ireland at least were entering a new phase within a moral nation. Their first leaders and their entries in the annual editions of the *Newspaper Press Directory* speak of measures of reform within the rule of law, and they assume that changes in legislation for Ireland are not going to be made by a parliament in Dublin.

Well before the defection of Keogh and the Sadleir scandal, many Irishmen had been disillusioned by party politics and party politicians. While the *Sligo Chronicle*

---

13 *The Celt*, July 1858; R.F. Foster 'Anglo-Irish Literature, Gaelic Nationalism and Irish Politics in the 1890s' in J.M.W. Bean (ed.), *The Political Culture of Modern Britain. Studies in Memory of Stephen Koss* (London, 1987), p. 97.   14 *Tipperary Leader*, first issue, 27 January 1855. It is worth comparing the shamrock image with the similar masthead of the New York Irish paper, *The Emerald* which serialised Charles J. Kickham's *Knocknagow* in 1875.   15 Comerford, *New History of Ireland*, pp 372–3.

noted in 1850 that 'A more liberal and elevated style of discussion is being introduced into politics and religion', it agonised over Ireland's future prospects, and reflected that its present state was 'most deplorable'. It attributed this condition to Irish politicians themselves, 'interested political charlatons' [*sic*], who were responsible for the masses depending too much on government and too little on themselves, and this dependency made them open to 'wild physical-force doctrines'. The only remedy for this condition was to educate the middle classes, and direct their attention to business and an interest in their own localities.[16] The moderate policies of the *Sligo Chronicle* would have Ireland advance crab-wise to self-determination, rather than seize power by force; thus by retrenching, the country could work to deserve recognition. Party politics were not the answer. When the *Waterford Chronicle* called for the elevation of Ireland's social and moral condition, at the same time it spoke of independence from party politics as 'a new feature in Irish Journalism', describing the discussion of all party politics and polemics as 'alien to its purpose ...'[17] In 1853, the newly-revived *Carlow Post* believed that independence from party was the only basis for national prosperity and good order. In 1859, the *Roscommon Herald and Boyle and Leitrim News* launched itself to meet a need for an independent journal to influence 'enlightened' public opinion. One of the reasons for this wish to take Irish issues out of party politics was the lack of an specifically Irish party at Westminster which could have lobbied for the issue of land, and this became explicit during the tenant right movement.

Although tenant right was acknowledged to be the main political issue, at least before 1856, it was paralleled by pressure for free trade and the industrialisation of Ireland. In 1850, politicians' election addresses published in the local press advocated free trade and 'cheap food for the industrious poor'.[18] In 1852, the liberal Cork newspaper proprietor and member of parliament, John Francis Maguire, organised the 'Great Exhibition of the Works of Industry of all Nations' in Cork. His motive was not just the encouragement of industry; he also hoped that the exhibition would open a new era in by showing the world what Ireland could do. He believed that the country had become 'imperialised' to such an extent that it no longer had the self-confidence necessary to succeed. While Irish politicians complained about the tendency of the government to enact legislation which tightened the central grip of Westminster, Maguire said that Irishmen themselves were the worst offenders in their failure to remedy this situation. Their lack of self-confidence encouraged this process, and the result of this surrender of their own power was a 'system of slow but effectual suicide'. The Cork exhibition was one of a number of national efforts during the 1850s which tried to change the public image of Ire-

16 *Sligo Chronicle*, 17 April 1850.   17 *Waterford Chronicle*, 17 April 1850.   18 The election address of Francis William Russell in the *Limerick Reporter and Tipperary Vindicator* on 8 January 1850 specifically referred to the need to turn away from repeal as the major political issue for Ireland, where there were 'other objects of great national importance'.

land in Westminster from that of an uneducated, dangerous country to a country
with important industrial and cultural institutions.[19]

The encouragement of Irish industry was just one route to gain power and respect in Britain, but this goal could only be achieved through publicity. The *Munster News*, first published in Limerick in 1851, justified the role of the newspaper as
public educator and as a spur to greater ambition: 'Our chosen agency ... will be the
encouragement of industry in all ranks; industry without which no modern Nation
can be prosperous and strong ... industry by which England, an ocean-speck, over-
rules and over-shadows an Eastern world [and] influences Kingdoms...'. The *Sligo
Chronicle* believed that 'as men become educated, this feeling of confidence and
esteem must prevail, and as a necessary consequence the public mind, so long de-
bauched by party strife, will be directed to the pursuits of business ... [thus] we
shall no longer be the slaves, but the equals of those are now our masters.'[20]

Evangelicals saw post-Famine Ireland as a country ripe for regeneration through
industrial effort, and printing and reading could act as a redemptive force. When
W.H. Smith appointed Charles Eason in 1856 to run the Irish side of his newspaper
distribution business, he chose the evangelical Eason first and foremost for his religious views.[21] The Revd David Doudney was one of a number of observers who
believed that the Famine was one of the greatest benefits that had befallen Ireland.
It had taken men 'away from dependence on the potato and made them see Protestantism in a new light' through the work of 'active, self-denying ministers'.[22] Doudney,
who had begun life in London as a printer, had travelled throughout Ireland during
the Famine distributing both relief and tracts. When he was appointed to the living
of Kilrush, Co. Clare, in 1847, he was impressed by the poverty and ignorance of
the people and decided to establish industrial, infant and agriculture schools at
Bonmahon, Co. Waterford. Three compositors and a press man joined him to teach
destitute boys a trade, by printing a commentary on the Old Testament. This effort
at evangelical industrial enterprise was hailed by the English press as an 'extraordinary production' produced 'in a wild village on the Irish sea-shore, by the hands of
the village boys'. Waterford was a 'moral wilderness', where enlightenment could
be spread in what was described as 'dark regions of Romish idolatry and supersti-
tion'.[23]

The feelings of dislocation and loss which are discernible in the press and in the
fiction of the 1840s and 1850s are constants in Irish literature going back to the

19 *Cork Examiner*, 11 June 1852. The Irish Industrial Exhibition in Dublin in 1853, the visit of the
Queen and Prince Albert in the same year, the statutory provision for a National Gallery of Ireland in
1854 and the 1855 Public Libraries (Ireland)Act are other examples.   20 *Sligo Chronicle*, 17 April 1850;
Munster News, first issue, 7 June 1851.   21 Cullen (1989) pp 33–4. In fact, as Cullen points out (p. 11)
Eason was an eccentric man with independent views who had been commissioned in the 1860s by the
Catholic clergy to publish prayer books.   22 'Old Jonathan', *Try: A Book for Boys* (London, 1857)
includes as an appendix 'A Pictorial Outline of the rise and Progress of the Bonmahon Industrial Infant
& Agricultural Schools, Co. Waterford'.   23 *Morning Advertiser*, 18 July 1853.

eighteenth-century, but at the half-century they can be linked not only with changes brought about by the Famine, but also with increased levels of emigration, which were additional motives for atonement.[24] The sins that were believed to have caused this disaster were debated both in Britain and Ireland. The Irish provincial press wrote of a need for the Irish people to seek redemption through self-improvement was debated in Ireland also.

An awareness of impending disaster which had existed in the 1840s had been deepened by their experience of the palpable evidence of God's wrath, and the years both before and after the Famine formed the moral background for the founding of the Total Abstinence Society and the extension of the work of the Repeal Association. These movements have been described as essentially revivalist, and revivalism depends on publicity for success.[25] Education, and especially reading, was included in the programme of societies for social improvement and political change, with the founding of new reading rooms and libraries. Gavan Duffy claimed to have founded the temperance and repeal reading rooms movement by '... inducing Father Mathew to engraft popular education on Teetotalism'. But Duffy had a greater vision which accorded with the modernising spirit of the 1850s, and addressed the question of reform through education in terms also of atonement, when he referred to the 'indulgence of our passions'. Temperance societies were 'not only associations for the diffusion of total abstinence principles, but for improving the morals and cultivating the understanding of the people ... I do not doubt of seeing the day when every town will have its Temperance Hall and every Temperance Hall its school-rooms, its reading-rooms, its lecture-rooms, its exhibition-rooms, and even its public baths and gymnasium, for the operative classes ... the way to happiness is not through the indulgence of our passions, but through their regulation and restriction.'[26] The ideal towns in this new Ireland would possess all the self-improving institutions necessary for an educated and sober nation.

Thus, the changes in attitude towards political reform evident in Ireland in the 1850s and early 1860s were indeed a product of the disruption produced by the Famine, but they were also a recognition that the issue of repeal was increasingly irrelevant. Rather than continue to press Westminster for reforms in the constitutional relationship between the two countries, many in Ireland now believed that economic changes must be made to create a strong and productive nation, worthy of respect. The press found a natural place in providing the necessary encouragement to improve education, and publicity for industrial enterprise.

---

24 In *The Ancient Music of Ireland* published in 1855 George Petrie spoke in apocalyptic terms of the loss of the collective memory of the past that was a result of the catastrophe which had struck Ireland, citing death and emigration as the causes. Cited by Thomas Flanagan, 'Literature in English', *New History of Ireland*, v, pp 495–6.   25 Emmet Larkin, 'The Devotional Revolution in Ireland 1850–1875' in *American Historical Review*, 77, no. 3 (June 1972), p. 637, reprinted in Emmet Larkin, *The Historical Dimension of Irish Catholicism* (Dublin, 1997).   26 C. Gavan Duffy, *My Life in Two Hemispheres* (London 1898), pp 53–5, 66–8.

The local press was itself supported both politically and financially by the development of towns, with markets, shops, roads and railway stations, and the publication of articles and advertisements in support of parliamentary and local elections. Advertisements for the sale of estates, for tenders for Boards of Guardians and Grand Juries, and for emigration agents and railway and steamship timetables – all were dependent on the provincial press and were the essential basis of its rapid growth during this period. In order to understand the close relationship between the development of the provincial press and social and political events it is necessary to know something of the newspapers published and the people that founded them.

2

The newspaper business, 1850–65

'Father, what does printers live on?'
'Why child?'
'You said you had not paid him for two or three years and you have his paper every week.'
'Take that child out of the room, what does he know about right and wrong?' *Belfast Vindicator*, 24 February 1844.

NUMBERS, PRICES AND CIRCULATION

The growth of the provincial press after 1850 was stimulated by increased urbanisation, by fiscal reforms and by improved transport links. It was limited by legislation which demanded capital to purchase stamped paper and to provide sureties against libel. There is one constant underlying the growth of the provincial press between 1850 and 1865 – the size of the town. The size of towns together with the growth of literacy acted together to trigger the founding of new titles. Mid-nineteenth-century census figures on the population are inexact,[1] but in 1850, outside Dublin no town had more than 100,000 people. Belfast and Cork had more than 75,000 people; Belfast had 4 papers in 1850 and Cork had 3. Three towns had more than 20,000 population: Galway, Limerick and Waterford. Galway had 2 papers, Limerick 3 and Waterford 4. Seven towns had more than 10,000 people and all of these had at least 2 papers; Clonmel had 3. It looks as though as soon as a town's population reached 3,500 people, a newspaper was founded. Where papers already existed in growing towns, new papers were founded; Cavan, where the *Anglo-Celt* remained the only paper, is the sole exception to this crude rule. On this basis, towns whose population should have warranted the founding of a newspaper, but where a paper never in fact appeared, were those which are close to major centres of population which had two, three or even four papers. The Cork towns – Bandon, Clonakilty, Mitchelstown, Midleton all come under the influence of newspapers published in Cork itself, and a similar effect can be observed in the hinterlands of Dublin, Waterford and Limer-

1 The introduction to Vaughan and Fitzpatrick (p. xix) is explicit on the inherent inaccuracies in the census figures during this period as exact statements of fact, pointing out that such events as the presence of passenger ships in ports, fair days and movements of military detachments may have affected the size of a town considerably on census days.

ick. This crude analysis does not take account of the idiosyncrasies of proprietors, and there are factors which go against the trend. It is true that William Johnston's militant Protestant paper, the *Downshire Protestant*, was founded in 1855 in Down-patrick, a town with less than 3,000 people, but Johnston's policies had a wider appeal, and his political and religious circles were used to effect in spreading his gospel.

At the beginning of 1850, 65 newspapers were in print, by 1865 there were 103. About 48 papers were founded between 1850 and 1865, and 21 papers seem to have ceased publication.[2] Reconciling these figures, the total numbers of papers published in each year between 1850–65 can be estimated as follows:

Table 1: *Estimated numbers of Irish provincial papers, 1850–65*

Year	No.	Year	No.	Year	No.
1850	65	1856	88	1862	104
1851	69	1857	91	1863	107
1852	69	1858	96	1864	102
1853	72	1859	98	1865	103
1854	74	1860	102		
1855	81	1861	103		

Fiscal reforms had a profound effect on the size of the newspaper press in the 1850s and 1860s with the abolition of taxes on knowledge. The tax on advertisements was repealed in 1853; the obligation to stamp newsprint prior to publication was abolished in 1855 and the tax on paper was repealed in 1861.

Until 1855, all newspaper publishers were obliged to print on stamped paper which was bulk bought in advance from the Stamp Office in Dublin. The number of stamps sold to any title is not a guide to the number of copies printed or sold at any one time. It can only be treated as a general guide to the amount of stamped paper bought at any one time. The *Connaught Patriot* bought stamped paper greatly in excess of the amount initially required. 'The Journal started on 6th August ... and 10,000 sheets stamped and unstamped, came to us from Messrs Ryan, Great Strand Street, Dublin, of these 7,500 were stamped. The weekly average circulation has been 500, though more than 600 were struck off some weeks, and on Monday after

2 Statistics on the numbers of papers at any one time have been taken from the *Newspaper Press Directory*. *Newsplan* only notes those papers held in archives. If copies of a paper did not survive, they do not appear in the *Newsplan* data. The problem here is that the information on dates of newspaper publication in *Newspaper Press Directory* is not reliable.

Table 2: *Newspaper stamps bought in 1850*

Newspaper	No. bought	Newspaper	No. bought
Anglo–Celt	20,000	Londonderry Standard	97,000
Armagh Guardian	34,750	Longford Journal	9,000
Ballyshannon Herald	2,500	Mayo Constitution	10,500
Banner of Ulster	123,000	Meath Herald	12,500
Carlow Sentinel	15,000	Nenagh Guardian	20,000
Castlebar Telegraph	15,000	Newry Telegraph	110,000
Clare Journal	19,000	Newry Examiner	27,500
Clonmel Chronicle	10,000	Northern Standard	15,000
Coleraine Chronicle	42,000	Roscommon & Leitrim	
Cork Constitution	180,000	Gazette	3,500
Cork Examiner	161,000	Roscommon Weekly	
Downpatrick Recorder	20,000	Messenger	9,525
Drogheda Argus	25,000	Sligo Champion	7,500
Drogheda Conservative	7,500	Sligo Chronicle	16,000
Dundalk Democrat	22,500	Sligo Journal	5,000
Fermanagh Reporter	22,500	Tipperary Free Press	24,000
Galway Vindicator	34,000	Tralee Chronicle	16,250
Kerry Evening Post	17,500	Tuam Herald	12,500
Kilkenny Journal	20,000	Tyrawley Herald	10,000
Kilkenny Moderator	25,000	Tyrone Constitution	18,000
King's County Chronicle	17,500	Ulster Gazette	11,500
Leinster Express	31,000	Waterford Chronicle	10,000
Leitrim Journal	2,500	Waterford News	10,000
Limerick Chronicle	165,000	Western Star	12,500
Limerick Reporter	37,000	Westmeath Guardian &	
Londonderry Journal	26,000	Longford Newsletter	18,000
Londonderry Sentinel	60,000	Wexford Independent	6,500

Source: HC 1866 (491) xl.113.

issue a copy could not be had for any money.'[3] Table 2 gives the number of stamps sold in 1850 to 52 Irish provincial newspapers. After 1855 and until the Income Tax Repeal Act 1870, a postal concession made to Ireland alone. Newspaper publishers bought stamped paper to enable copies to be sent free through the post.

The drive to abolish taxation on newspapers was a natural cause for those liberal campaigners working for the advancement of working-class education.[4] In Britain, the conservative arguments on the dangers of educating the poor through the press had blown out by the 1830s;[5] by the mid-century, working-class literacy and the improvement of working-class skills was the next battle for reformers. In Ireland, however, debate on educational reforms still suffered from an association between literacy and revolution, dating back to the events of the 1790s.[6] Tension persisted between those who believed that education was a defence against anarchy, and those who believed that education would tend to unsettle the poor who might wish to change their station in life. Evangelicals like the Revd Doudney thought that instruction should be limited to religious education and to what could be socially useful. Ireland had a special place in parliamentary debates. Many politicians believed that the country could be united with England by the widespread distribution of London-based newspapers to spread what was called 'national tone'. The argument was that the union would be reinforced by binding people to their natural rulers. Discussing the effect of the abolition of newspaper stamps on the development of the press in Ireland, the Select Committee on Newspaper Stamps received no evidence from the Irish newspaper proprietors themselves and a mixed amount of prejudice from men who in the main had a hazy and somewhat biassed idea of Irish affairs. Frederick Hunt, the sub-editor of the London *Daily News*, told the committee that the removal of duty would result in a proliferation of papers in country market towns. Although these might be supported by local advertisements, he was unable to see the value of the small Irish provincial paper which was 'written as to excite and foment antagonistic opinion ... and local antipathies'. He therefore supported the view that newspapers circulating from the larger towns – and especially the London papers – would 'give more than ever a tone to national opinion ...'. Instead of 'entering into little local bickerings ... you would have distributed throughout the breadth of England and Ireland papers with national views ... there

3 *Connaught Patriot*, 14 January 1860.   4 It was also a natural home for those advocating what Cobden called 'moral power' – a resonant phrase of this period – which would be advanced by what he called 'steady sober middle-class reformers' advocating 'free trade, temperance, education, peace': Richard Cobden to C.D. Collett, secretary of the People's Charter Union and secretary of the Newspaper Stamp Abolition Committee, quoted in Lee, op. cit., p. 45, fn 3.   5 By reducing stamp duty on the press in 1836 the government effectively conceded that the press should be made available, if still expensive, to the working-classes: Lee, op. cit., pp 42–9 deals with the history of the agitation for a cheap press.   6 Linda Lunny, 'Knowledge and Enlightenment: attitudes to education in early nineteenth-century East Ulster' in Mary Daly and David Dickson (eds), *The Origins of Popular Literacy in Ireland: Language Change and Educational Development 1700–1920* (Dublin, 1991), pp 100–2 outlines the debate on education in Ireland in the period.

would be little papers to give local news, but papers emanating from large towns, such as London, Manchester and Liverpool ... would circulate all over the country ...'.[7] But elsewhere Hunt had written on the value of a thriving and diverse press: 'Where Journals are numerous the people have power, intelligence and wealth; where the Journals are few, the many are in reality mere slaves.'[8] Sir T.F. Lewis, who had had some experience of Irish affairs, agreed with the committee's view that if remote counties such as Donegal, Sligo and Antrim had to depend solely on their local newspapers, the union would be endangered. Prejudice would ensue and the 'general spread of national feeling through one part of the country and another' would be prevented.[9] A more realistic view of the value of the provincial press in Ireland was expressed by William Edward Hickson, who knew the country through his membership of Nassau Senior's 1841 commission of enquiry into the condition of handloom weavers. Hickson held that provincial papers met a specific need by publishing local market prices, and he put forward a powerful additional argument on the important role of Irish newspapers in persuading the people to emigrate. Because the poor knew no geography, the press was crucial in providing information about the movement of ships carrying the families of agricultural labourers and in convincing them that emigration was in their own interest.[10] The *Limerick Reporter and Tipperary Vindicator* illustrated the role to be played by the press in unifying England and Ireland when they expressed wonder at the transmission of the Queen's Speech in 1856 by electric telegraph which, before she had left the House of Lords for Buckingham Palace, had been printed in Limerick, Cork, Waterford, Clonmel and Dublin. Her words had 'come hundreds of miles under and over ground ... and the Londoner possesses no greater facility for obtaining information than the humblest artizan in the most distant locality from the Great Metropolis to which the magnetic wires reach'.[11] It seems not to have occurred to the newspaper, which at that time supported the repeal of the union, that there was a certain irony about this closer link with Westminster made possible by science.

The abolition of the stamped press did not, however, result in the beneficial results for the strength of the union that had been envisaged by witnesses to the Select Committee. Cheaper newsprint brought the rise of the 1*d.* press. In England cheaper newspapers increased support for the Liberal party; in Ireland the rise in the cheap press after 1860 coincided with the rise of nationalism, and over time the number of papers that expressed nationalist ideas began to increase.

Newspaper proprietors had to register the title and the place of printing and publication with the Stamp Office. They also had to provide the name and address of the printer, together with that of the publisher. Information was also required

7 Loc. cit., QQ 2355, 2360.   8 Frederick Hunt, *The Fourth Estate* (London, 1850), ii, p. 272.   9 Loc. cit., Evidence of Hunt, QQ 2356–60 and Sir T.F. Lewis, Q 1497. Lewis had served on an enquiry into Irish revenue in 1821 and on a commission into Irish education in 1825. *DNB*.   10 Loc. cit., Q 3203.   11 *Limerick Reporter and Tipperary Vindicator*, 1 February 1856.

about the names and addresses of the proprietors and their occupations, including the names of proprietors resident outside the United Kingdom. The number of shares issued if there were more than two proprietors had to be given, and two sureties had to stand for the paper in cases of blasphemy or seditious libel. Bonds, £400 for Dublin papers and £300 for country papers, had to be lodged. Those willing to stand surety had to provide referees to testify to their own solvency and they in turn had to be approved by the Stamp Office.[12] The Post Office regulations after 1855 were strict to ensure that free postage was available only to the stamped press.[13] These requirements were occasionally the subject of litigation. Some enterprising publishers made attempts to undercut the stamped press by printing unstamped papers almost entirely filled with advertisements in order to avoid having to buy stamped paper. When he was president of the Provincial Newspaper Society in 1866, Joseph Fisher of the *Waterford Mail* corresponded with the Board of Inland Revenue and the Attorney General about the 'constant and persevering disregard of the law by a number of persons publishing unregistered papers', and he appealed for action to be taken against them. Fisher, who was himself an expert on newspaper law,[14] went to the length of comparing the entries in the *Newspaper Press Directory* with the official returns, and claimed that there appeared to be 'a vast number of Papers claiming to be Newspapers which have not complied with the law'. He believed that there were 14 unregistered papers in Ireland: 'One of the unregistered and unsecured papers has attracted a rather unenviable notoriety of publishing articles which many legal subjects regard as libellous.' Although told by the Board that their solicitor had called upon the papers to comply with the law, Fisher remained dissatisfied.[15]

A local excise officer in Ennis found himself engaged in a provincial farce when he was asked by the Stamp Office to deal with a complaint against an unregistered paper, the *Clare Advertizer or Kilrush Gazette*. Instructed to buy copies, he went to the newspaper office in Kilrush and was told that they had none. The proprietor, John Carroll, was himself asked for three copies but Carroll said that there was no

---

12 Circular issued by the Stamp Office PRO IR 56/3. Richard Pigott, proprietor of the *The Irishman*, was threatened with legal proceedings in 1865 and had previously incurred penalties for publishing a newspaper without sureties. Pigott pleaded ill-health but was nevertheless served with a writ: Commissioners of Inland Revenue to Richard Pigott, 15 September, 2 October, 5 October, 11 October 1865. PRO IR 57/45.   13 Newspapers were closely defined: they had 'to contain public news, intelligence, or occurrences and be published periodically at intervals not exceeding 28 days.' Commissioners of the Board of Inland Revenue memo, 12 July 1858. PRO IR 5745. They had to be 'made up in covers open at the sides, have the stamp exposed to view,... must be posted within fifteen days of publication, have no marks or writing (other than the address) thereon or anything enclosed which would subject them to letter postage ... They are forwarded from one part of the Kingdom to the other free ...': *Thom's Directory* (Dublin, 1864), pp 1049–50.   14 Joseph Fisher and James A. Strahan, *The Law of the Press ...* (London 1891) which went into three editions.   15 PRO IR 57/45 Fisher to Board of Inland Revenue, 8 September 1866; Board of Inland Revenue to Fisher, 31 December 1866; Fisher to Board of Inland Revenue 16 January 1867.

such paper, although three copies were later bought by a Mr William Clohissey who, discovering that he had been caught up in prosecuting the newspaper, then declined to help further. Another excise officer, a Mr West, was then asked to purchase copies, but he refused as he was a personal friend of Mr Carroll. It became apparent that there were two Carrolls: John A. Carroll the publisher, and his son Joseph, aged 12, whose name appeared at the foot of the newspaper. Many attempts had been made to take legal action against the *Gazette* but without success, because its existence was always denied. One local solicitor had been trying to bring an action against John Carroll for some time without success, and wrote in disgust to the solicitor of the Board of Inland Revenue: 'This paper, I am afraid, is a perfect nuisance in Kilrush.'[16] Given the prejudices and passions expressed during parliamentary elections and the amount of money earned by the provincial press, especially before the Ballot Act in 1872, it is not surprising that there was pressure for the legal requirements on registration and sureties to be enforced.

The law governing sureties against libel were rigorous. Gerald McCarthy, the proprietor and editor of the *Dundalk Democrat*, ran into difficulties in supplying suitable sureties to the Stamp Office and for a while it looked as though it might be impossible for his paper to continue. In August 1864, one of his sureties, Arthur Johnston, had withdrawn and the other, Arthur Matthews, had to make an arrangement with his creditors. Two new sureties had to be provided. Competitors were not long in hearing of McCarthy's difficulties, and not only the law began bear hardly on him. The proprietor of the *Newry and Dundalk Examiner*, Patrick Dowdall, wrote to the Treasury Solicitor in June 1865 complaining that McCarthy had continued to publish the *Dundalk Democrat* without sureties. Dowdall had reason to complain, saying that some years before he had brought an action against McCarthy, who had been sent to gaol and was forced into insolvency. As McCarthy had lodged no sureties with the Stamp Office, Dowdall had no remedy. Until 1865, repeated applications were made to McCarthy by the Stamp Office but although several names were offered as sureties, they were rejected as 'insufficient' and he was reduced to putting forward his original names, but the near insolvent Arthur Matthews was again rejected. Legal proceedings were instituted, further sureties rejected and McCarthy was told by the Treasury Solicitor that, if he did not enter an appearance, he would be arrested. On 25 October 1865 he was gaoled for contempt of court, and from gaol he succeeded in submitting two suitable sureties to the Stamp Office (one of them a Poor Law Guardian) and he was released. It was then found that his arrest and imprisonment had been the result of an error by an official of the Board of Inland Revenue.[17]

To survive at all, a provincial paper had to be able to count on a loyal core of

16 PRO IR 57/65 George McGown to Solicitor, Board of Inland Revenue, 15 December 1863, 1 January 1865, 25 January 1865; J.B. Kennedy to Solicitor, Board of Inland Revenue, 13 August 1863. 17 PRO 56/43 Memorandum, 30 August 1864; Patrick Dowdall to Treasury Solicitor; memorandum, 1 June 1866; 16 October 1866.

readers on its doorstep. The introduction of the 1*d*. press was instrumental in creating this essential commercial base. Table 3 shows that with the introduction of the 1*d*. press into Ireland between 1860 and 1870, 22 out of 33 1*d*. papers were based in the north-east. This underlines the dependence of the cheap newspaper on industrial towns where sales could be made through a variety of outlets – newsboys, newsagents and shops as well as subscriptions.

Table 3: *Newspapers which lowered their prices to 1*d., *1860–70*

1857	Belfast Morning Post
	Lurgan Gazette
1864	Ballyshannon Herald and North Western Advertiser
	Banner of Ulster
	Belfast Morning News
	Bray Gazette
	Carlow Weekly News
	Cork Daily Herald
	Dundalk Express
	Kingstown Journal
	Londonderry Journal
	Londonderry Sentinel
	Protestant Watchman
	Ulster Observer
1865	Drogheda Conservative
	Londonderry Standard
	Newry Commercial Telegraph
	Newry Herald
	Portadown News
	The Watchman (Enniscorthy)
1867	Fermanagh Mail
1868	Ballymoney Free Press
	Belfast News Letter
	Cavan Weekly News
	Cork Examiner
	Newry Standard
	West Cork and Carbery Eagle
1869	Cork Constitution
	Ulster Examiner
1870	Belfast Evening Telegraph
	Connaught Witness
	County Tipperary Independent
	Londonderry Guardian

Source: *Newspaper Press Directory*

Cheaper newsprint made more frequent publication possible. Four existing Belfast papers went over to daily publication in the years following 1855: the *Belfast Mercury* (renamed the *Belfast Daily Mercury*) in 1857, the *Belfast Northern Whig* in 1868, the *Ulster Examiner* in 1870 and the *Belfast Morning News* in 1872. This had its consequences on the distribution of the press. Charles Eason, who had gone from Manchester to manage W.H. Smith's Dublin business in 1856, reported to Smith in 1859 on the economic consequences of the rush to the cheap press:

> We are suffering from an entire change in the Newspaper business under which the Penny papers have almost entirely taken the place, in the country, of the old established and dear papers. The profit derived from the Newspaper business may be said to have disappeared, as the Public buy in the Streets the papers which now take the places of those they is obtained through the Newspaper Agent and at the Bookstalls.[18]

With the exception of towns like Limerick, Waterford and Cork, it is unlikely that many sales were made in the street (with the possible exception of market days) until later in the period.[19] The wholesalers had another effect on the sale of newspapers and journals – they could be selective. Smiths, with their monopoly on railway station bookstalls, could and did refuse to sell certain papers. The Kilkenny monthly, *The Celt* wrote, 'Several ... correspondents have written complaining that the "Celt" is not to be had at the Railway stations. The fault is not ours; an Englishman rents the right of having his bookstalls exclusively at each terminus, and he, with what we must conclude to be a thorough Saxon hatred of everything Irish, peremptorily refuses to permit the "Celt" to be sold at Irish railway stalls!'[20]

Statements made by proprietors on the size of circulation were based on the annual parliamentary returns of the number of newspaper stamps sold.[21] One of the problems about these circulation claims is that it is impossible to gauge how important the transfer from subscription to direct sale may have been for each paper, because the returns after 1855 only give the number of sheets of stamped paper used to print copies for postal subscribers. For example, was the growth in the number of stamps bought by the *Fermanagh Reporter* from 7,500 in 1864 to 10,000 in 1870, due to the paper's greater absolute popularity, or the preference of its readers to receive the paper by post, or the fact that more readers as a proportion of the whole

---

18 Ibid., Eason, Dublin to G.E. Ilherry, Great Southern and Western Railway, 14 January 1864.   19 In 1872, Lewis Ferdinand, proprietor of the *Galway Vindicator* told the Galway County election petition hearing that the paper was posted to subscribers the same night it was published and that they had a 'regular list of subscribers, and very frequently papers are ordered separately': HC 1872 (240–I) xlviii, Minutes of Evidence to the Galway County Election petition hearing, Q12333.   20 *The Celt*, 10 October 1857.   21 'Shown by the latest Government returns to be the *most widely circulated Journal in Ireland*': Advertisement for *Belfast Northern Whig, Newspaper Press Directory, 1851.*

lived at a distance from Enniskillen and were unable to buy the paper direct? The *Reporter* claimed to circulate not only all over Ulster and also in Leitrim (where it had a special edition, the *Leitrim Journal*), the United Kingdom and the colonies. If these claims were true, then by 1870 the paper must have had a large number of subscribers.

Middle-class households tended to buy newspapers by subscription, and in rural areas these were delivered by post. Newspapers were used as a free means of telling the recipient that you had arrived safely at your destination: Carlyle and his brother posted newspapers to each other when Carlyle was touring Ireland in 1849.[22] Newspaper proprietors expected high standards of delivery from a relatively new postal service. Anthony Trollope, then a surveyor of posts in Ireland, assured the Select Committee on Postal Arrangements in 1855 that letters posted in the morning in Dungarvan could be delivered in Waterford the same day by using the railway, and that by July 1855, there were two daily deliveries in Dungarvan.[23] Joseph Fisher of the *Waterford Mail* gave evidence as secretary of a committee formed to put the case of local newspaper proprietors to the Postmaster-General. He told the Committee that, despite paying for stamped paper which guaranteed early delivery, newspapers destined for Dungarvan had to be printed in Waterford four hours earlier than similar papers published in Dublin. The Revd Doudney of Bonmahon, who published two journals, one monthly and one bi-monthly, found that he was obliged to pay to send them to Waterford for distribution elsewhere. This was despite their being printed on stamped paper which entitled them to special treatment.[24] But by 1865, the mechanics of publication and distribution which lasted for at least the next 75 years were in firmly place.

PEOPLE: PROPRIETORS, EDITORS AND REPORTERS

The commercial background of editors and proprietors did not make a good impression on some visitors. When Carlyle travelled across Ireland in 1849 with Charles Gavan Duffy, he dined in Kilkenny with Dr Robert Cane of *The Celt* and there met 'Snuffy editors, low-bred but not without energy, once "all for repale", now out of that; – have little or no memory of what they said or did.' In Cork he talked to Michael Joseph Barry, who wrote poems for *The Nation* and for a while had been a Young Irelander but had recanted after 1848. Carlyle described Barry of the *Cork Southern Reporter* as an 'editor of songs, of newspapers'. In Galway Carlyle met 'an editor', Edward Butler. Carlyle's account of his politics connect Butler with the

22 'Your newspaper I returned last night for a sign': Thomas Carlyle to John A. Carlyle, 17 July 1849, in C. de. Ryals (ed.), *The Collected Letters of Thomas and Jane West Carlyle*, 244 (Durham, 1995), p. 129.   23 Select Committee on Postal Arrangements, HC 1854–55 xi [445], QQ 2603–12 and 2629–32.   24 Ibid., QQ 274 and 1010–51.

Galway Mercury, 'Maynooth pupil this editor, a burly thick-necked, sharp-eyed man – couldn't be a priest; in secret counter works M'Hale (Archbishop of Tuam] as I can see, and despises and dislikes his courses and him.' Dr Thomas McKnight, who edited the *Belfast News-Letter* and later the *Londonderry Standard* was the sort of man that Carlyle preferred: 'an honest kind of man, tho' loud-toned and with wild eyes, this McKnight; has tobacco too, and a kind little orderly polite wife'.[25]

One hundred and sixty-nine men in the 1851 census said they were newspaper editors, reporters and proprietors. From the information we have they were working on about 70 newspapers. In 1851 the census details were extremely brief in their description of occupations; later censuses are more helpful in their analysis of education and religion.

By 1861, the numbers of proprietors, reporters and editors had increased sharply; there were 238 in total, of whom two were women. The religious profession of those involved in newspaper production and distribution in the 1861 census throws some light on education levels of the period. Roman Catholic proprietors, editors and reporters were still in the minority.

Table 4: *Occupations by religious profession, 1861*

Newspaper proprietors, editors and reporters:	male	female
Established church	77	2
Roman Catholics	107	–
Presbyterians	34	–
Methodists	11	–
Independents	3	–
All other	4	2
Total:	238	
Protestant	131	
Roman Catholic	107	

Source: Census of Ireland 1861: Pt. IV. Reports and Tables relating to Religious Professions, Education and Occupations. HC. 1863 [3204.III] lx.1

Later census figures also reveal the number of proprietors who ran papers together with other professions or trades.[26] In the smaller towns they tended to com-

25 Thomas Carlyle, *Reminiscences of My Irish Journey in 1849* (London, 1882), pp 85, 120, 190, and 255.
26 The varied background of a number of nineteenth-century Ulster editors included Amyas Griffiths of the *Belfast Mercury* (1851–61) who had been an excise officer; Samuel Neilson of the *Northern Star* (1868–72) a draper, Hugh McCall of the *Banner of Ulster* (1842–69) a pawnbroker: cf. Aiken McClelland,

bine publishing the local paper with running a general store or a book selling and general printing business.[27] In 1851, the eclectic nature of their employment appeared in their advertisements. A leaflet published in 1851 by John Thompson, proprietor of the *Armagh Guardian* said he was an 'agent for the Norwich Union Life and Fire Insurance; Stephens Unchangeable Blue and Blueblack fluid inks sold, Teas of the China Tea Company, Bewley and Evans Perfumes, and Family Medicines; R. & L. Perry & Co's, Morrison's and Holloway's Pills and Ointments, Stationery &c. sold. Typography neatly and expeditiously Printed'.[28] John Hackett of the *Tipperary Free Press* was a bookseller, stationer and patent medicine vendor; he also sold musical instruments, tea, and coffee 'ground by powerful machinery'. Of the 16 agents for a patent medicine, 'The Silent Friend' in 1848, ten were either booksellers or newspaper proprietors.[29] John Hackett dabbled in politics; he was a town councillor, and there is a passing reference to him in the enquiry into the Tipperary County election in 1867, where the *Tipperary Free Press* was alleged to have given publicity to the clergy on the nomination of Captain White, and to their subsequent resolutions, and to have printed placards publicising these resolutions. Hackett also acted as agent on polling day for Captain White.[30] John Hackett must have had considerable influence: contributors to the newspaper included Richard Lalor Sheil (1791–1851) the lawyer and one of the founders of the Catholic Association; Dr Cooke Taylor (1800–49) the writer and educational reformer; General Thomas Perronet Thompson (1783–1869) proprietor of the *Westminster Review*, politician and supporter of Catholic emancipation; and Michael Doheny (1805-63) the Young Irelander and writer of *In the Felon's Track*.[31]

One of Hackett's contributors was his cousin Maurice Lenihan, who ran the *Limerick Reporter and Tipperary Vindicator*. Proprietor and editor of the paper for over 50 years, Lenihan was born in 1815, the son of a prosperous Waterford draper and woollen merchant, and one of 15 children. He was educated at a dame school and went on to St. John's College, Waterford and Carlow College. When his father died, he helped John Hackett by reporting the local assizes, and was urged to take up journalism. After two years on the *Tipperary Free Press*, Lenihan went on to the *Waterford Chronicle* and reported the tithe war in Munster. His articles made that paper's reputation. In 1841 Lenihan moved on to the *Limerick Reporter* and then to the *Cork Examiner* under its liberal proprietor, John Francis Maguire. Daniel O'Connell and Bishop Power of Killaloe urged Lenihan to start a paper in Nenagh

'The Ulster Press in the eighteenth and nineteenth centuries', *Ulster Folklife*, 20 (1974), pp 89–99; unfortunately he does not give their exact dates. **27** Booksellers in the provinces in eighteenth-century England often combined the sale of books with maps, prints, fire insurance and fishing tackle. As in Ireland, they also sold patent medicines and groceries. Cf. John Brewer, *The Pleasures of the Imagination: English Culture in the Eighteenth Century* (London, 1997) pp 174–6. **28** Advertisement leaflet in Madden Papers, Dublin City Library Ms 274. **29** *Tipperary Free Press*,14 June 1848. **30** *Newspaper Press Directory*, 1851; Select Committee on the Tipperary Election Petition, HC 1867 (211) viii. **31** Madden papers, Dublin City Library.

advocating repeal, and O'Connell announced the founding of the *Tipperary Vindicator* in Thurles in 1844. In 1849 Lenihan bought up the *Limerick Reporter* which in January 1850 was amalgamated with the *Tipperary Vindicator*. Although Lenihan had been intimate with the leaders of Young Ireland he was cautious about their politics, prudently steering a course between his patron, O'Connell and his friend Thomas Meagher. He was urged by a fellow journalist, M.G. Conway of the *Newry Examiner* to dissociate from the views of the Young Ireland party expressed in *The Nation* which were (Conway believed) 'extravagant eulogies and assumptions'.[32] Lenihan himself believed that the Young Ireland movement would 'end in smoke or worse'. But despite this, he was friendly with Meagher, and dined with him in the condemned cell in Clonmel, and although he attacked Michael Doheny in his paper, he stood bail for him and went some way towards protecting his reputation.[33] Lenihan was a friend of the antiquarian George Petrie, and in 1858 himself became a member of the Society for the Cultivation of the Irish Language, and in 1863 of the Kilkenny Archaeological Society. He was proposed for membership of the Royal Irish Academy (also in 1863) by the Earl of Dunraven. The entry for the *Limerick Reporter and Tipperary Vindicator* in the 1851 *Newspaper Press Directory* demonstrates the intellectual plane on which the provincial press in the larger towns could now operate. Describing itself as a liberal paper, it boasted 'Its original translations from the foreign journals are a novel feature. Its reviews [are] elaborate. It is a political, literary and family newspaper and is generally replete with matter of the deepest interest to all classes in Ireland.' Leniham assumed a level of literacy and breadth of interest far removed from the small papers of the 1840s. It is a pity that Carlyle never met him.

After the abolition of stamp duty in 1855, nationalists became editors and active in literary societies. William Kenealy, Peter Gill, P.J. Smyth, Martin O'Brennan and Denis Holland became proprietors of new papers advocating nationalist policies founded between 1855 and 1859.[34] Their readers were the 'respectable' wage earners, the skilled workers and the urban lower-middle class described by Comerford in his study of those who were active in Fenianism in the mid-1860s. They were part of the increased numbers of newly-literate in the census figures of 1861. These were the National School masters, the town shop-boys, mechanics, nailors, shoemakers and tradesmen who figured in the constabulary reports on Fenian activity in the 1860s.[35] The demands of this new readership were an essential part of the changing press over the next twenty years.

---

32 Conway to Lenihan, 8 October 1845: Lenihan papers, NLI Ms. 5859. 33 Meagher used Lenihan to correct false reports that he had attacked his friends including Michael Doheny 'nothing could have been more false than this ...': Meagher to Lenihan, October 23, 1848 NLI 4184. Meagher kept in touch with Lenihan when he arrived in America, asking him to reprint a speech he had made from a text in the *Irish News*: Meagher to Lenihan, 13 October 1857, NLI Ms 4184. 34 Editing the *Tipperary Leader* (1855), *Tipperary Advocate* (1857), the *Waterford Citizen* (1859) the *Connaught Patriot* (1859), and the *Galway American* (1862). 35 R.V. Comerford 'Patriotism as Pastime: the Appeal of Fenianism in the

PROSPECTUSES, ADVERTISING AND READERSHIP

This Roman Catholic organ is conducted with much talent and energy. It is more political than polemical and is one of those journals so long remarkable for the patriotic lyrical effusions, which, like those of Tyrtaeus, find an echo in so many 'Irish Hearts'.[36]

Writing a prospectus was the first task for the proprietor of a new newspaper. The purpose of a prospectus was to make the political, literary and commercial programme of a newspaper immediately clear to prospective readers and advertisers. In *Pendennis*, written between 1848 and 1850, Thackeray's prospectus for the proposed *Pall Mall Gazette* touches lightly on the elements essential for success of a newspaper: its politics, the breadth of its news-gathering, the influence it can command both through its proprietor and shareholders and the social standing of its readers, and how it will deal with competing journals. Thackeray's observation of the newspaper prose style of the 1850s and the use of capital letters is acute.[37]

The first entry of the *Carlow Post* in the *Newspaper Press Directory* echoes this mode when it announced that it was

Edited by a gentleman of well-known abilities ... strenuously but temperately advocates an Equitable Adjustment of the Landlord and Tenant Question, the Extension of the Franchise, the Non-payment by the State of the Ministers of any religious denomination and Equality in civil and Religious Rights ... also filed in the principal News Agency Offices, Coffee Houses and Hotels of Dublin.[38]

As the epigraph for the *Castlebar Telegraph* at the beginning of this section shows, early prospectuses employed flights of prose that extended beyond mere commercial transactions. Later entries were more mundane and limited themselves to hard facts. A prospectus was printed separately before the paper began publication and formed part of its editorials for some months after the paper appeared. Once written, a prospectus was circulated widely as a leaflet, and an extensive knowledge of local people and institutions was essential to the attraction of business, and without such a network, the successful launch of a newspaper was problematical. When John St George Joyce became editor of the *Galway Express*, he had only recently

mid-1860s' in *Irish Historical Studies* xxi, no. 87 (1981).   **36** Entry of the *Castlebar Telegraph or Connaught Ranger. Newspaper Press Directory* 1851. Tyrtaeus was a seventh-century BC elegaic writer of patriotic songs sung by the Spartans. William Drennan was called the Tyrtaeus of the United Irishmen. Cf. Norman Vance, 'Celts, Carthaginians and constitutions: Anglo-Irish literary relations, 1780–1820', in *Irish Historical Studies*, 22, no. 87 (1981), pp 224–5.   **37** *Pendennis*, p. 331.   **38** Loc. cit., entry for 1857.

returned to Galway from America, and did not appear to have the necessary local connections. Joyce sent circulars to names drawn from 'a very complete list', using the previous year's *Slater's Directory*, the Grand Jury panel and the 'long panel'. But '... very few of the circulars were answered, and I then sent a paper; some of the papers have been returned; and in the case of those which have not been returned, I assume they will take them'. However, Joyce's lack of local intelligence told against him when he admitted that some of his potential subscribers were later found to have died. Despite these difficulties, by 1872 the paper was being published twice a week and had about 300 subscribers from 'all classes', 240 of whom lived in Galway.[39]

The text of prospectuses also formed the basis of proprietors' entries in the *Newspaper Press Directory* which were directed to potential advertisers. The circulation area that they declared to be covered by their paper was an important part of their claim that they had a large and influential readership. A paper's readership was dependent on residents' prosperity, on local industry and on local transport links. In the early years a number of papers asserted that they were read overseas. Between 1850 and 1892, 216 papers in the *Directory* made specific claims to circulation areas, which are analysed in Table 5.

Table 5: *Circulation areas, 1850–92*

Local within a ten mile radius of publication town	45
Province	72
Neighbouring counties (not Dublin)	53
England	22
Scotland	14
America	10
Canada	5
Australia and Colonies	6
India	3
Europe	3

Source: *Newspaper Press Directory*. (The circulation areas claimed overlap; the total here does not correspond to the total number of newspapers surveyed.)

Papers defined their circulation areas politically, geographically, and socially. According to the *Limerick and Clare Examiner* in 1851, it only 'circulated in those districts favourable to repeal'. Other papers confirm the demand for the Irish provincial press by emigrants to the industrial North of England: in 1851 the *Cork*

39 Loc. cit., QQ 12373–424.

Examiner cited readers in 'Manchester and other English towns'. It is possible, however, that some of these readers were not individual subscribers but saw the paper in a reading room.

Comerford has drawn attention to the way that the pre-existing features of industrialisation – land-holding, the devotional revolution and the decline of the Irish language prior to 1850 – were then 'cast in new combinations and a new order of precedence' as a reaction to the famine and a response to conditions in the world outside. The enormous increase in newspaper reading should be seen in the context of an improvement in communications throughout Ireland.[40] The development of the Irish railway system was undoubtedly important for the commercial success of provincial papers. Railways brought readers, and railways brought advertisement business. In an advertisement in the *Newspaper Press Directory* in 1857, the *Armagh Guardian* pointed to the town's 'Direct Railway Communication with the leading Commercial Towns' which made the paper a 'suitable medium for advertisements'.

The parliamentary procedure that preceded the construction of a railway line also affected the development of newspaper business; papers were founded in anticipation of the business that would be brought when the line was completed. The prospectus for the Great Southern and Western Railway which was to serve Athlone was published in 1846, and the route and the towns to be served were outlined, thus encouraging proprietors to open new papers. The *Westmeath Independent*, which started publication in Athlone in 1846, claimed in 1851 that its geographical position and its prospective connection to the railway system was the reason for its being one of 'the First mediums for Advertising ... superseding the necessity of advertising in Seven other papers'.[41] The service did not reach Athlone until August 1857, six years later.[42] By comparing the dates when newspapers began publication with the announcement of the construction of new railway lines and stations, it is possible to make some connection between the two commercial enterprises. The Wexford, Carlow and Dublin Junction Railway Company was incorporated in 1846; Carlow station opened in 1850 and the line to Wicklow opened in 1855. The *Carlow Post*, which started in 1853, claimed to circulate in Kildare, Kilkenny, Wexford and Wicklow. The Waterford and Limerick Railway Company was announced in 1845; it opened in stages between 1845 and 1854, and Limerick station opened in 1848. The *Limerick and Clare Examiner* started publication in 1846 and the *Munster News* in 1851, claiming circulation in 'Limerick and Munster generally'.[43] Clonmel station opened on this line in 1846, and the *Clonmel Chronicle* (1848) claimed in 1851 to circulate in Tipperary, Dublin and King's County. Dundalk station, on the Dub-

---

40 At the same as noting the increase between 1850 and 1870 in the number of letters delivered, he also notes the increase in the receipts for goods traffic which multiplied in size five times; by 1870 over 400 towns and villages had a telegraph office, and newspaper circulation had increased 50% in the twenty years after 1850. At the same time there was a decline in the trading of west coast ports. Cf. Comerford, *New History of Ireland*, p. 373 and 375.   41 *Newspaper Press Directory*.   42 H.C. Casserley, *Outline of Irish Railway History* (Newton Abbot, 1974), p. 30.   43 Casserley, op. cit., p. 78.

lin and Belfast Junction Railway, was opened in February 1849, and the *Dundalk Democrat* began publication in October 1849, claiming to circulate 'all over Ulster'.[44] There is evidence that even after 1870 newspaper proprietors continue to rely on the post, which could only be made possible and expanded by the developing railway network.

Newspapers in Galway urged the particular advantage of being connected with a large port. Between 1864 and 1867, the *Galway Express* claimed to write about 'everything connected with the Galway packet station'.[45] The *Galway American* combined local shipping interests with nationalist propaganda. In its first edition, it spoke of its 'opportunity to help in the development of the great Resources of Ireland's most Western seaport ... an Organ is needed to make known its capabilities. It will not fail, at the same time, to uphold the great National interests of Ireland ...'[46] By covering the American Civil War in detail, it urged Ireland to look west for aid towards its independence. In 1862, the newspaper attacked those Irish who sympathised with the Confederates, referring to the 'Strong bond of union between the Northern States and Ireland ... in the event of America becoming a great military and naval power, Ireland's long night of tribulation would assuredly come to a speedy end.'[47]

Sligo, Ballina, Westport, Galway and Tralee all suffered from a decline in shipping trade, and this increasing isolation can be seen in the fortunes of the local press. Between 1850 and 1892, Ballina, Co. Mayo, had seven papers in print. Although a port, the town was physically isolated and badly affected by the agricultural depression of the early 1860s and from 1879 onwards. Of the seven papers, three belonged to Thomas Ham, a general printer: the *Ballina Chronicle* (1849) which, having amalgamated with the *Connaught Watchman* in 1851, lasted until 1863; the *Tyrawley Herald* (1844) which became the *Ballina Herald* in 1870. In 1850 all three were published weekly at 5*d*. Ham's policies in the papers may have led to their failure: they were conservative and Protestant. In the absence of the railway, the early Ballina papers may have had problems in finding a big enough circulation base. Although the Ballina railway link had been proposed in 1856, the line did not arrive until 1873. The Ballina press only came into its own during the Land War.

Public institutions – poor law boards, railway boards, petty sessions and the Encumbered Estates Courts – used the local press to place advertisements. Their business was the bread and butter of the local newspaper proprietor, and contested hotly.[48] Not just advertisements, but placards and leaflets in elections, and the printing of Poor Law Guardian minute books and cess receiptbooks, all helped run the presses

---

44 Casserley, op. cit., p. 169.   45 Entry in the *Newspaper Press Directory*.   46 *Galway American*, 12 April 1862.   47 Ibid., 10 May 1862.   48 An advertisement for the sale of a Jobbing Office which comprised 'Letters for Posters, Fancy Type for Cards, Circulars, Shop Bills, & Frames, Cases & in great variety with Double Crown Metal Albion press' adds 'Proprietors of Newspapers, Booksellers & those who have not already an office of this description attached to their establishments would much consult their interests by purchasing the above': *Limerick Reporter and Tipperary Vindicator*, 15 January 1850.

of a weekly paper in between publication days. The Ulster Printing Co., publishers of the *Belfast Daily Mercury*, carried out an enormous variety of miscellaneous printing jobs – 'Dog Lost' notices, railway timetables for the Ballymena railway, testimonials for clergymen, parcel labels, trade cards, handbills and reports for the Belfast Town Council.[49] Contracts awarded by local institutions such as the Boards of Guardians were extremely valuable. The *Belfast News-Letter* was 'one of the county Advertisers for Antrim and Down' in 1851. The *Anglo-Celt*, which circulated over a wide area of county Cavan claimed to be the "established advertisement organ of Poor Law Boards' in 1857. Custom brought by new institutions and the increasing importance of the role of the Catholic church in provincial life brought with it new and distinctive Irish business. The *Galway Vindicator* advertised itself in 1857 as 'the "primal" and only two-day journal published in the West of Ireland' which had the contract for legal and public advertisements including those of the Encumbered Estates Court. The *Tralee Chronicle* (1843) which aspired to be read by the gentry and tourists, gave information about local sports (including deer hunting) but they too had the contract for advertisements by the Roman Catholic clergy.

The clergy's appeal as a literate and increasingly politically active group became more frequently heard. The *Tralee Chronicle* was 'the medium by which the Catholic clergy advertises'. The *Tuam Herald* in 1851 claimed it was the 'special organ' of the Roman Catholic church. Observers like Sir Francis Head made a strong connection between the Roman Catholic priesthood and some parts of the newspaper press. Head believed that the reader of Irish newspapers would be able to 'perceive that the *Irish Priests* Press ... not only openly preaches ... hostility to everything bearing the name of British but sympathy and alliance with every offender against British laws' and he quotes the '*Munster Citizen*' (not a title in print at the time) as a 'specimen of the delusions practised on the Irish people'.[50] In this period, however, the influence of the clergy, important in the 1870s and 1880s, was relatively muted.

It is difficult to classify the types of readers to whom newspapers claimed to appeal; in their own interest most papers would cite commercial readership in order

---

49 Ulster Printing Co. Ltd. Job Book: PRONI D.2450/3/5 1858–1861. The jobbing printing in Darius Clayhanger's shop gives a fair idea of the kind of work done by a provincial printer. He too published a newspaper. 'Auctions, meetings, concerts, sermons, improving lectures, miscellaneous entertainments, programmes, catalogues, deaths, births, marriages, specifications, municipal notices, summonses, demands, receipts, subscription-lists, accounts, rateforms, lists of voters, jury-lists, inaugurations, closures, bill-heads, hand-bills, addresses, visiting-cards, society rules, bargain-sales, lost and found notices: traces of all these matters, and more, were to be found in that office; it was impregnated with the human interest; it was dusty with human interest ...'. *Clayhanger*, p. 103.   50 Sir Francis Head, *A Fortnight in Ireland* (London, 1852). Head's entry in the *Dictionary of National Biography* admits that he was not entirely accurate in his observations. Referring to the 'fictions and mendacious narratives of passing events' which made the establishment of a liberal paper so necessary, the first edition of the *Carlow Post* called Head an 'imaginative tourist': 15 October 1853.

to attract the healthy advertising revenue which was essential to underpin the successful paper. Table 6 analyses the readership claimed in the *Newspaper Press Directory* by newspapers published between 1850 and 1865.

Table 6: *Occupations of readers cited by newspapers, 1850–65*

Commercial	58
Agricultural	55
Family readership	15
Clergy	14
Public institutions: Poor Law Boards, Encumbered Estates Court, Petty sessions, railway boards	7
Professions	4
Military	4
Tourists (Bray, Kingstown and Tralee)	3

Source: Entries in *Newspaper Press Directory*

There were numerous variations on the commercial theme. Local events, local industry, particular groups of readers, all had their attraction.[51] Protection as a political policy lingered in Ireland much longer than at Westminster, and protection allied to nationalism was advocated by some newspapers well into the 1860s. At the beginning of the period, agricultural protection was advocated by the *Londonderry Sentinel*, and the *Londonderry Standard* remained 'always the farmers' friend' in 1851. Local events were commercially attractive: in 1851 the *Western Star* rightly believed that the 'Great National Fair' at Ballinasloe 'gives an importance to the Journal it might otherwise not possess. [The paper has] unusual facilities for the Advertisement of Lands, Stock, Agricultural implements and everything connected with husbandry.' Cork's position as the third most important town in Ireland and the largest port on the south-western coast made all the Cork papers of the period concentrate on commerce, and in addition Cork opened a National Exhibition in June 1852. The *Cork Examiner* in 1865 said that 'It has taken the initiative in the recent industrial movement in the South and is the chief organ of all new undertakings which spring from it.' By 1867 the paper said it had 'made the Irish industrial movement a speciality.' The *Cork Evening Echo* had a special edition for Queenstown where reporters were 'permanently employed' to deal with shipping news.

Citing the high social class of its readers as a reason for both advertising and buying a paper was a practice particularly redolent of the 1850s, and disappears later in the century. At the beginning of the period, readers among the gentry and

51 The *Wexford Constitution* in 1873 announced that 'The numerous shipping disasters which take place on the dangerous Wexford coast are promptly, correctly and fully recorded in its columns'. Pessimistic information useful both to travellers and insurance companies.

nobility were claimed by the conservative *Western Star* and *Belfast News-Letter*, and the then neutral *Cork Daily Herald* spoke of its being read by the 'wealthy and influential classes' in the south of Ireland. The *Banner of Ulster* in the same year said its readers came from 'the best classes of society'. The *Londonderry Guardian* in 1858 claimed the support of the landed gentry. Cork papers, in particular, empha-sised money: the *Cork Herald* in 1857 published fiction and 'the fashions with occa-sional explanatory woodcuts, domestic economy and general household matters' which it believed would interest 'the wealthy and influential classes'. The *Irish Daily Telegraph* (formerly the *Southern Reporter*) was a liberal free trade paper in 1851 and had become 'moderate liberal' by 1872. It presciently described its readership as 'the upper and middle class, viz. those who have something to lose'. Their prob-lems, although anxiously analysed in the 1850s, tended to disappear with the in-crease in nationalist feeling and alliances. Imperceptibly the nobility and gentry lost ground to a wider audience.

   In the 1850s papers claimed to be read by the military: the *Westmeath Independ-ent* of Athlone pointed out that it was published in 'one of the largest garrison towns in Ireland'; the *Roscommon Gazette* had a column for naval and military appoint-ments and the *Cork Constitution* claimed to be 'a favorite in the messrooms of the Sister Isle, not less than the attention paid by it to the state and all prospects of military affairs'.[52] Claims like these were not seen later in the period. However, as will be seen later, the mess rooms in Ireland continued to read the provincial press.

   The question of the social class of readers of the provincial press was not only the concern of the press proprietor, however. In 1872, the Galway County Election petition hearing spent some time worrying about the corruption of Galway news-paper readers whose political judgement might have been affected by the vast quantities of material published in newspapers (particularly the *Tuam Herald*) and circulated as leaflets all over the county. The editor of the *Galway Express* told the enquiry that the paper had a large circulation in the county among all classes, in-cluding publicans and farmers. Pressed on the type of farmers who took his paper, he did not understand what was meant by the phrase used by barristers appearing at the hearing: 'the frieze-coated class'. His subscribers, who might have been shop-keepers or tenant farmers, were not his acquaintances. However, he knew that he had three hundred subscribers as he bought 12s. 6d. worth of halfpenny stamps twice a week in order to post 300 copies of each edition. The proprietor of the *Western Star* of Ballinasloe told the hearing that his paper, which had been esta-blished for 25 years, had an 'average circulation' in the county among all classes. Certainly the gentry subscribed but he did not know whether or how many 'frieze-coated men' bought the paper. Lewis L. Ferdinand, proprietor of the *Galway Vindicator*, was asked:

52 *Newspaper Press Directory*, 1851.

I take it for granted that the chief circulation of your paper is amongst the gentry of the county, and the shopkeepers, and respectable persons?
– It has a wide circulation; it is circulated in Dublin, and London and many places.
Q. But I presume you do not send it to the humbler classes of voters in Connemara, the frieze-coated voters, as they have been called here?
– Not one.

Later in the enquiry he was pressed further and said that he believed that 80 subscribers to the *Vindicator* were farmers.

Q. And that includes every class of farmers from the highest to the lowest?
– No, the gentry are all farmers, properly speaking, too; but these men are far removed ... above what you call the frieze-coated people, the peasantry of the county; they are gentlemen farmers. [There are] ... no regular subscribers among the peasant farmers, but a great many of them purchase the paper to send it to America.[53]

The fact that only 15 of the papers which were extant in 1850 failed to survive for the next 40 years can probably be attributed to their successful commercial management and their geographical location. Of the 21 papers that disappeared between 1850 and 1865, 12 went under between 1862 and 1865. 86 papers in total closed between 1850 and 1892, but this was the largest number over the shortest period of time. The causes may have been competition, or a shake-out of under-capitalised papers begun in the mid-1850s after the abolition of newspaper stamps, or a reflection of the state of the Irish economy. An examination of the papers that failed is suggestive. The *Galway Mercury* (1844–60) competed with two other Galway papers also describing themselves as 'liberal': the *Galway Vindicator* and the *Galway American*, though the latter was really crypto-nationalist. Tralee had a small local population, never above 6000. The railway did not come to Tralee until 1859 and its relative isolation and dependence on seasonal tourism may have made it difficult for the town to sustain many newspapers. Fluctuations in seasonal trade may have accounted in part for the failure of the *Kerry Star* (1861–3) and competition probably forced the *Kerry Examiner* (1840–56) out of business. The closure of the *Kingstown Journal* (1863) may also have been caused by unpredictable seasonal trade (it claimed to have 'news of the watering place with a list of visitors')[54] and it was in competition with Dublin papers. The fine balance between an attractive price to the customer and financial viability proved the downfall of a number of papers. In 1864 the *Banner of Ulster* (1842) reduced its price to 1*d*. and by 1869 it had gone.
The Belfast papers showed resilience because their circulation areas were, in the

---

53 QQ13969–975.   54 *Newspaper Press Directory*, 1863.

main, confined to the industrialised north and they had on their doorstep the essential ingredient of a successful press: a literate public in an industrialised city with the newspaper-buying habit. However, the effect on the press in the surrounding countryside of the distribution of newspapers published in the larger towns can be seen here. The smaller Ulster papers seem to have been vulnerable for two reasons. Industrial development encouraged development of the transport infrastructure within Ulster. Belfast, Carrickfergus, Lisburn, Londonderry, Lurgan, Newry and Portadown all had railway stations before 1850. By 1860, Ballymoney, Banbridge, Cavan, Coleraine, Dungannon, Enniskillen, Monaghan and Omagh were connected to the railway network. All the Belfast papers in 1850 claimed to circulate throughout Ulster, and this may account for the decline in circulation of the *Coleraine Chronicle*, the *Downpatrick Recorder* and the *Newry Examiner*. The *Ballyshannon Herald* disappeared in 1884. There were four Belfast papers in circulation in 1850; by 1865 there were seven; three papers had started and died between those dates. This seems to suggest that the Belfast sales were hard won. The *Banner of Ulster*'s liberal politics, and competition, may have been factors which led to its disappearance in the wake of Ulster revivalism in the late 1860s. Four further existing papers went over to daily publication between 1857 and 1872: the *Belfast Mercury* in 1857, the *Belfast Northern Whig* in 1868, the *Ulster Examiner* in 1870 and the *Belfast Morning News* in 1872.

In Limerick City the population declined slightly between 1841 and 1891 (from 40,205 to 37,155) and two papers quickly opened and closed between 1848 and 1858. Both the *Limerick and Clare Examiner* (1846–55) and the *Limerick Observer* (1856–7) failed to hold their own against the established grip of the *Limerick Chronicle* (1766) and the *Limerick Reporter* (1839) which in 1850 amalgamated with the *Tipperary Vindicator* founded in 1844. Some towns certainly had too many papers. With a population of around 12,000 between 1861 and 1891, Wexford had nine papers. In the thirty-four years from 1858 to 1892 it had five papers publishing simultaneously and, for a short while between 1880 and 1883, it had six papers competing together. It is not surprising that four papers ceased publication between 1858 and 1888. The need for competition might have accounted for the high profile of Edmund Walsh, who took over the *Wexford Guardian* (1847–57) and became proprietor of *The People* and the *Wexford Standard* (1879–?88). The gradual decline of particular political allegiances in certain parts of Ireland led to problems if a district was geographically isolated. The *Sligo Chronicle* and the *Sligo Journal* suffered in consequence of their conservatism in an area which was already liberal and was tending to nationalist politics. The *Sligo Journal* disappeared in 1866. The *Sligo Champion* claimed in 1851 that it was the 'recognised political organ of the Roman Catholic clergy of Elphin and Achonry'; the association of politics, the press and the Roman Catholic church was borne out particularly strongly in the development of the Connaught press. Political polarisation grew; increasingly in the 1850s papers describing themselves as 'independent' declined in popularity.

3

Land reform and the politics of the 1850s

'The Newspaper is nowadays what the preacher was some two or three hundred years ago. It is the guide, counsellor and friend. It is our best moral police ... It exposes abuses, unmasks jobs, censures vice, lashes tyranny ... such is the newspaper! in all free countries, the great agent of political education, the chief bulwark of liberty, and the most active pioneer of public intelligence' *Belfast Vindicator*, 15 May 1844.

Two issues in the 1850s, the tenant right movement and the events that led up to the suicide of John Sadleir, were used by groups of newspaper proprietors to focus the attention of their readers on the consequences of Ireland's continuing dependence on England. The tenant right movement and the founding of the Tenant League failed because Irish representatives at Westminster were unable or unprepared to persuade parliament of the urgency of Irish land reform. The episodes which involved William Keogh and John Sadleir were a demonstration to Irish people that when their representatives at Westminster turned their backs on their country, Ireland suffered. They were part of the political reasons for a marked growth in the number of newspapers which advocated the policies which characterised Irish nationalism in the 1860s: protectionism, the Irish language and the implicit rejection of English interference with Irish affairs.

After 1855, the link between nationalist policies and the Catholic church began to grow closer: key issues and key images, centring on the Irish language and literature and the importance of Ireland's natural resources, recur in newspapers founded after 1855 which called themselves liberal and Catholic. (Outside Dublin, they were not yet describing themselves as nationalist.) As a hostile move, Irish protectionism opposed the concept of peace through free trade. William Kenealy believed that 'the minerals of Ireland are not less national than the shamrock on its soil'.[1] Maurice Leniham warned that protectionist policy was unsuitable to Ireland, as it would only be advantageous to landlords.[2] The political theories formulated by the Kilkenny journal, *The Celt* in the mid-1850s were, once again, at least ten years ahead of their time. In 1857, it stated that its policy was: 'To stir up past memories. To develope [*sic*] existing energies and resources ...'; and in successive articles the pa-

1 *Tipperary Leader*, 27 January 1855.   2 *Limerick Reporter and Tipperary Vindicator*, 18 January 1850.

per explored the qualities essential to define nationhood. In 1858 a writer interpreted nationhood in terms of a common national language: language united Italy and is 'the only preservative of German unity'.[3] The difficulty for Ireland to embrace the idea of a nation based on the Irish language was the reality that those who wished to advance in the world spoke English.[4] But *The Celt* gave America as an example of a nation where emigrants had newspapers in their own language, and attacked the Irish press for failing to publish articles in Irish.[5] This, however, was a false comparison: emigrants to America from central Europe *ipso facto* were unlikely to speak English, and unlike the Irish did not have English as the language of government and again, unlike the Irish, did not look to England as a source of employment.

When Keogh and Sadleir accepted government office in 1852, newspapers, especially in their own localities of Limerick and Tipperary, saw their faithlessness as another reason to propel Ireland towards re-embracing nationalism, and Sadleir's subsequent disgrace was cited as driving a wedge between England and Ireland. The failure of his Tipperary Joint Stock Bank in 1854 meant hardship for the small farmers who had placed their savings in Sadleir's care, and the local press counselled their readers to place their trust in Ireland alone. The *Tipperary Leader*, under the brief editorship of William Kenealy before he went to the *Kilkenny Journal*, announced in its first edition in January 1855 that its mission would be 'to rescue this noble country from the disgrace of political corruption in its representatives. The *Tipperary Leader* complained that the Irish press had 'strangely neglected the aid of Literature in building up and informing national opinion' and believed that 'men have been made mere village politicians'.[6] The outbreak of the Crimean War, the Indian Mutiny and, in the late 1850s, the real possibility of a war with France were opportunities for some elements in Ireland to make moves against the British government. *The Celt* saw the corruption of men like Keogh and Sadleir as the beginning of the end of the old decencies.[7]

One political issue dominated the early 1850s: land reform through tenant right and the three Fs, fixity of tenure, fair rents and free sale. Repeal was dead. In his address to the electors of Limerick in 1850, Francis William Russell believed that a single policy of repeal for Ireland was 'not within the reach of attainment at least for the present'.[8] Indeed, if repeal was to be the main end of legislation for Ireland, Ireland's energies might be diverted from seeking the successful resolution of other issues of great national importance. The *Limerick Reporter and Tipperary Vindicator*

3 *The Celt*, August 1858.   4 Even in the remotest parts of Ireland, this held true. An Inspector of National Schools in Inishboffin in 1850 saw adults attending school for 'one prominent desire, the desire to learn English.' Quoted Mary Daly 'Literacy and Language Change', in Daly and Dickson, *Origins ...*, p. 155.   5 *The Celt*, July 1857; August 1858.   6 Ibid.   7 In September 1857, *The Celt* believed that there was reason to believe that the middle classes in Ireland were not only losing their nationality but also 'in too many instances, losing the public virtue and the public integrity ...'.   8 *Limerick Reporter and Tipperary Vindicator*, 8 January 1850.

gave a platform to politicians thrashing about seeking policies and solutions which would satisfy all interests. It reprinted a letter from the *Cork Examiner*, written by a Revd Cornelius Corkran, the parish priest of Tracton, and headed 'Suppression of the Repeal Association and the Alliance – Coalition of New Organisation' which advocated a federal solution for Ireland. This new Association aimed to terminate Ireland's 'provincialism and restore her once more to the rank of a nation under the British Crown'.[9] A week later, the paper had turned to tenant right, welcomed Sir William Somerville's Landlord and Tenant Bill and the Ulster tenant right campaigners, whose movement was spreading southwards. A week later again, the paper rejoiced that the issue of tenant right was every day 'more active, zealous and efficient'.[10] In a manner not seen before in Irish politics the press backed the campaign for tenant right. In 1850, at a moment when the county electorate had risen by 125 per cent with the extension of the franchise to tenant farmers, the Tenant League's dependence on newspaper support and coverage critical became critical.[11] Newspaper owners who espoused the cause seized the opportunity to influence voters and tried to bring about, by varying means, a united Irish parliamentary party backing a single cause.

Gavan Duffy had perceived that the need was for an Irish party with a single issue of land reform as its main platform – the success of the single-issue Anti-Corn Law League was still very recent – and to him this meant persuading Members of Parliament who had party commitments elsewhere to come over in support. As Comerford points out, this decision meant contested elections, which in turn meant extensive propaganda in meetings and petitions.[12] In his study of the Tenant League, J.H. Whyte cites newspapers as his most important source material, because of the party's open proceedings in the eighteen-fifties and because several of its most important decisions were taken at conferences organised and reported by newspaper proprietors.[13] At stake were issues of common experience and public concern and the role of the press in keeping tenants informed on the progress of the campaign was crucial. Clark and Donnelly make the point that 'The League challenged the idea that the relationship between landlord and tenant was a strictly private affair.'[14]

The 1852 conference which founded the Tenant League was organised by newspaper owners: John Gray of the *Freeman's Journal*, Gavan Duffy of *The Nation*, and Frederick Lucas of *The Tablet*. John Francis Maguire of the *Cork Examiner* and James M'Knight of the *Banner of Ulster* were strong supporters. John Francis Maguire was a product of the mid-century Irish middle class. Born in 1815, the son of a Cork merchant, he was called to the Bar and founded the *Cork Examiner* in

9 29 January 1850.   10 8 February and 12 February 1850.   11 R.V. Comerford, 'Churchmen, tenants, and independent opposition 1850–1856' in *New History of Ireland*, v, p. 400, fn 1.   12 Ibid., p. 400. 13 J.H. Whyte, *The Independent Irish Party 1850–9* (Oxford, 1958), p. 187.   14 Introduction to Part III 'Changing Lines of Cleavage and Cohesion' in Samuel Clark and James S. Donnelly (eds), *Irish peasants: Violence & political unrest* (Dublin, 1983), p. 273.

1840. A close friend of Father Mathew (he wrote his biography), Maguire was later credited with the introduction of linen manufacture to Cork and building the Cork Spinning Mill with 1200 spindles.[15] The entry for the *Cork Examiner* in the 1851 *Newspaper Press Directory* encapsulates the change that had taken place in the politics of the paper after the death of O'Connell. Although in 1851, the paper said that it had backed repeal, it also said that it was 'now the advocate of the "Tenant Right League" and lends its warmest support to the advance of Irish agriculture, Irish commerce and manufactures.'

Another newspaper owner involved in the movement was James M'Knight,[6] proprietor of two liberal Ulster papers, the *Londonderry Standard* and the *Banner of Ulster* between 1846 and 1876. M'Knight was described by his fellow newspaperman Thomas MacKnight of the *Belfast Northern Whig* as 'one of the greatest authorities on the Ulster land question from the tenants' point of view' and the 'undisputed leader of the radical tendency from 1846 until his death in 1876',[17] M'Knight centred his campaigns on Donegal and in Derry, which before 1872 was the only county in the north to elect a Liberal MP who supported tenant right. M'Knight's argument for tenant right was based on his interpretation of the grants made to the original plantation undertakers, which he said were in trust, and did not make the landlords proprietors. Their tenants had created the estates by reclamation of the land, and their rent was therefore a confiscatory tax. M'Knight's approach to the problems of land reform centred on the 'Three Fs' pressed by the Tenant League. But M'Knight did not see land reform just as a local issue: the extension of a legalised 'Ulster custom' he believed would unite north and south behind the same policies.

The inherent danger to British interests in M'Knight's programme, and consequently its attraction to Irish interests, was precisely because it sought to bring the whole country together behind one cause. Hitherto liberal landlords in Ireland had worked through the Whig party in Britain while building up local supporters and, as Bew and Wright point out, an anti-landlord agitation led by Whigs was most unlikely.[18] Indeed, agrarian agitation of any kind tended to push 'good' liberal landlords into the arms of the Tories.[19] But a new crisis diverted the attention of Irish politicians. The introduction of the Ecclesiastical Titles Bill in 1851 and the formation of the Catholic Defence Association began to divert Irish MPs away from tenant right. Although it formed an alliance with branches of the Tenant League, the Association was based mainly in the south, and thus destroyed the possibility of action in unison with the north. This, and improved agricultural conditions after

15 Obituary of J.F. Maguire, *Freeman's Journal*, 2 November 1872.   16 His name is spelt variously M'Knight, McKnight and MacKnight. The spelling used by T. MacKnight in *Ulster as It Is* (London, 1896) is used here.   17 MacKnight, op. cit., p. 99; Paul Bew and Frank Wright, 'The Agrarian Opposition 1848–1887', in Clark and Donnelly op. cit., p. 194.   18 Bew and Wright, op. cit., p. 197.   19 *Banner of Ulster*, 2 April 1852.

1853, removed the urgency which had earlier propelled the Tenant League and supported James M'Knight's policies. A campaign which was no longer advocating a single issue, and the organisation of the Tenant League with both Catholic and Presbyterian clergymen as its leaders embodied fissiparous tendencies.

Maurice Lenihan, as a veteran of both the repeal movement and Young Ireland, would have been well aware of the difficulty in reconciling such diverse aims, and the unlikelihood of a coalition being formed. By 1852, on the eve of the founding of the Tenant League, the *Limerick Reporter and Tipperary Vindicator* supported 'any and every collateral measure by which the passing of this grand object can be protected'. It worried, however, about the possibility that English liberal politicians who supported tenant right might be diverted away in their parallel advocacy of free trade – the issue of protection threatened the integrity of tenant right.[20] Additionally, the problems raised by the Ecclesiastical Titles Bill and the formation of the Catholic Defence Association were recognised to be unwelcome diversions away from the main issue in Irish politics.[21] Strength of feeling against a liberal party which was not prepared to put Irish land at the head of its programme for reform, hardened in the General Election of that year, when the paper attacked the party as 'unprepared, unarmed, uncombined ... We have had Members of Parliament, but their business is not ours.' The newspaper demanded MPs whose conduct will be 'guaranteed a plighted word as binding as an oath ...'[22] Frederick Lucas was accused by the earl of Shrewsbury of being a communist for advocating the right of the Irish to live on the soil of Ireland and enjoy its benefits. Shrewsbury told Cardinal Wiseman that this was '*their* notion of tenant right – of fixity of tenure'.[23] Facing up to the charge that the policies of the tenant right movement subverted the rights of property, Maurice Lenihan appealed to Irish landlords to take part in the Tenant Right Conference later in the year, which 'will clear away the delusion (by) which the Tenant cause is obscured by the enemies of Tenant Right ... (the) movement is not tainted by communism'. In fact, as Sheridan Gilley points out, the object of the tenant right movement was to make the Irish peasant so satisfied with his lot that he would have no wish to engage in revolutionary movements or emigrate to the slums of England, there to be infected by violent extremism.

The disparate aims of the tenant right movement were highlighted on the eve of the Tenant League conference in September 1852 by M'Knight's *Banner of Ulster*, which believed that the conference was 'not a tenant right, or Tenant League affair, though the leading men connected with the latter will be present – it is a national display in honour of Liberal principles generally ... its importance is consequently far beyond that which belongs to any merely sectional expression of opinion'.[24] By

---

20 23 January 1852. 21 Ibid., 30 January 1852. 22 Ibid., 13 April 1852. 23 Quoted in Sheridan Gilley, 'Frederick Lucas, *The Tablet* and Ireland. A Victorian Forerunner of Liberation Theology' in Stuart Mews (ed.), *Modern Religious Rebels: Presented to John Kent* (London, 1993), pp 73 and 75–6. 24 Op. cit., 10 September 1852.

the time the conference took place, the *Banner of Ulster* saw it as not just the co-operation of north and south in reform of the land law, but as an expression of the changing face of Ireland. After the conference it wrote: 'The Southern deputies who attended on this occasion were actuated by sentiments of intense earnestness – the tenant community in the Southern districts is rapidly disappearing from the face of the earth, so that there is now no time for trifling with the industrial question, unless the rural population is to be exterminated altogether.'[25] What Ulster was teaching tenant right supporters was that the country could and should no longer depend on agriculture as its first industry. M'Knight's views in Belfast coincided with those of J.F. Maguire in Cork – that rapid industrialisation must supervene. A dispossessed and dependent peasantry embodied within it a threat to the economic well-being of both north and south; if that element disappeared or became a lesser threat as a proportion of the whole of Ireland, unity between north and south was more likely, based as it would be on a different, and successful, industrial base.

The newspaper could act as an effective watchdog on the activities of Members of Parliament. Just as the meetings of the Tenant Right conference and the branches of the Tenant League were public, the meetings in the House of Commons were public also, and when Irish MPs deserted the cause in 1856, the *Limerick Reporter and Tipperary Vindicator*, published the voting record of Irish Members of Parliament in thirty divisions, commenting 'The above return ought to convince every friend of Tenant Right who are their true friends and no mistake. The most vehement among the ultra advocates of the question out of Parliament, appear to have taken no part whatever in relation to the cause in the place to which their confiding constituents elected them.'[26]

The year 1856 began with the suicide of John Sadleir and the collapse of the Tipperary Joint Stock Bank, which hit hard the small farmers who read the *Limerick Reporter and Tipperary Vindicator*. In the face of their own financial disaster, their support for the Tenant League disappeared and, at the end of the year, the paper rounded on the League, alleging that from the first it never augured well: 'Suspicion always haunted it like a shadow. It became extreme and impracticable ... Public confidence was withdrawn ... all because men shuddered at the, idea of contact with an association conducted, not to promote Tenant Right, but to victimise individuals who had made themselves obnoxious to a small knot of noisy, self-constituted newspaper leaders, influenced throughout by selfish antipathies and unchristian malevolence.'[27]

Lenihan, the veteran of repeal and friend of Meagher and Doheny, expressed his bitterness that the cause of land reform had failed to unite both politicians and tenants. For those newspaper editors who were interested in nationalist ideals or the

25 *Banner of Ulster*, 10 September and 14 September 1852.   26 25 January 1856.   27 19 February and 14 November 1856.

constitutional reform of the law and institutions, the events of the 1850s were a reminder that both inside and outside Westminster they remained powerless. The failures of the recent past reminded them that within Ireland there was a long way to go to mobilise public opinion behind change and repeated betrayal by their representatives at Westminster were further evidence that they could not look there for reform either. The quest for solutions to these two problems underlay the work done by the Catholic nationalist press during the 1860s and 1870s.

4

Reading rooms and newsrooms

'Went with Grandfather, as is the usual custom, to the Newsroom'
William Johnston of Ballykilbeg.[1]

In her work on attitudes to education in east Ulster, Linda Lunny points out that the very existence of news sheets increased the desire to be able to read.[2] Gavan Duffy believed that the greatest supporters of Young Ireland had been 'the reading men', the tradesmen, clerks, and shopkeepers educated in the reading rooms of the Repeal Association.[3] James Grant had thought that 'No person in this country [England] could have any idea of the denseness of the mental darkness which prevails in Ireland'. Even though there was no way of buying books and no means of doing so, nevertheless 'a taste for reading was now spreading ... among the better class of peasantry'.[4] Increasingly after 1840, people bought books, subscribed to circulating libraries, read newspapers in public houses, listened to others reading newspapers aloud, rented newspapers and went to reading rooms and newsrooms.[5] Thomas Hogg, the secretary of the Leeds Mechanics' Institute told the Select Committee on Newspaper Stamps of the popularity of newspaper reading: 'Certainly ... [at present] there are many of them who prefer to go to a public house, where they can have a sight of the paper ...'. But if the supply were larger at mechanics' institutes they would go there for preference, although one of the advantages of the public house was that readers could 'talk and discuss the subjects of the day, which is not allowable in a public news-room'.[6] William Edward Hickson told the committee that reading newspapers would stimulate reading in general and he regretted that many mechanics' institutes had failed because they had no newsroom. In the north of England, institutes' newsrooms had proved the greatest attraction.[7] He strongly advocated that newspapers should be made available in mechanics' institute newsrooms all over the country. Again, Thomas Hogg gave strong support to this view quoting further evidence on the mechanics' institute reading rooms in the north of

1 18 January 1855, PRONI D.880/2/7. 2 Lunny, in Daly and Dickson, op. cit., p. 105. 3 C. Gavan Duffy, *Young Ireland: A Fragment of Irish History* (London, 1896), p. 175. 4 Grant, op. cit., pp 171–2. 5 In *He Knew He Was Right*, in her exile in Nuncombe Putney, Devon Priscilla Trevelyan rents a newspaper from the landlady of the Stag and Antlers, paying a penny a week for half a day's reading: Anthony Trollope, *He Knew He Was Right* (1869; Penguin edition, 1985), p. 135. 6 QQ 1034, 1036. 7 Evidence to the Select Committee on Newspaper Stamps, HC 1851 558 QQ 3260–5.

England. Nearly all these institutes had newsrooms and were sited near factories; indeed in 'some of the small towns there is no other good room in the place'.[8] He thought that the working classes would attend the institutes in greater numbers if the price of papers were lower and the supply greater. In their discussion the committee took it as axiomatic that reading rooms and newsrooms were to be found in towns for skilled workers.

The impulses of redemption and renewal already seen were part of pressure from landlords and employers for better education and better understanding by their tenants and workers. Lord Roden founded a library for his tenants at Bryansford in 1836, believing that it would be 'spiritually uplifting'; Murlands founded a library and reading society at Annsborough in 1865, and the Hillsborough Linen Company established reading and recreation rooms for its employees in 1888.[9] In the 1830s and 1840s, newsrooms had accounted for two-thirds of the business of a retail newsagent in Dundalk.[10]

In his history of the teetotal movement, Brian Harrison has pointed out the numbers of prominent teetotalers in Britain who also involved themselves in mechanics' institutes, Sunday schools, educational voluntarism, ragged schools, a free press, and public libraries.[11] When James Grant attributed the growing taste for reading in Ireland to the prevalence of teetotal principles,[12] he was only part right. Self-improvement for patriotic reasons was also a major factor. The repeal movement enrolment certificate stated that 'Our first principle is to preserve and increase the VIRTUE of the people.'[13] The repeal movement saw the programme of the temperance movement as a model to influence potential supporters through reading and debate. In 1844 the repeal Association adopted rules for the establishment of repeal reading rooms which were to 'afford a source of rational occupation for the leisure hours of the industrious classes, where they may be instigated to increased patriotism, temperance, and virtue'.[14]

Father Mathew was thus a guiding light and model for change. A contemporary observer of his work defined it as wider than temperance alone: 'His object in establishing the temperance rooms was to afford the teetotals a place of meeting for the purpose of weaning them from a public house, supplying them with good books ... [this] ... had been accomplished in many parts of the country that had at this moment libraries in which were to be found the Sacred Bible, historical and geographical works and works of all kinds for the improvement of the operative.'[15] At the

8 Ibid. QQ 1029–31.   9 J.R.R. Adams, *The Printed Word and the Common Man: Popular Culture in Ulster 1700–1900* (Belfast, 1987), pp 128, 39.   10 L.M. Cullen, 'Establishing a Communications System; News, Post and Transport', in Brian Farrell (ed.), *Communications and Community in Ireland* (Dublin, 1984), p. 22.   11 Brian Harrison, *Drink and the Victorians* (London, 1971), pp 111, 112 and 174.   12 Grant, op. cit., pp 250–1.   13 Quoted in H.F. Kearney, 'Father Mathew: Apostle of Modernisation' in Art Cosgrave and Donal McCarthy (eds), *Studies in Irish History presented to R. Dudley Edwards* (Dublin, 1979), p. 166. Kearney describes the active Mathewite as middle class.   14 Margaret Barnes, 'Repeal Reading Rooms', *An Leabharlann*, 23, no. 2 (1965) p. 55.   15 Kearney, in Cosgrave and McCarthy, p. 167.

height of the temperance and repeal movements, teetotal journalists founded papers. John Francis Maguire started the *Cork Examiner* in 1840 as a teetotal newspaper; Maurice Lenihan, after working with Maguire, himself became a teetotaller. As a corollary to their work for the closure of public houses, the temperance movement in the first half of the century encouraged the opening of mechanics' institutes, libraries and reading rooms, and the reduction of duties on reading material. 'Respectable' members of society in various towns established reading rooms which in their turn made the provincial press more generally available. Literacy – in English – was one of the aims of the movement. In its prospectus, the *Cork Examiner* claimed to be read in 'various reading rooms throughout Ireland and to some extent in Manchester and other English towns'.[16] After Father Mathew's death, commitment to self-improvement through reading rooms continued in many of the towns where his influence had been strongest. James Grant had described Cork as 'an intellectual place. Its inhabitants are a reading people'.[17] Cork, Limerick, Clonmel, Kilkenny and Ennis, which had founded reading rooms through the Repeal Association,[18] were among the first to found public libraries. When newspaper stamps were abolished in 1855, in the same year towns were allowed to charge a 1*d.* rate to found libraries; in October 1855 a meeting in Ennis resolved to levy a halfpenny rate to have a library and £356. 2*s.* was subscribed. A meeting of Cork ratepayers resolved unanimously to establish a school of design by levying a halfpenny rate. With a free library of 250 volumes on art, the school opened in January 1856 to 170 students 'chiefly of a mechanic class'.[19]

The Repeal Association Committee noted that just as the temperance movement had opened up an opportunity to recruit members to their cause, the establishment of reading rooms encouraged patriotism. In Cashel, Co. Tipperary, card-playing was said to have been entirely given up, dance houses were less frequented in Trim, Co. Meath, and examinations in history and general sciences ... are sufficient proof that useful studies are preferred to all the inducement of the public houses'.[20] The Association optimistically decided that reading rooms should be opened in districts where there were 2,000 enrolled repealers who regularly subscribed 1*s.* each, and £1 6*s.* 0*d.* a year was to be allowed for newspapers which were to be filed for future reference. By 1845, the Association had opened 71 reading rooms; by the end of 1845 there were 85 in operation.[21] The hopes of temperance supporters were confirmed when it seemed that the attraction of reading rooms had proved greater than the attractions of drink.

The paucity of surviving records of mid-century mechanics' and literary institutes in Ireland gives a misleading idea of the numbers of reading and news-rooms

16 *Newspaper Press Directory*, 1851.   17 Grant, op. cit., p. 9.   18 Kearney, in Cosgrave and McCarthy, pp 171 and 172.   19 Return from Ennis, Cork and Limerick in Ireland, as to the Establishment or Rejecting of Public Libraries, Museums or Schools of Art, HC 1856 (221.I) LIX, 367.   20 Margaret Barnes, op. cit. p. 55.   21 Ibid., p. 54.

at the height of their activity in the mid-century. From the available evidence, it would appear that, in the 1850s at least, their number was considerable. The *Belfast Daily Mercury*, edited by James Simms (a former editor of the *Belfast Northern Whig*), became in 1857 the first provincial daily paper in Ireland. By 1859 it was read in 23 reading rooms and newsrooms in Ulster:

Table 7: *Reading rooms and newsrooms supplied by the* Belfast Daily Mercury *in 1859*

Ballymena	Newsroom
Ballymacnutt	Newsroom
Belfast	Broomfield newsroom
	Commercial newsroom
	Journeyman Tailors' Association newsroom
	Newsroom
	People's newsroom
	Presbyterian Young Men's Association
	Queen's College newsroom
	Ulster Club
	Young Men's Christian Association
Dundalk	Guildhall newsroom
	Chamber of Commerce
Dungannon	Newsroom
Gilford Mill	Reading Room
Lisburn	Conservative Newsroom
	Newsroom
Londonderry	Library Association
	Newsroom
	Victoria Exchange Newsroom
Lurgan	Mechanics' Institute
Newry	Commercial Coffee Room
Stewartstown	Newsroom

Source: Audited accounts Ulster Printing Co. Ltd (PRONI D.2450/3/4 ff 1-30)

Reading rooms and newsrooms were a congenial daily meeting place for town workers interested in current affairs, but they were not provided free. Subscribers paid one subscription to the library and another separate one for the use of the newsroom. The Belfast People's Reading Room and Library, founded in 1845, charged 2*s*. 6*d*. a quarter to the 'Working Classes' and 4*s*. a quarter to all other readers.[22] The Belfast Mechanics' Institute opened in 1825, 'to promote the knowl-

22 *The Belfast and the Province of Ulster Directory, 1863–1864* (Belfast, 1863).

edge of the arts and sciences; to found a Library; to establish and support lectures on subjects useful to the working classes of the community'. Readers paid a subscription of 12s. a year to use the library, reduced in 1865 to 6s.[23] The directors of the Belfast Mechanics' Institute in 1865 included two engineers, a machinist, an engraver, a printer and a lithographer.[24] The objective of the constitution and laws of the Belfast Mechanics' Institute was to instruct mechanics 'in the scientific principles of the arts which they practise'. The Belfast People's Reading Room and Library had lectures 'by several eminent gentlemen', and proceeds from the lectures were used to improve the library.[25] Although the Institute excluded books of 'religious controversy, or party politics, of an immoral character or impugning the Christian religion', there was no reference to excluding newspapers.

In the 1840s parts of Ireland saw the influence of the press on the working class suspicious. One example of a town where newspapers were regarded by some as a manifestation of immorality was Clonmel. The Clonmel Mechanics Institute was founded in 1842 by principal townspeople to improve the commercial life of the town, to benefit both employer and worker alike and to supplement workers' skills. Like so many other institutions, it also hoped to rescue Clonmel workers from drink. In 1843 it had 211 members, increasing to 367 by 1867.[26] Publicity for the Institute in the *Tipperary Free Press* in January 1842 emphasised the need for political neutrality. It forbade books or discussions of a religious and political kind, and the Rules and Regulations of 1845 stated that 'Newspapers and works of an acknowledged Theological or Political character or such as have an immoral tendency [were] not to be taken into the Rooms, or received as donations'.[27]

Five years later, however, the same newspaper began advocating a programme of reform for the Institute which included the provision of newspapers in the library. In a swingeing attack on what it saw as the incompetent and self-serving management committee, the paper printed an 'Address to the Inhabitants of Clonmel'. It drew attention to the decrease in membership – 415 members in 1845 had reduced to 241 in 1846 and 194 in 1847, and of the present 194 members, 90 were found to object to the way the Institute was run by a nine-member committee in 'a manner ... that would do no discredit to Russian despotism and intelligence'. In the past year, the committee had only spent £8 12s. 6d. on 'Literature and Science works'. The article continued sarcastically:

> Rule 12 states that the Institute is exclusively devoted to the diffusion of Scientific Information, including of course such Works on Science as 'Paul Clifford',

23 Belfast Mechanics' Institute and the Belfast Working Men's Institute Correspondence, rules and agreements concerning amalgamation with the Belfast People's Reading Room: PRONI D1769/24/2. 24 Constitution and laws of the Belfast Mechanics' Institute: PRONI D.1769/24/2. 25 *The Belfast and the Province of Ulster Directory for 1863–1864*. 26 Byrne, 'Mechanics' Institutes in Ireland before 1855', p. 174. 27 Ibid., p. 392.

'Jack Hinton', 'Sorrows of Werther', 'Hadjii Baba' and 'Tristram Shandy' ... Yet this despotic Committee ... cannot see any connection between the Newspaper Literature of the day and such works as the following: Allison's Political History of Europe, Drapier's Letters, Junius, Irish Parliamentary Debates, Edinburgh Review, Quarterly Review, Dublin Review, Letters to the Morning Herald. In a word, the multitudinous array of History that crowds their Library, and which any man either of intelligence or impartiality will at once admit to be neither more nor less than the Newspaper Literature of the 'olden Times', abridged, analyzed, and carefully preserved for the instruction and benefit of posterity ... we give [these examples] as an illustration of the consistency of the Committee which excludes the Press while it admits Political Literature ... while the Wealthy may indulge either at the Club or the Newsroom in all the variety of information which the press of Europe can afford, the Mechanic is not in his humble hall, to dare to cast an eye over those papers, which day after day first chronicle the triumphs of science and art.

The paper criticised the reading room of the Institute as being 'cold and cheerless'. It demanded the admission of 'the Press' into the reading room, on condition that each subscriber who paid 5s. (to be reduced from 10s.) subscription to the Institute Library should pay an extra 1s. 3d. half yearly in advance to be 'exclusively devoted to the purchase of Newspapers'.[28] In 1848 there was increasing pressure at the Annual General Meeting for the Institute to introduce newspapers. The Revd Mr Orr urged the meeting 'to keep pace with the liberality and enlightenment of the times by admitting the newspaper press from which so much literary and scientific information was to be obtained'. His opponents expressed fears that, should newspapers be introduced, the Institute would lose money, and they alleged that the introduction of newspapers had been the cause of the decline of the Cork Mechanics' Institute.[29] By 1867, the political and social barriers had been broken down, and newspapers had been made available. The Annual Report noted that the Institute subscribed to the *London Times*, the *Irish Times*, the *Freeman's Journal*, the *Cork Examiner*, the *Tipperary Free Press*, and the *Clonmel Chronicle*.[30]

But there were problems. Writing of the public library movement, Altick has noted an inconsistency between contemporary views of the working population as a rabble and their concurrent desire for intellectual improvement. Reading rooms were seen as dangerous; it was 'not healthy' for working men to have to go to public places to read newspapers, where 'discussion could so easily get out of hand'.[31] If this were perceived in England in the 1850s it was doubly so in Ireland. When Resident Magistrates sent reports of unrest to Dublin Castle, these were supported

28 Byrne, p. 193 and *Tipperary Free Press*, 18 December, 1847. 29 *Tipperary Free Press*, 18 January 1848. 30 Byrne, p. 193. 31 R.D. Altick, *The English Common Reader* (Chicago, 1957), p. 331.

with copies of seditious ballads, threatening letters and newspapers. Maura Murphy's work[32] on Dublin Castle's view of the seditious ballad is based on material sent to the Castle between 1801 and 1881 by RMs and police, and these reports echo the views also expressed on the influence of the provincial press, and the rise and fall in the level of their concern is the same.[33] When the repeal reading rooms were closed by the authorities in 1849, there were protests that patrons had in consequence transferred their custom to the public houses, but the reasons that led to their closure were rooted in the governing class's fear of the effects of education on the peasants. A Resident Magistrate in Cork complained that the suppression of the press had had 'The happiest results ... [the peoples'] imagination being no longer deceived by delusive expectations (and seductive and poisonous doctrine).' However, he went on to draw attention to the social problems that had subsequently arisen:

> Habits of drunkenness having set in amongst some of the artisans, who heretofore spent their time in the newsroom instead of the Public House ... I have been applied to by the Roman Catholic clergyman to enquire if I would be opposed to his getting up a newsroom to be open to the Police and authorities. I told him I was for the present opposed to reading rooms among the lower orders. When I gave him my reasons he did not press the matter.[34]

A Resident Magistrate in Limerick welcomed the suppression of *The Nation* and *The Irishman* 'and such publications ... It is impossible to overestimate the injury inflicted upon a mercurial People by these inflammatory and seditious essays. Their circulation in this City and County was enormous'. His colleague in Thurles, Co. Tipperary echoed him on 'those poisonous publications [which] were read at all the Public Houses, and cheap reading rooms on Sunday'.[35] The anxieties expressed by Resident Magistrates in 1848 which had induced the punitive measures taken against reading rooms had receded by the 1850s, and until the mid-1860s, government was less willing to intervene in freedom of expression in Ireland, or did not publicly see the need to do so.

In 1848, Lord Clarendon (Lord-Lieutenant 1847–52) had attempted to support a loyalist newspaper to deal with the influence of both the Tory and nationalist press but with disastrous results to himself personally and to the credibility of the government. Noting that that there was no unionist or loyalist paper to counteract 'the diatribes of The Nation and other seditious prints', he had decided, with the advice

32 Maura Murphy, 'The Ballad Singer and the role of the Seditious Ballad in Nineteenth-Century Ireland: Dublin Castle's View', *Ulster Folklife*, 25 (1979); K.T. Hoppen, *Elections, Politics and Society in Ireland 1855–1885* (Oxford, 1984), pp 424–9. 33 Murphy, op. cit., p. 80. There was a high level of concern between 1829 and 1848; between 1865 and 1879 and, in the case of the press, in the 1880s. 34 PRO CO 904/9 1849 Confidential report on the state of the lately disturbed districts. 35 Ibid.

of his Chief Secretary Sir William Somerville, to secure an editor for a journal which would be modestly subsidised by the government. Unfortunately 'in an evil moment' he chose a journalist who had served six months in prison for blackmail. The upshot was that the editor (Birch of *The World*) extracted vast sums of money from Clarendon himself and from the secret service fund, allegedly to pay agents in country towns and then to pay himself.[36]

Was there any justification for the belief, both before and after the rebellion of 1848, that there was a link between learning to read and an involvement in nationalist movements? In Trollope's *The Macdermots of Ballycloran*, written in 1847, the heroine, Feemy Macdermot, read romantic fiction: 'she was addicted to novels, when she could get them from the dirty little circulating library at Mohill ...'[37] Her priest, Father John McGrath, read Charles Lever, Charles Dickens and the fathers of the Church. St Omer-educated and of 'good family', Father John represents the older generation of Irish priests. Trollope conveys that he was moderate in politics, a gentleman and well-educated, and he is contrasted with his curate, Father Cullen, who is Maynooth-educated, son of a 'little farmer' and a man of 'violent politics'. The association of the 'little farmer' with 'violent politics' underlines the popular association between a lack of education and extremism, that side of the Irish propaganda coin, where stupidity is linked with violence. While Father Cullen supported repeal, he was 'perfectly illiterate'.[38] Emmet Larkin makes the point that the devotional revolution after the Famine 'satisfied more than the negative factors of guilt and fear'; fears of a loss of Irish identity came to mean that to be Irish was to be Roman Catholic,[39] and this led the younger Maynooth-educated priests of the 1850s to a deeper involvement in local politics than their seniors.

Thus, the developing 'taste for reading' noted by James Grant particularly favoured the history and present condition of Ireland. Grant observed that those who could not read assembled to hear the repeal press read aloud. In Cork and Kerry, Grant noticed that in the repeal reading rooms 'the most zealous repeal papers' were regularly read to listening groups of illiterate men; in the country, peasants assembled on Sunday afternoons (in the summer out in the open air and in the winter in the school-room) to hear the weekly repeal papers. 'The persons so in-

36 Herbert Maxwell, *The Life and Letters of George William Frederick Fourth Earl of Clarendon* (London, 1913), pp 316–17. In 1850 Birch sent Clarendon a bill for £4700 for 'suppressing the Irish rebellion' and, despite Clarendon attempting to hush the matter up by paying Birch further money out of his own pocket, Birch took the Chief Secretary to court and Clarendon was forced to admit his involvement in the affair.   37 Anthony Trollope, *The Macdermots of Ballycloran* (1847; Oxford, 1989), p. 122. Feemy Macdermot's taste in literature was similar to the contents of the Clonmel Mechanics' Institute anathematised by the *Tipperary Free Press* and the romantic fiction published by the local newspapers. The book she had borrowed from the Mohill circulating library was 'The Mysterious Assassin' which Robert Tracy, the editor of the Oxford edition locates as possibly Isaac Crookenden's *The Mysterious Murderer, or, the Usurper of Naples, to which is prefaced the Nocturnal Assassin, or Spanish Jealousy* (London, 1806).   38 *The Macdermots of Ballycloran*, p. 44.   39 Larkin, (1972), p. 649.

structed repeat ... the principal points of what they have heard. In this way the
peasantry of Ireland are systematically instructed in the principles of repeal; and
hence the amazing progress which that question has made'.[40] This passion for listening to the printed word was reflected in Irish nineteenth-century genre paint-
ing: Howard Helmick's 'News of the Land League', Erskine Nicholl's 'The Ryans
and Dwyers, Calumniated Men' and Charles Lamb's 'Spreading the News' are three
paintings of groups of peasants reading or listening to newspapers being read. To
the neurotic Resident Magistrate, watchful for every nuance of social change and
political involvement, it is perhaps not surprising that there was a strong reaction
against such organised self-improvement.

The politically-involved clergy were therefore working on a field already tilled.
When Dr Croke of Cashel founded the Charleville Reading Society in 1850, he
spoke of his motives in a speech which makes the link between popular education
and nationalism crystal clear:

> I was not actuated alone by motives of a local character; I had, moreover, in view
> the general interests of our country. I felt convinced that agitation in one shape
> or another would be practised here until the great bulk of the people ceased to be
> discontented ... no system of agitation can succeed, except by mere accident,
> amongst a people ignorant of their duties, and almost heedless of their rights as
> citizens ... That a system of popular education with a view to the improvement
> of our national character might well be looked upon as the most powerful auxil-
> iary to a national movement and that all who are solicitous about the success of
> the movement should labour to impress upon the people a due sense of their
> weight and importance in the State ... I founded this Society to be sure for edu-
> cational purposes but I confess, with the ulterior design of helping on, in due
> season that great national struggle, on the success of which the peace as well as
> the prosperity of this island most palpably depends.[41]

By the mid-1850s, the influence of temperance as a motor for self-improvement
seems to have declined, but the reading rooms continued. Dr John Forbes, travelling in Ireland in 1852, noted that although the adherence to teetotal principles had
diminished, the habit of reading in the rooms founded by the movement was surviving. In Killarney he saw that members of the Temperance Hall assembled every
evening to read the newspapers and books from a library of nearly 400 volumes.
Despite the fact that membership of the movement in Tralee had sunk from nearly
600 to about 60, there was a Temperance Hall with 40 members which took five
newspapers. The Temperance Hall in Limerick had 300 members and a library
which took newspapers, but cautiously they did not 'admit any discussion or dis-

40 Grant (1844), pp 200–1.   41 *Limerick and Clare Examiner*, 11 September 1850.

putes on politics'. While the Temperance Hall in Athlone was in debt, in Killarney there were three halls where the members assembled every evening.[42]

The minute books of the Kilkenny Circulating-Library Society give some insight into the working of a literary institute and its committee and how a newsroom was run. The Society was founded in 1811 by 'a number of gentlemen': including the proprietor of the *Kilkenny Moderator*, the headmaster of Kilkenny College, and John Prim, general printer and stationer and father of John Prim the antiquarian.[43] It survived for a hundred years, until the establishment of the Carnegie County Library in 1910. At its beginning the Society seems have been a literary institution with a library which stocked novels and instructive works. Their alphabetical catalogue, which has no date but was probably written in the 1830s, has many of Sir Walter Scott's novels. The Society was run by shareholders, called Proprietors, and the funds were supplemented by a local Kilkenny charity, the Evans Trust. The political sympathies of the Proprietors before 1850 varied from the conservative Abraham Denroche of the *Kilkenny Moderator*, to the repeal politics of Cornelius Maxwell at the *Kilkenny Journal*. Its chairman for many years was Dr Robert Cane of *The Celt*. Cane's political makeup was eclectic: he was a catholic nationalist married to a Protestant and his patients were the Protestant gentry. As a repealer he remained on good terms with Young Ireland. *The Celt* commissioned articles from influential nationalist figures like C.J. Kickham and William Kenealy.[44]

In 1844, there seems to have been some concern about the condition of the Society, and Cornelius Maxwell moved to restore it 'in conformity to the spirit of its original foundation'. There was pressure to move the reading room from its original site in the Coal Market to the Tholsel, which was more central and 'where it could be conducted in a more respectable manner and on a more extended scale of utility'. It seems also to have declined in quality, and was used as a newsroom rather than as a circulating library. Robert Cane clearly felt that a newsroom did not provide the breadth of knowledge and culture necessary to a city of Kilkenny's size and importance. He wrote to the Library Committee: 'I feel deeply anxious upon the subject … as a citizen anxious to see Kilkenny's only Literary institution restored – to see its present mere Newsroom reorganised as a Library and book institution – to make it an instrument of the further spread of knowledge in a City … since that period [twenty years ago] it has been nearly valueless – certainly valueless as a library, and used only as a newsroom.'[45] But by 1846 the Society seems to have regained its self-confidence, and like the Clonmel Mechanics' Institute it considered reducing its subscription. The popular appeal of newspapers reading was gaining ground:

The News-Room of the Institution is now in such an improved state as coupled with its abundant supply of newspapers and periodicals will it is hoped produce

42 John Forbes, *Memorandum made in Ireland in the Autumn of 1852* (London, 1853). 43 Kilkenny Library Society Minutes, book 1, 6 April 1811. 44 Comerford (1985), p. 44. 45 Minutes of the Kil-

an increased number of yearly subscribers. Should the late improvements in the News-Room fail of producing this favourable result the Committee feel no doubt that the proprietors will see the wisdom of further assisting in its accomplishment by lowering the yearly subscription to a standard commensurate with the demand of the time for cheap information ... We are sure it is [the Proprietors'] wish to diffuse the taste and advantages of reading as widely as possible.[46]

By 1869, the opening hours were from 8 a.m. to 10 p.m., those most convenient for working men. The minutes of the Society increasingly refer to the newspaper and periodical press, rather than to their purchase of books, and it seems possible that the main reason for this dependence on newspapers may have been because of a continued shortage of money.

For the cost of running a reading room was not cheap. Thomas Hogg, the secretary of mechanics' institutes in Leeds, told the Select Committee on Newspaper Stamps in 1851 of the problems faced by institute newsrooms: in small towns they had 'the greatest difficulty in getting a good supply. They have to beg from all the friends of the institution to give them a secondhand copy of *The Times* [and other papers] ... their own funds being too low to buy them at cost price, and at first hand'. Some institutes, he said, bought papers a day old or had two newsrooms, one expensive for the day's papers and the other cheaper for the papers of the day before.[47] In Kilkenny, Cornelius Maxwell supplied newspapers free to the Circulating Library Society in return for two subscriptions, one in the name of his editor.[48] The Marquis of Ormonde and the county Members of Parliament were asked to donate parliamentary papers.[49] Weekly papers remained in the newsroom for two days and all other papers for a day only, and they were then sent to those people who had bought particular titles at an annual auction the previous year. This was advertised in the local press and on placards.[50] Selling back-numbers of newspapers was a valuable addition to the Society's funds; the sale of a year's supply of eleven papers in 1850 raised £17 11s. 6d.[51]

When newspaper tax was abolished in 1855, existing financial difficulties increased as, although the cover price of a single copy was less, some popular newspapers were published more frequently. In 1857 the *Belfast Northern Whig* began to come out three times a week at 1d. a copy. While its cover price had been reduced, its annual cost rose from 12s. 6d. to 16s. od. By 1858, the Kilkenny Proprietors found that the *Northern Whig* was 'of no practical utility to the Society and was scarcely ever read in the Rooms'. The propriety of substituting '*The Ulsterman* ... was dis-

kenny Circulating-Library Society, 1 November 1844, 17 December 1844 and 3 February 1845.   **46** Minutes, 30 March 1846.   **47** Loc. cit., QQ. 1031 and 1059.   **48** Minutes, 28 September and 4 December 1854.   **49** Minutes, 3 March 1845 and 31 July 1845.   **50** Minute, 30 September 1850, and advertisement in *Kilkenny Journal*, 5 October 1850.   **51** *Kilkenny Journal* advertisement, loc. cit.
52 Minute, 2 March 1858.   **53** Minute, 13 December 1847 and 18 March 1848.

cussed [and] it was finally Resolved unanimously that the *Northern Whig* be discontinued and *The Ulsterman* ordered'.[52] This change from the liberal *Belfast Northern Whig* to radical nationalist *Ulsterman* was a straw in the wind. The proprietor of *The Ulsterman*, Denis Holland, had taken part in the 1849 rising and worked on *The Irishman*, another radical paper. Holland then became involved in the National Brotherhood of St Patrick and later ran the *Galway American*.

The numbers and titles of newspapers seem to vary according to funds available and geographical location, and to political persuasion. In October 1845 the newsroom took 15 papers: the *Sunday Times, Chronicle, Tablet, Mark Lane Express*, the daily *Freeman's Journal*, the *Mail, Post, Pilot, Packet, Cork Southern Reporter, Waterford Chronicle, Waterford Day Note, The Nation*, the *Farmer's Gazette*, and the *Illustrated London News*. In 1847 they resolved to take 'the Kilkenny Papers', and the *Times, Tablet, Illustrated London News*, daily *Freeman, Evening Mail, Evening Post, Pilot* and *The Nation*, but no magazines or reviews. This decision to have a majority of London and Dublin papers and no magazines seems to have caused protests, and in December 1847 the Proprietors had a special meeting to discuss the choice of newspaper subscriptions, and they decided to take 'only one London paper' in addition to the *Times*, together with the *Liverpool Mercury*, the *Evening Packet, Cork Reporter, Punch* and the *Mark Lane Express*. The extra London paper was the liberal *Morning Chronicle*. Their papers were in the main politically unexceptionable, tending toward liberal politics, a tendency which continued; there is a whiff of controversy when a move in 1848 to take John Mitchel's *United Irishman* was dealt with by assigning the proposer, the Revd Mr O'Flynn, to be personally responsible for the cost.[53]

The sense that Kilkenny wished to keep itself at a slight distance from metropolitan affairs was continued in 1856, when the Society again debated the papers to be ordered for the succeeding year, and they decided on a Liverpool paper, a Waterford paper, and a Limerick paper and were divided on whether to take a Dublin weekly paper. The weekly *Nation* was decided upon instead of the *Telegraph*; the liberal *Waterford News* in preference to the conservative *Waterford Mail*, and the neutral *Limerick Chronicle*. The Society's members reading tastes tended to be liberal (though some conservative journals were taken), to be constitutional, to be educated. They read the *Quarterly Review*, the *Edinburgh Review, Household Words*, the *Dublin University Magazine, Blackwoods* and *Fraser's Magazine*. In 1847 they subscribed to *Punch*, but by 1856 they had stopped it, again a move away from London. Another indication of a change in political temper was in 1861, when the Proprietors of the Society resolved to buy 'works having reference to Kilkenny' either through their authors or their subjects, such as Dr Robert Cane's *Williamite Wars*, the *Transactions* of the Kilkenny Archaeological Society and John Banim's works. (John and

54 Minute, 10 September 1859.   55 Mary Kenealy, 'Finn's Leinster Journal', *Old Kilkenny Review*

Michael Banim had been born in Kilkenny.) Irish politics and Irish history began to dominate the Society, with subscriptions taken out to the Irish Archaelogical and Celtic Societies and to the Ossianic Society. Many books were sold, including all the Scott bought in the 1820s and 1830s and topographical guides to English counties. One reason for this realignment may have been in part that William Kenealy had become the editor of the *Kilkenny Journal* in 1857, and by September 1859 he was a Proprietor of the Society.[54] When Kenealy had worked on the short-lived *Tipperary Leader* he had been gaoled for libel. He applied from gaol to be editor of the *Kilkenny Journal* in competition with Charles Kickham. Either because of his earlier connection with Dr Cane's *The Celt* or because he had married the daughter of the proprietor, Kenealy was successful.[55]

Reading rooms and news rooms were popular until the end of the century. Ports like Belfast continued to have newsrooms for sailors who were unable to read newspapers regularly. In 1877, the Belfast Sailors' Institute and Workmen's Reading Rooms in Dock Street had a circulating library and reading room 'liberally supplied with newspapers and periodicals'.[56] As Table 9 has shown, 4.49 per cent of the subscribers to the *Belfast Daily Mercury* in 1859 were newsrooms. The abolition of the newspaper stamp and the creation of the 1*d.* press may well have influenced a move towards individual subscriptions, but not necessarily towards the daily purchase of a newspaper on the street; as Cullen points out, casual news sales in Ireland lagged behind England, and most newspapers were still sold on the basis of quarterly or half-yearly subscriptions. National papers were distributed by wholesalers and sold through newsagents and newsvendors located in large towns, who dealt mainly with the national press, but the local press was still sold direct by the proprietor.[57] Throughout the whole century, however, the combined influence both of a cheaper press and improved communications worked to widen both the numbers of subscriptions and individual copies bought.

The ideals of the moral nation remained, even if in the three decades after 1860 they were increasingly submerged by nationalist politics. A series of letters in *The Nation* in 1876 revived the link between temperance, nationalism and the provision of reading rooms. Among these, a writer from Killucan, Co. Westmeath advocated reading rooms as a 'source of instruction to Irish youth who are not versed in their country's history; and secondly it would tend to further the National cause by infusing a patriotic ardour'. This theme was taken up by another reader from Kells who regretted the incidence of drunkenness among young men in the town, and who believed that 'The establishment of popular reading rooms would improve the education of our people, foster and strengthen their patriotism'.[58]

The writers of these letters subscribed to the same values as Dr Croke. In his

new series 1, no. 5 (1979).   **56** *The Belfast and Province of Ulster Directory for 1877.*   **57** Cullen (1984), pp 23 and 27.   **58** *The Nation*, 12 August and 2 September 1876.

speech founding the Charleville Reading Society, Croke made the necessary cross-over between the purposes which lay behind post-Famine morality and the development of nationalism when he referred to the 'improvement of our national character' as an 'auxiliary to a national movement'. These ideals underlay the philosophy of those who ran the press from the late 1860s up to the eve of the Land War.

5

The emergent nation, 1866–79

> The minds of the Irish people are in the hands of the Irish priests. They
> have a platform where no other voice is heard. They have a press which
> supports their views. Their newspapers are extensively read, & the people
> read no other ... the clergy [are] the intermediate class between the gentry
> and the people.[1]

In November 1861, William Kenealy of the *Kilkenny Journal*, Peter Gill of the *Tipperary Advocate*, and Martin O'Brennan of the *Connaught Patriot*, followed the cortége of the Young Irelander, Terence Bellew McManus, to his second funeral in Dublin.[2] Ten years later, in April 1872, five Galway newspaper proprietors, John McPhilpin and Edward Byrne of the *Tuam News*, Richard Kelly of the *Tuam Herald*, Lewis Ferdinand of the *Galway Vindicator* and John St. George Joyce of the *Galway Express*, were summoned to appear before the Galway County election petition hearing to give evidence about their papers' alleged involvement in corruption. The network of relationships which developed between nationalist proprietors is characteristic of the 1860s and 1870s. The new men who entered provincial journalism after 1860 came with the fixed purpose of having a voice in politics. This was expressed, not just through their newspapers, but through their own presence at important events. John McPhilpin told the Galway County election petition hearing that he had attended every meeting held by Captain Nolan, the Home Rule candidate, not for the purpose of recording the meeting (that was done by his editor, Edward Byrne) but to watch the proceedings: to see and be seen.[3] Growing numbers of nationalists saw journalism as a respectable way to live because, unlike landowning or shopkeeping, it did not depend on exploiting others and unlike law, it could not be not seen as supporting the government.

Benedict Anderson's perceptive analysis of the development of nationalism touches both on the growing links forged between the writers of nationalist ideas and nationalist images and on their readers.[4] Anderson speaks of the 'deep horizon-

---

1 Moriarty to William Monsell MP, 2 March 1868, in J.H. Whyte 'Select Documents: Bishop Moriarty on Disestablishment and the Union 1868' in *Irish Historical Studies*, 18 (1956–7), p. 195.   2 McManus, who had been transported to Tasmania after his part in the 1848 rebellion, escaped to San Francisco where he died in 1860.   3 Evidence of John McPhilpin, QQ6944, 6968–72; evidence of Edward Byrne, Q7200.   4 Benedict Anderson, *Imagined Communities* (London, 1983), p. 9.

tal comradeship' among nationalists, who worked to create their 'imagined political community'. He quotes Ernest Gellner's theory that nationalist propaganda was not so much the arousing of the consciousness of nationhood, but rather the 'invention of a nation'.[5] This section examines the contribution of particular newspaper proprietors to this work. Anderson goes on to define the intellectual and social development of the readers of newspapers who, observing other people reading the same paper, were 'continually reassured that the imaginary world is visibly rooted in everyday life'.[6] This is an important insight into the exchange between the publisher and the reader of newspapers. In Ireland, 'print-capitalism' (Anderson's phrase) played a vital role in both spreading and fixing the idea of the nation. In nineteenth-century Ireland, the invention of a Gaelic nation peopled by men and women descended from a race of heroes, was sustained on two levels, by the scholarly rediscovery of legends and by the publication of tales of past deeds. Especially in the west of Ireland, the Irish language and the re-telling of Gaelic history began to be a force within nationalism. Nationalist writers advocated the encouragement and protection of Irish industry against Saxon competition. If this work had been carried out only on the scholarly plane, it is possible that its influence would have ossified. But mid-century nationalist journalists used their newspapers to recount the lives of heroes, and projected the nation as looming out of an immemorial past, and they played their part in turning 'chance into destiny'.[7]

Newspapers in the 1860s took their mission seriously. 'We look upon the Press as a legion engaged, more or less consciously, in an earnest incessant warfare against darkness – a march without halt – a battle with no decisive or irretrievable issue.'[8] In his description of *The Jupiter* in *The Warden* (1855) Trollope encapsulates the mid-century newspaper's view of its powers. The press is always right, parliament is always wrong, and compared with editors, politicians are mere puppets. *The Jupiter*, directed by its editor Tom Towers, is omnipotent:

> Such is Mount Olympus, the mouthpiece of all the wisdom of this great country. It may probably be said that no place in this 19th century is more worthy of notice. No treasury mandate armed with the signatures of all the government has half the power of one of those broad sheets, which fly forth from hence so abundantly, armed with no signature at all.[9]

Provincial newspapers saw themselves as increasingly influential in local affairs. The *Connaught Patriot* said roundly, 'The greatest check on fraud is the dread of public opinion, of which the Press is the vehicle.'[10] Martin O'Brennan stated that 'We hold it to be the first – the chief – almost the only duty of a Provincial Newspaper to deal with local things. Failing in this it is but the tool of cliques, the shield of

5 Anderson, loc. cit.   6 Anderson, pp 39–40.   7 Anderson, p. 9.   8 *The Times*, 14 December 1869.   9 Anthony Trollope, *The Warden* (1855; Oxford 1980), p. 183.   10 24 March 1860

jobbery and a public cheat ... our duty is to expose all tyranny; and, in this province, there is a great deal of it'.[11] In a period of growing urbanisation, newspapers had much to report. Towns competed with each other to be linked to the railway, and to instal gas lighting in the streets. The *Tuam Herald* published a map of Tuam, advertising it as useful for property owners, solicitors and barristers, and antiquarians, literary clubs and local public offices.[12] Politics became more sharply defined. Ulster politics, particularly urban working-class politics, lost their liberal dimension. The patent medicine vendors and grocers who had founded newspapers during the previous twenty years began to die out and by the end of the 1870s, men who later became nationalist Members of Parliament were increasingly involved in the provincial press and greater numbers of newspapers claimed to have nationalist politics.

Communications continued to improve; more people could read and read increasing numbers of newspapers.[13] The electric telegraph, permanently installed in 1866, brought news from abroad faster. Illiteracy continued to fall and dropped particularly fast in the west and south:

Table 8: *Levels of illiteracy, 1871*

	Percentage illiteracy	*Percentage drop since 1851*
Ulster	26	– 9
Leinster	27	–12
Munster	39	–17
Connaught	49	–17
Ireland	33	–14

Source: W.E. Vaughan and A.J. Fitzpatrick, *Irish Historical Statistics.*

The introduction of the electric telegraph brought faster reports of debates at Westminster, and there was an increased desire to know about the work of Irish Members of Parliament.[14] Even in the smaller papers, the space devoted to report of parliamentary debates was enormous. In 1878 the proprietor of the *Freeman's Jour-*

---

11 8 February 1862.   12 *Tuam Herald*, 19 March 1864.   13 Railway journeys per head of the population were 0.9 in 1851; they rose to 2.9 by 1871; letters delivered per head of the population rose from 5.5 in 1851 to 13.3 in 1871: cf. Comerford (1989), pp 374–5.   14 The development of the electric telegraph also led some of the English provincial papers to set up branch offices in Fleet Street, but by the end of the 1870s only the *Belfast News-Letter* had a Fleet Street office. The Speaker told the Select Committee on Parliamentary Reporting that the introduction of the electric telegraph made the Irish press more dependent and anxious to have their own reporters in the Press Gallery; previously they had taken their reports from the London papers. *Kelly's Commercial Directory* for 1879; Evidence to the Select Committee on Parliamentary Reporting, HC 1878 (327) xvi, QQ 1712–14.

nal, Edmund Dwyer Gray, told the Select Committee on Parliamentary Reporting that questions affecting Irish readers arose in parliament two or three times a week.[15] Complaining about the lack of accommodation for Irish reporters in the Press Gallery, he pointed out that, especially in relation to Scotland and Ireland, there were issues which were of great importance to the provincial Irish press, but which were of no interest to metropolitan papers:

> Irish questions of primary importance are constantly discussed in the House; matters are discussed which are said by opponents to be of an almost revolutionary tendency; they are of such importance; they are of great interest to the Irish people, and they naturally desire to see the views of their representatives on such questions of great importance, Home Rule, the Land question, the Education question, Grand Jury reform, and similar matters, reported at length. No such vital questions ever arise with reference to any particular locality in England.[16]

Irish MPs had complained to him about the inefficiency of parliamentary reporting, saying that 'reporters do not understand Irish subjects as well as they do English subjects', and that, while English papers *didn't* report Irish subjects, Irish papers *couldn't* report them.[17] Irish papers were no longer dependent on lifting pieces of news from the London press: they began to have their own London correspondents. In 1880, Wemyss Reid wrote that '20–30 years ago', the London correspondent column of a provincial paper had its 'ridiculous and contemptible side ... No wonder Thackeray jibed at him.' New and better communications had led to a 'new order' of London correspondents and the 'tawdry rubbish' of *Pendennis* ceased to be marketable.[18]

In the 1860s, the debate within the Catholic church on the involvement of the priesthood in politics separated nationalists like John MacHale of Tuam from what J.H. Whyte has called ecclesiastical unionists like Cardinal Cullen in Dublin, and this division was reflected by some newspapers. The Catholic church itself became involved in newspaper investment and newspapers used the church's patronage to further their commercial ends. The readers of Catholic newspapers ranged from the intensely conservative to the extreme radical and this posed their editors with problems. In 1871, the *Tuam News* asked 'Can Cheap Literature Pay?' The writer (possibly the proprietor, John McPhilpin, himself) complained that Catholic newspaper readers were 'particularly captious' in their choice of paper. 'If the paper cost a penny, the cry was "Oh, it is a pitiful penny trumpet, it will never do a day's good till its size and price are changed".' If this advice was taken 'in a weak moment', and the newspaper was doubled in size and cost, the circulation was cut by more than a

15 Evidence of Edmund Dwyer Gray, Q 2434.   16 Ibid., Q 2412.   17 Ibid., Q 2410.   18 T. Wemyss Reid, 'Our London Correspondent' in *Macmillan's Magazine*, 43 (1880), pp 18–26.

half. If the paper spoke of Home Rule it was 'dubbed Fenian on the spot', while other readers would protest 'it was not hot enough'. Either the paper had nothing but religious news, or 'not Catholic news sufficient'.[19]

In the 1860s there was an extra dimension to the external perception of Irish nationalism. Campaigns waged by newspapers were said by government and British popular opinion to influence a population thought ignorant and easily led. Ministers and officials were uncomfortably aware that the lack of dependable local leadership and a defective education system could be, with the extension of the franchise after 1868, an incendiary combination. Bishop Moriarty, coadjutor Bishop of Kerry, quoted at the beginning of this chapter, had some reason for feeling apprehensive at the influence of some of the priests and some of the newspapers, and his fear that 'no other voice is heard' was echoed by other observers.

Officials in London and Dublin took the simplistic view that the Irish people could not and did not discriminate between political parties and factions but also had an innate tendency to combine in secret societies, to follow charismatic leaders and to indulge in violent action. The government's anxieties were intensified by what they saw as foreign influence, most particularly from Irish–America, on some sections of the Irish population. At the same time, liberal governments were faced with the problem of having to use powers and policies in Ireland that they had denounced in successive countries in Europe. Radical and nationalist politicians were quick to compare the stated beliefs of liberal statesmen like Gladstone and their practice in coercion legislation. For Poland, Hungary and Italy, freedom of speech and the self-determination of peoples were extolled as the first principles of liberalism. In Ireland in the 1870s, these principles were seen to be denied. The authorities in London and in Dublin Castle viewed with increasing concern the way the press pursued nationalist ends. With the introduction of a clause in the Peace Preservation Bill of 1870 to limit the freedom of the press, the government took the first step to attempt to control the influence of newspapers in Ireland.

19 *Tuam News*, 16 June 1871; reprinted from the *Catholic Times*.

6

The newspaper business, 1866–79

The Irish press demands more spirited management from the fact that their political and religious differences are serious and intricate in that country.[1]

By 1879, there were about 16 more papers than in 1866 and 55 more than there had been in 1850.

Table 9: *Numbers of Irish provincial papers in print, 1866–79*

1866	104	1873	108
1867	104	1874	107
1868	110	1875	110
1869	111	1876	112
1870	111	1877	114
1871	113	1878	117
1872	111	1879	120

Source: *Newspaper Press Directory*

In 1863, the *Dublin University Magazine* had predicted a great slump in the newspaper industry, because of the abolition of stamp duty. The 'wanton and un-provoked tinkerings of a certain class of statesman' had created an over-supply of papers. The records of the bankruptcy court held 'a terrible catalogue of casualties' by which a quarter of a million pounds had been lost in newspaper enterprises in Great Britain. It is certainly true that there was a high casualty rate in the years after 1855.[2]

Writing about the factors had which governed the success or failure of newspa-pers in Sunderland in the nineteenth-century, Maurice Milne has identified a number

1 J.A. Scott, 'The British Newspaper: the Penny Theory and its Solutions' *Dublin University Magazine*, 361 (March 1863), p. 363. Scott (1832–99) was sub-editor of *Dublin University Magazine*.   2 Scott, loc. cit., pp 363–4.

of key criteria which ensured the success of a provincial newspaper.[3] These can usefully be applied to the Irish press. First, a newspaper had to adopt the political stance of the majority party of the area. In Ulster between 1866 and 1879, the failure of a number of liberal papers reflected the increasing polarisation of loyalties in the province. Here liberalism collapsed in the face of the advance of nationalism, and political parties became increasingly polarised. Milne's political point may be relevant to the demise of the *Banner of Ulster* (Belfast), the *Carrickfergus Freeman* (Antrim) and the *Londonderry Guardian*. Here commercial considerations may also have taken their toll: the conservative *Lurgan Gazette* was said to have suffered from a 'lack of advertising revenue' which in the end proved fatal, and the *Ulster Observer* and *Northern Star* engaged in damaging internecine strife.

Milne's second criterion is that the successful weekly newspaper needed to share the overheads by publishing a companion daily paper. This stratagem could only be successful in the larger cities: W. and G. Baird began the *Belfast Evening Telegraph* in 1870 as the first halfpenny evening paper in Ireland and three years later this was partnered by the *Belfast Weekly Telegraph*. The fact that both papers survived into the mid-twentieth century confirms the commercial good sense of this arrangement. The *Cork Evening Echo* was started in April 1872 by Daniel Gillman and Frederick P.E. Potter, proprietors of the Irish *Daily Telegraph*, formerly the *Southern Reporter*. However, here they may have over-reached themselves, because both papers ceased publication in 1873.[4] The expenses of publishing more frequently in paper, wages and distribution were great. This may have been one reason why the *Connaught Patriot* never achieved the triweekly publication hoped for in the first number.[5]

PEOPLE: PROPRIETORS, EDITORS AND JOURNALISTS

Milne's third point is that the proprietor had to be a person with political standing in the community, a condition that was increasingly evident in Ireland in the last quarter of the nineteenth-century. New papers were started, not by small shopkeepers, but by politicians with manifestos expressed in their main editorial leader. Nevertheless, newspaper editors still doubled up with other jobs into the late 1860's.[6] A competitive price and a good advertising base ensured commercial success; and the printing contracts supplied by local boards and institutions were useful in maximising the return from capital investment. Auctioneers, emigration agents, printers and the law courts all took space in the provincial press.

3 Of the 25 newspapers founded in Northumberland and Durham between 1856 and 1865, nine had ceased publication by 1865: Maurice Milne 'Survival of the Fittest? Sunderland Newspapers in the nineteenth century' in J. Shattock and M. Wolff (eds), *Victorian Periodical Press: Samplings and Soundings* (Leicester, 1982), pp 193, 214–16.   4 The *Cork Evening Echo* does not appear in *Newsplan*.   5 *Connaught Patriot*, 27 August 1859.   6 Census of Ireland 1871 HC 1876 [C1377] lxxxi.

Table 10: *Occupations and religious persuasion 1861 and 1871*

Newspaper Proprietors, Editors and Reporters:	Males	Females
Total 238	236	2
Roman Catholics	107	
Established Church	77	
Presbyterians	34	
Methodists	11	2
Independents	3	
All other Persuasions	4	
Newspaper proprietors only	144	4
(Total 148)		

Source: Census of Ireland for 1861 HC 1863 [3204.III] lx.1

The social status of newspaper proprietors changed. The proprietors and editors of the provincial press, wrote Edward Dicey in 1868, never aspired to work for the metropolitan press. The editor of a local paper was either a local man who owned the paper in whole or in part and worked it with the view of pushing himself forward in his business, or else he had drifted into journalism or risen into it from being a reporter. Their social status was unclear: in England it was impossible for an editor to associate with the landed gentry, but he was superior to shopkeepers, because editors tended to assert their own importance.[7]

The type of man who went into provincial journalism, wrote a 'Conservative Journalist' in 1886, explained why the provincial press had radical tendencies. In his analysis, the writer hypothesised that most provincial newspapers owed their origin to country stationers, who were advertising agents for city printers. With the development of the town, the jobbing printing business grew, and the stationer would start a press of his own, later employing a man and then an apprentice to assist him. However, the workload was irregular and, in order to use his capital to the full and keep his employees in regular work, the stationer would issue a weekly sheet of

7 [E. Dicey,] 'Provincial Journalism' in *St Paul's Magazine* III (1868), pp 61–73. Edward Dicey, the author and journalist, was the brother of Albert Venn Dicey, the jurist. They were both sons of Thomas Edward Dicey, a pioneer of the Midland Railway and, importantly for this purpose, owner of the *Northampton Mercury*. When he wrote this article, Edward Dicey was on the *Daily Telegraph*. He became editor of the *Daily News* and then of the *Observer*.

advertisements and local gossip, police cases and meetings. He would then realise that at least 10 per cent of his customers were buying London papers, and that this 10 per cent were educated and upwardly mobile citizens who had become dissatisfied with present day institutions. The astute stationer/printer was prosperous enough to take the risk of expressing this dissatisfaction, so his newspaper's politics were radical, tempered by the commercial realities of his stationery business. Although his upwardly mobile readers might eventually become dissatisfied with his radical paper, and might indeed establish a conservative paper themselves to denounce change, the 'representatives of capital' would nevertheless continue to advertise in the radical paper and to promote its interests.[8] The interpretation of the 'Conservative journalist' partly explains why the older provincial papers moved over to radical politics in the last quarter of the century. New papers began as radical because they had a new kind of owner and more men went into journalism as a means of expressing radical opinions.

These opinions were expressed through the growth of Catholic nationalism: the major political characteristic of the new newspapers of the 1870s, and this trend continued to accelerate over the next decade. The need for a Catholic newspaper in the Tuam district was recognised in 1870 when *Tuam News* referred to the 'totally inadequate Newspaper representation of our community'. Their aim was for a 'truly representative paper ... we own no party but country'.[9] Outside Dublin, the first newspapers that described themselves as 'nationalist' were all started in 1876. These were the *Western News* (Ballinasloe), *The Celt* (Waterford) and the *People's Advocate* (Monaghan), the last paper run by Daniel MacAleese. MacAleese, who began life as a shoemaker in Co. Antrim, was a self-educated man who became a printer's reader, then a journalist and ended his career as MP for North Monaghan.[10] He came to Monaghan from editing the *Ulster Examiner* in Belfast, a newspaper begun in 1868 by bishop Dorrian. The bishop spent thousands of pounds in order to crush A.J. McKenna, a former editor of the *Ulster Observer*, which was a liberal catholic paper. McKenna, a Maynooth-educated man, went on to found the Belfast *Northern Star* in 1868, also a liberal catholic journal, which held 'advanced views', but lasted only four years. The *Ulster Examiner* of bishop Dorrian and Daniel MacAleese was nicknamed the 'Vatican Juggler and Star of Purgatory' and claimed particular circulation amongst the Catholic clergy in the province. MacAleese's *People's Advocate* was a cheap (1*d.*) paper, addressing national and Catholic questions, which lasted until 1906.

Some newspapers initially claimed liberal politics and later embraced outright nationalism in the full flood of the movement in the 1880s. The *Mayo Examiner* and

---

8 'Why is the Provincial Press Radical?' by 'A Conservative Journalist' in *National Review*, 7 (1886), 678–82.   9 Reprint of circular issued by the Proprietors of the *Tuam News*, 9 December 1870, in issue of 23 June 1871.   10 J.S.Crone, *Dictionary of Irish Biography* and *Who's Who of British MPs*.

the *Kerry Sentinel* both began as liberal papers. The *Mayo Examiner* changed to nationalism in 1888,[11] and the *Kerry Sentinel*, founded by Timothy Harrington in April 1878 was undoubtedly nationalist, although it never changed its insertion as 'liberal' in the *Newspaper Press Directory*.

Claims to direct or indirect links with the Catholic church became increasingly common. The *Tuam News* advertised that it contained 'special information concerning the Catholic church'. Its great strength was in its association with St Jarlath's College, and its publication of Irish history and columns in Irish were due to the work of Father Ulick Bourke, who from the start was associated with the newspaper. The *Clare Independent*, founded in 1878 as a Catholic newspaper by Thomas S. Cleary had the motto 'Vox populi vox Dei'. Born in Dublin in 1851, Cleary contributed bad poetry to various Irish and American papers, including *United Ireland* and the *Boston Pilot*, under the pseudonyms 'Denis O'Dunn' and 'Free Lance' and in 1882 published 'Shin-Fain, or Ourselves Alone a drama of the Exhibition'. His *Songs of the Irish Land War* (1888) was dedicated to William O'Brien MP 'whose generous recognition has so often stood me in good stead in the hard struggle of Press life ...' and he wrote an 'Elegy on the Death of Parnell' which was distributed along the route of Parnell's funeral.[12] *The Celt*, a Waterford paper published in 1876, announced that 'Our patent of Nationality comes direct from Heaven'. Although it published a column in Irish, Waterford appears not to have been an area receptive to this kind of material, for the paper lasted only ten months. Newspaper mottoes are again a useful indication of the true allegiance of the paper. The *Leinster Independent*, where 'a special letter from Rome is made a feature', claimed to be independent in politics, but its motto was 'Faith and Fatherland'.

FINANCING THE PROVINCIAL PRESS

> ... *libera scripta manet*. The paper has no memory, and it has no conscience. In that case it has no body. I will not for the honour of journalism say that it has no soul ... How gratified would the good and worthy electors of Galway be to hear that in the exuberance of Mr Nolan's generosity, he provided 6,000 of the Archbishop's letter, printed at the *Tuam News* at great price for a constituency.[13]

The scarcity of archives on the provincial press makes difficult to give a coherent account of the financial realities of newspaper production. The capital cost of setting up a newspaper were considerable. A French printing machine cost as much as

11 *Newspaper Press Directory*. 12 John Wyse Jackson and Peter Costello, *John Stanislaus Joyce: the Voluminous Life and Genius of James Joyce's Father* (London, 1997), p. 166. 13 Judge William Keogh, delivering his judjment on the Galway County election petition.

£750–£800, and even a second-hand machine could cost £650.[14] Maurice Milne, in his article on the *Sunderland Daily Echo* in 1875, says that there the total wage and salary bill averaged about 58% of the total running costs; the money spent on paper, ink and type 27%, and 15% was spent on 'intelligence' and fees to newsagencies. Twenty per cent of the money raised from selling the paper was spent on distribution and newsagents' commission. John Bright told Richard Cobden that, after the abolition of duty, newspaper politics became more violent in order to attract readers.[15] The surviving archives of the Ulster Printing Co. Ltd, publishers of the *Belfast Mercury*, provide a brief view of the income and expenditure of publishing the paper in August 1860, and the minutes of the Galway County election petition hearing are eloquent on the mass of work provided during one by-election in 1871.

During the three weeks between 2 August and 21 August 1860, the Ulster Printing Company sold 593 unstamped and 221 stamped copies of the *Belfast Daily Mercury*. The income from miscellaneous sales and advertisements and from sales in the printing office was twice as much as the revenue from newspaper sales alone. Set against the total income, the office and the press only just stayed in the black:

Accounts of the *Belfast Mercury*, 2–21 August 1860[16]	£	s.	d.
Income			
Unstamped copies (593)	54	7	2
Stamped copies (221)	33	3	0
Sales	8	4	8
Advertisements	88	7	4
Printing	265	14	3
Office	81	12	1
Expenditure			
Cost of running Office, Press, etc	250	18	0
Balance	14	16	3

14 Bright to Cobden, 26 October 1855: BL Add. Mss 43,384 f.22. I am grateful to Dr James Sturgis for referring me to Bright's papers.   15 Bright to Cobden 20 May 1860: BL Add. Mss 43,384 f.199; 21 September 1855, f.12.   16 Cashbook of *Belfast Mercury* 1858–1860: PRONI D.2450/3/1.

The cost of running the office included small but crucial payments to the suppliers and distributors of news:

Subscription: Magnetic Telegraph Co	£ 2 10s. 0d. p.w.
Fee *Belfast News-Letter* for Dublin reports	£ 3 3s. 3d. p.c.m.
Delivery of paper to country districts (Antrim, Lisburn, Newtownlimavady, Downpatrick, Dromore, Lurgan, Carrickfergus, Ballymena, Ballymoney, Coleraine, Londonderry, Larne)	£13 1s. 0d. p.c.m.
Railway Co. carriage	£ 5 0s. 0d. p.c.m.

With such a small profit over three weeks, it is not surprising that, in the following year, 1861, the *Belfast Mercury* was sold to the printers, W. & G. Baird.

Milne's analysis, and the figures from the *Belfast Mercury*, confirm that running a provincial paper was not the way to make a fortune. Journalists, too, found the going hard. Richard Pigott pressed many friends for funds, including Isaac Butt and John Matthews, the proprietor of the *Down Independent*, to whom he gave the reason for a loan to meet a pressing creditor as:

As a national journalist I am denied the ordinary Banking accomodation [*sic*] which the smallest trader can obtain without difficulty. Irish bankers no doubt consider that the conductor of national journals is so liable to government prosecution and the confiscation of his property that he is an unsafe person to whom to give credit ...[17]

Pigott was not a shining example of financial probity, but Matthews did send him £2 10s. 0d.

But local newspapers had one certain source of income. As the journalist Andrew Dunlop put it, they 'had a good harvest at election times', and many proprietors depended on income from this source to enable them to 'live from one election to another'.[18] Large sums of money were to be made from a candidate who was able to spend freely on the publication of favourable reports of meetings, both public and private. Leaders and letters were then reprinted as circulars and leaflets and circulated throughout the district.

The by-election for Galway County which was held on 8 February 1872 was caused by the resignation of one of the sitting members, Viscount Burke. The candidates were the ultra-Tory, Captain the Hon. William Trench and the Home Ruler,

---

17 Pigott to Matthews, 6 May 1872: NLI Ms 5762. In the light of Pigott's examination in front of Sir Charles Russell (a friend of John Matthews) at the hearing of the Special Commission, the spelling mistake is significant.   18 Andrew Dunlop, *Fifty Years of Irish Journalism* (Dublin, 1911) p. 20.

The editor of the *Tuam News* asserted that its circulation was quadruple that of the *Tuam Herald*. In the Union debate, the *Tuam Herald* was thought to be the 'fittest', but the *Tuam News* was 'in the habit of publishing the advertisements and getting the greatest publicity'. Despite the fact that its price was higher (and its circulation apparently less) the *Tuam Herald* was awarded the business.[25]

The placing of contracts with mainly politically sympathetic papers was general practice. The liberal government in July 1880 followed this when the Board of Trade approved the Irish newspapers for official advertisements. Their list had 12 liberal papers, 5 conservative, 2 independent-liberal, 1 moderate-conservative and 1 radical paper.[26] With the delicately balanced parliament after the General Election of 1892, the placing of advertisements under the new liberal administration was possibly a reflection of the size of the Irish party and of continued support for Home Rule. Of the 24 Irish provincial newspapers on the official Home Office list in January 1893, 15 were nationalist, 3 Liberal, 3 independent, 2 Conservative and 1 Protestant. Of the nationalist papers, 10 had been prosecuted for publishing the illegal resolutions of the Irish National League in the previous ten years.

The increasing polarisation of politics, whether within Ulster, with the loss of the liberal middle ground, or in the south west and west, with the growth of nationalism, was reflected in the success or failure of newspapers. The introduction of the Ballot Act (1872) and the Corrupt Practices Act (1883) probably curtailed newspapers' rich pickings during elections,[27] and it is possible that these limitations in part helped to involve the press and journalists in direct involvement in the development of political parties. With the beginning of the Land War, the activities of provincial newspaper proprietors, both in the way they used their newspapers and by their own personal involvement in national politics, demonstrated the immense harvest to be reaped by the provincial press.

BIRTH AND DEATH OF AN ULSTER NEWSPAPER: WILLIAM JOHNSTON OF
BALLYKILBEG AND THE 'DOWNSHIRE PROTESTANT', 1855–62

> The great leading principle of Mr Johnston's mental nature is, the *entireness of his consecration to the cause with which he is identified*: and all the other elements of which it is composed may be said to be various developments of this one great principle.[28]

The 'Band of Literary Photographers' who wrote this panegyric of William Johnston

25 *Tuam News*, 27 October 1871.   26 PRO BT/11/E4748.   27 Although, as Hoppen has pointed out, the small numbers of electors in many constituencies after 1872 made it difficult for voters to conceal their intentions. Op. cit., p. 73.   28 'A Band of Literary Photographers', *Descriptive and Critical Sketches of Thomas M'Clure, William Johnston, and M.R. Dalway* (London, 1869), p. 10.

when he was first elected to Parliament in 1868, observed his physical make-up as 'the faithful representation of his mind, comparatively massive, robust and symmetrical'.[29] Within the Orange Order, he had a reputation for complete dedication to the Protestant cause; he was said to be a popular speaker and able to stand clear of local squabbles and concentrate on great national issues'.[30] In an attempt to distance Johnston and his supporters from the charge of rabble rousing, the authors of the pamphlet drew attention to Johnston's serious nature, his freedom from dogma and his unwillingness to sacrifice anything for the sake of personal popularity. Johnston's opponents naturally took a rather different view and attempted to discredit him and his cause; and his detractors were not necessarily Roman Catholic. In the context of an account of a march of 100,000 Orangemen in 1860 which was encouraged by Johnston's paper, the *Downshire Protestant*, the *Belfast Northern Whig* described the ideal Protestant by citing the agent to the Hertford estate, who: 'amidst his Protestant principles and Conservative politics, he does not forget he has the character of a Christian and a gentleman to sustain ... respectable men never desire to excite disorder and riot.' To many Tories, Johnston was no gentleman.

William Johnston of Ballykilbeg was born in 1829, the son of minor Ulster landed gentry. He was a member of the Church of Ireland. Educated at Trinity College, Dublin, he was called to the Bar in 1872.[31] He came of age at a moment when orangeism was experiencing profound changes in its membership. Throughout the 1850s, an alliance was being forged between the Orange Order and conservatism and county grandees began to use the lodges as a means by which they could make contact with the industrial classes. Hoppen[32] highlights the growth of lower-class respectability in the Belfast lodges in the twenty years after 1850, when commercial travellers, artisans, shopkeepers and farmers were elected officers of the Order. One of the 'Band of Literary Photographers' writing about Johnston describes himself as 'A Draper in Castle Place'. From the evidence of advertisements in the *Downshire Protestant*, these were the men to whom William Johnston wished to address his message.

Johnston went into politics early. At 16 he had a printing press on which he published a weekly broadsheet, the *Ballykilbeg Newspaper*, which appeared for four years in various forms and sizes. He joined the Orange Order in 1848 at the age of 19. In 1850, when he was 24, his father died and he inherited Ballykilbeg House, Downpatrick and estate with rentals of £950 a year. In 1854 he founded the Down Protestant Association, whose aims included the abolition of nunneries, the withdrawal of all grants from Maynooth and the enforcement of the Ecclesiastical Titles Act. He first stood, unsuccessfully, for parliament in 1857, aged 28.

29 Op. cit, p. 5.   **30** Ibid., essay by 'The Author of literary feats in Belfast under freezing difficulties', pp 28–9.   **31** Aiken McClelland, 'Johnston of Ballykilbeg' M.Phil. thesis (New University of Ulster, 1977).   **32** Hoppen, op. cit., p. 325.

One of the legacies of the tenant right movement was the recognition by some Ulster groups that Catholics had demonstrated that they were capable of political organization across the country. This fact increasingly brought Presbyterians and Anglicans together and it forms the background to the founding of the *Downshire Protestant* in 1855. As a member of the Established Church, Johnston stood apart from the general run of those proprietors of Ulster Protestant newspapers who were in the newspaper business to further and consolidate Presbyterian doctrine. What separated them from Johnston was not necessarily dogma but his popular politics. As David Miller has said, the Orange Party interpretation of the constitution was that it was the 'once for all contract' undertaken with William III. The maintenance of the establishment of the Church of Ireland was an important element of that contract.[33] Discounting Johnston's extremist rhetoric, the evidence of the *Downshire Protestant* is that Orangemen in Downpatrick felt isolated and vulnerable.

Johnston's life was full of political and quasi-political activities, divided between church and Sunday school, the Protestant and Orange Associations and judicial duties. He served on a committee of the Protestant Orphans' Association, and was a member of the Grand Lodge and the District Lodge of the Orange Order, of the Grand Jury and the Down Infirmary governors. He wrote reviews and articles for Protestant magazines and newspapers, including the *Dublin Morning Herald* and the *Londonderry Sentinel*. Downpatrick had a number of reading rooms with Protestant affiliations. In 1851, the Downpatrick Mechanics Institute was reported to be flourishing, with a newsroom 'furnished with a respectable assortment of English, Irish and Scotch papers'. Workers could spend their leisure time 'in a becoming and rational way ... in reading and improving their minds'.[34] The Down Protestant Association united with the Young Men's Christian Association to found a reading room and library there in 1855,[35] and further Protestant reading rooms were founded in 1864 and 1877. In March 1855 Johnston began discussions with the Down Protestant Association about the possibility of starting a local newspaper dedicated to the maintenance of the Protestant cause. Johnston considered calling the paper 'The Downshire True Blue', but he named it the *Downshire Protestant*. In April 1855, he and his Association 'Had much talk about the newspaper and believe it is likely to take'.[36] The drop in newspaper prices after the abolition of newspaper stamps in June 1855 made cheap radical propaganda possible and Johnston's new newspaper was priced at 2½*d*., within the reach of small town artisans and shopkeepers. This compared with 3*d*. for the *Downpatrick Recorder* and the *Newry Commercial Telegraph*.

Johnston used his extensive Protestant network both to provide the legal securities required before the paper could be published, and to publicise the paper through-

33 David Miller, *Queen's Rebels* (Dublin, 1978), p. 62.   34 *Downpatrick Recorder*, 27 September 1851.   35 *Downpatrick Recorder*, 13 January 1855.   36 Diary of William Johnston of Ballykilbeg: PRONI D.8809/ 2/7, 26 April 1855.

out Ulster. He had to borrow £500 at 6 per cent interest to provide a bond to provide security against possible libel actions. (He was never good with money, and his
diaries are full of notes of his borrowing large sums at high interest. By 1864 he had
amassed debts of £10,000, and these were due largely to his political activities.) In
May he bought an office and shop in Downpatrick, and by 30 June he saw 'with
pleasure everything getting in to order in the office'.[37]

In April 1855, Johnston received the printed prospectuses for the newspaper,
and over the succeeding weeks he and his wife Hattie sent copies out to prospective
subscribers. Johnston wrote to all the District Masters of the Orange Lodges, and
his wife to a number of Presbyterian ministers. Local newspaper proprietors, Conway
Pilson of the *Downpatrick Recorder* and James Henderson of the *Newry Commercial
Telegraph*, received prospectuses, and copies were sent to the *Belfast News-Letter*
and the *Coleraine Chronicle*. Circular letters were sent to members of the Grand
Lodge of the Order. A canvasser was hired to drum up support all over Ulster. After
the newspaper had been published, complimentary copies were sent to possible
readers.[38] 'The Grand Jury room members each received a copy and welcomed the
cheapness of the newspaper's advertising in comparison with other papers.[39] The
first number of the paper was published on 6 July 1855 and 125 stamped copies
were sold in the shop to 'General approbation – some grumbling'.[40] There were 423
subscribers by the end of the first week of August, and by October these had increased to 481. For some time after the newspaper started, Johnston kept a note in
his diary of the numbers of new subscribers gained each week.[41]

The paper's masthead is an epitome of the Protestant work ethic and fidelity to
the Crown. Printed in gothic type, the title is set between an industrial scene of
smoking chimneys with a linen worker at his loom and, on the other side, a plough,
a reaping hook and a rake. In the centre of the masthead a pile of books, a copy of the
Magna Carta and one entitled 'Lords Commons', signifying the constitution. Below a text from Oliver Cromwell enunciates the doctrine of liberty of conscience
opposed to the doctrines of the papacy. The first leader announces the importance
of commencing the newspaper at that moment 'at the present most important crisis
in the history of our country, the church, the world, we bear earnest witness for the
true Protestant's doctrine – justification by faith in a living Saviour ...' The object of
the newspaper is to put forward the policy 'that enlightened Protestantism is the
true foundation of individual happiness and national prosperity and glory'.[42] Adver-

37 Diary, 17 and 19 May, and 30 June 1855.   38 Diary, 15, 18 and 19 May and 7 June 1855. The practice
of sending out complimentary copies to possible subscribers was general: an advertisement in the *Kerry
Sentinel* on 28 April 1879 refers to specimen copies of their first issue being sent to those people that the
editor had not been able to canvass personally, and asking for their return with the wrapper if a subscription was not required. For further evidence of this practice, see the evidence of the editor of the
Galway Express to the Galway County election petition hearing above.   39 Diary, 16 August, and 17
September 1855.   40 14 April, 15 June, 16 Augst, 17 September 1855.   41 6 July, 4 and 7 August, and
17 September 1855.   42 *Downshire Protestant*, 6 July 1855.

tising covers the front page: in addition to the advertisements for local and Belfast firms: shipping, sales of estates, cabinet makers, patent medicines, there is a column headed: 'The *Downshire Protestant* Directory' and below are advertisements by drapers, life assurance firms and ironmongers. The implication here is that the firms listed are all guaranteed to be Protestant, employing Protestant labour. In the first issue, amongst the usual reports of local affairs, there are articles on 'Popery in Scotland', and 'The Chief Design of the Papacy in the promulgation of the dogma of the Immaculate Conception'.

The new paper did not have a particularly warm welcome from the rest of the Protestant local press, whose proprietors believed that Johnston's high profile did harm to their cause. Conway Pilson was hostile to Johnston, more especially after Johnston had gained the official printing contracts for the district from the *Recorder*. Pilson called him 'The Downshire Dunce' whose logic was as bad as his theology, and believed that he had done more to injure Protestantism in County Down than all its other enemies.[43] The *Belfast Northern Whig* used its report of a demonstration led by Johnston in Lurgan on 12 July, 1860 to urge the passing of the Party Emblems Bill. It condemned such processions as 'childish diversions, unworthy of any notice whatever'. The role of the *Downshire Protestant* as 'an organ of the Orange faction' was to unsettle the community in order to challenge the government.[44] In its description of the scene at Lurgan, the *Whig* relegated the Orange Order and Johnston's paper to the caves of prehistory: 'It will be a happier day for Ireland when Orangemen and Ribbonmen shall be extinct races of ferocious creatures ...'[45] The *Belfast News-Letter* dismissed Johnston as a 'rural buffoon'. But Johnston used his newspaper to reach national politicians. In March 1855, he sent 17 copies of the *Downpatrick Recorder* with reports of the proceedings of the Down Protestant Association to Derby and Disraeli, among others.[46] His radical populism was at least 10 years ahead of its time.

Newspaper owners had their tribulations. Johnston wrote and sub-edited much of the newspaper himself, spending one whole day a week at the printers. At the outset, he engaged a Mr Knox of Dublin ('brother to Mr Knox of the *Morning Herald*') as sub-editor, but the next day and again a week later he found he had to read all the page proofs himself because his new sub-editor never appeared. On 26 July he discovered that Mr Knox had been drinking and dismissed him at once.[47]

The 'heavy expenses' associated with running a newspaper made Johnston consider giving up in September 1859, but he carried on for another three years. In December 1859, J.A. Henderson of the *Belfast News-Letter* offered to buy the printing press and stock and carry on the title but when Johnston made him a formal proposal in January 1860, Henderson withdrew. By 1862, the circulation of the paper had fallen from 1200 to 750 copies per issue. In September 1862, Johnston arranged

43 *Downpatrick Recorder*, 28 February and 7 March 1857.   44 *Belfast Northern Whig*, 27 July and 3 August 1860.   45 *Belfast Northern Whig*, 3 August 1860.   46 Diary, 17 March 1855.   47 Diary, 18, 19,

with Conway Pilson to merge the paper with the *Downpatrick Recorder*, and the *Downshire Protestant* ceased publication on 27 September. The stock was valued, the type was sold by weight to Pilson and the books were handed over on 25 October.[48] The public reason given for the closure of the paper was Johnston's ill-health. This may have been the reason – his diaries have frequent references to days when he has to retire to bed with headaches and perhaps he suffered from migraine, not helpful to an active politician. Another reason was that a new Protestant paper was about to be published. The new *Downshire Standard* was advertised in the *Downpatrick Recorder* in October 1862.[49]

In 1868, Johnston was prosecuted and imprisoned for taking part in a march in contravention of the Party Processions Act. Groups of Protestant workers were annoyed that Disraeli's government had not intervened, and angry with the *Belfast News-Letter* which had refused to print advertisements for an 'indignation' meeting. As a result of his imprisonment, Johnston became the 'working man's friend' and with covert liberal support and the financial assistance of his old adversary, the *Belfast Northern Whig*, he was elected to parliament in 1868. The reason for the *Whig*'s about-turn was their desire to capitalize on Johnston's ability to bring liberals and conservatives to support parliamentary reform.[50] Once elected, Johnston's politics became less extreme, particularly after 1872 and the repeal of the Party Processions Act. Gradually abandoning his populist stance, he moved over to mainstream conservatism. He was even able to perceive the love of country present within Fenianism. Expressing solidarity with another politician who was imprisoned for his political views, Johnston sympathised with O'Donovan Rossa when, in 1870, Gladstone moved that Rossa should be disqualified from taking his seat.[51]

The *Downshire Protestant* was not Johnston's final experience of newspaper management. The *Belfast Times* had been founded in 1872 by radical Orangemen and edited by Nicholas Flood Davin, a drunken eccentric. He was described as unfortunate: 'one could hardly say whether his spasms of energy were more to be dreaded ... than his hours of idleness. In the former he probably produced a batch of libels, in the latter he artlessly cribbed the leading article of some English contemporary and had it printed as his own'.[52] Johnston was hired to edit a weekly edition of the paper. Davin did not agree with Johnston's politics, and thought him to be 'an Orangemen, honeycombed with Radical crochets, and with the Radical crochets of what may be called petticoated politicians'.[53] Not surprisingly, Davin soon became involved in a row in which he was alleged to have insulted the wife of one of his own

25 and 26 July 1855. **48** Diary, 24 September and 9 December 1859; 3 January, 22 July, 27 and 29 September, and 4 and 25 October 1860. **49** *Downpatrick Recorder*, 4 October 1862. The *Downshire Standard* was advertised as a 'political, literacy, commercial and agricultural journal' which would advance 'uncompromising Protestant principles and be devoted to the Political, Intellectual and Social improvement of its readers': advertisement in the *Downpatrick Recorder*, ibid. **50** Hoppen, op. cit., p. 317. **51** Ibid., p. 69. **52** A. Campbell, *Belfast Newspapers Past and Present* (Belfast, 1921). **53** Aiken McClelland, p. 78.

proprietors. The row had consequences, not just for Davin, who was dismissed, but for the newspaper. The publicity led to the backers of the *Belfast Times* to withdraw their support, and the paper closed in August 1872.[54]

Like many other men of his background and education, Johnston's interests were eclectic. He read widely and was an amateur astronomer, and his diary is full of notes on the progress of his garden.[55] He enjoyed Tennyson's *Idylls of the King*, a life of Hodson of Hodson's Horse, and Dickens, finding *Tale of Two Cities* 'an improvement on *Little Dorrit*, religiously and artistically - more thoughtful and serious'. Harrison Ainsworth's *Westminster Abbey* was 'an able and thoroughly Protestant story'. Johnston's diary is a good source to discover the day-to-day reading of the mid-century Ulster Protestant, and a foil to John Pope-Hennessy's analysis of rural Catholic reading in 1886 which is dealt with in Chapter 11.

Johnston's espousal of the politics of the extreme Orange Party and his advocacy of violence towards Catholics, are unattractive. Yet his diary shows him a man of great sensibility. In his tenderness for his family (his description of the death of his wife Hattie is moving) in his religious belief and his intellectual interests, William Johnston was a man of greater depth than a first glance at the *Downshire Protestant* would suggest. He appears particularly interesting in apposition to the subject of the next chapter, Martin O'Brennan.

54 Ibid., pp 78–9.   55 'Saw Jupiter plainly and Saturn dimly through McCan's telescope': Diary, 19 January 1858.

7

Gaelic nationalism: Martin O'Brennan
and the *Connaught Patriot*

> People of Galway, look upon the laws of days gone by and those of this
> day, and say which bear the impress of paternal hands and minds, thought-
> ful of a people's happiness, and a nation's strength![1]

Writers on the Gaelic revival have tended to assume that before Standish O'Grady
and Douglas Hyde, only antiquarian societies and individual scholars worked in
this field. In her study of nineteenth-century folklore, Mary Helen Thuente briefly
refers to the 'popularisers of Ancient Ireland' but she fails to analyse material that
appeared in the growing provincial press. Martin Williams asserts that until the last
decades of the nineteenth-century the Fenian and Red Branch sagas were 'not written down and published for an English-speaking Irish audience ... most educated
Irishmen, cut off from the oral tradition probably knew little even of the well-pre-
served tales'. He places Standish O'Grady's *History of Ireland,* published between
1878 and 1881, as the first 'popular' English version of Irish legends. In his dissec-
tion of the place of Gaelic history and culture in nineteenth-century publishing and
its influence on developing nationalism, Oliver MacDonagh has written that 'for
almost the entire length of the nineteenth-century the bulk of the pioneering work
for the preservation or restoration of Gaelic culture is attributable to Irish Protestants'.[2] There is a general belief that until the founding of the Gaelic League in
1893, the Irish language and Irish history were of little interest to popular readers.
But there is a link between the journalists who published popular versions of Fenian
tales and the founders of the Gaelic League.

In his examination of the intellectual background to Douglas Hyde's nationalism, Dominic Daly has looked at the young Hyde's library in the 1870s. He put into
context the formation of the founding of learned societies in the mid-century: the
Gaelic Society (1806), the Celtic Society (1840) and the Irish Archaeological Society (1845) who merged in 1853, and the Ossianic Society (1853) which had as its
object the publication of Fenian poems, tales and romances in Irish with literal

---

1 *Tuam News,* 27 October 1871. 2 Thuente, op. cit., p. 21; Martin Williams 'Ancient mythology and
revolutionary ideology in Ireland 1878–1916', in *Historical Journal,* 16 (1983), pp 307–10; Oliver
McDonagh, *States of Mind: A Study of the Anglo-Irish Conflict* (London, 1985), pp 108–11.

translations. Here there is a link between the popularisers of Ireland's past and the scholarly background of the 1890s Gaelic revival. Douglas Hyde bought Archbishop MacHale's translations of Moore's *Melodies*, edited and corrected by Father Ulick Bourke of the *Tuam News*; he had Bourke's edition of Dr Gallagher's *Sermons* and Bourke's own *College Irish Grammar*. Hyde also owned *Ancient Ireland* by Philip Fitzgerald Barron, founder of the *Waterford Chronicle*, and Martin O'Brennan's *Antiquities* and *Ancient Ireland*. But Hyde thought that much of the folk-lore of Ireland that had appeared in print was spurious and written only to make it saleable. Indeed, he sincerely thought that he was 'the first to collect folklore in Irish; the first to collect the poetry of the people from their own mouths'.[3] Hyde ignored the role played by newspapers and disliked the press as part of a modernising tendency started by O'Connell and the Catholic priesthood, whose 'more than indifference to things Gaelic put an end to all that was really Irish, and taught the people to speak English, to look to London and to read newspapers'. A man 'who reads Irish mss. and repeats Ossianic poetry, is a higher and more interesting type than the man whose mental training is confined to spelling through an article in United Ireland'.[4] Hyde's rigorous assessment of the genesis and quality of Irish folklore and history should not necessarily be applied to what appeared in the provincial press of the 1860s and 1870s but it is important to recognise that it appeared at all. Where Hyde may have most influenced modern writers is in his total rejection of the popular press for evidence of national consciousness through the recounting of history and as propaganda for the Irish language.[5]

The Gaelic past was plundered for a variety of political aims. Tom Dunne has shown that for Catholic writers and politicians this perception of themselves as heirs to a race of heroes was a tremendous boost to their self-confidence. After the 1820s, writers in Ireland had begun to recognise that there was an increasing middle-class Catholic readership for fiction and poetry, and by the mid-century this readership was swelled by the growth of the provincial press. The idea of an Irish nation defined by language led, in the 1830s and later, to what Dunne has described as the authorities' 'Spenserian preoccupation with the "Gaelic" threat and a strong distaste for Catholicism'.[6] This preoccupation was behind the prosecution of *The Nation* and the closure of the Young Ireland reading rooms in 1848. Anglo-Irish and English politicians and some contemporary observers regarded the calling in aid of Gaelic heroes and images and the Irish language as suspect and dangerous. The Irish belief that the pre-colonial past was better than their present condition was evidence enough.

3 Quoted in Conor Cruise O'Brien, 'Exorcizing the English Demon, Douglas Hyde and the politicization of the Gaelic League', *Times Literary Supplement*, 21 June 1991, pp 9–10.   4 Preface to *Beside the Fire* (London, 1890), pp xi, xxiii–xxiv.   5 Dominic Daly, *The Young Douglas Hyde* (Dublin, 1974), pp 28, 51 and Appendix II.   6 Tom Dunne, 'Haunted by History: Irish Romantic Writing 1800–1850' in Roy Porter and Mikula Teich (eds), *Romanticism in National Context* (Cambridge, 1988), p. 7.

Links began to be made between literacy, reading matter and action. In 1870, replying to a question by Arthur MacMorrough Kavanagh, who had quoted a passage from the *Wexford People*, the Chief Secretary Chichester Fortescue outlined the agrarian crimes which took the form of threatening letters and notices. Fortescue spoke of the impossibility of separating these outrages from the 'nature of those weekly publications which form the literature, too often the sole literature, of the classes from which those outrages proceed.' It was well known that this kind of literature taught a 'hatred of the constitutions and government of the United Kingdom' which 'poisons the mind' and 'inflames the passions of the people by rhetorical descriptions of the wrongs of other days'.[7]

In the provincial press Gaelic history was presented in two ways. First, there were scholars, who published histories and guide books of their locality, and collected folk tales and songs. John George Augustus Prim ran and edited the *Kilkenny Moderator*. Prim was one of the founders of the Kilkenny Archaeological Association, collected folk material and dirges and wrote a history of St Canice's Cathedral, Kilkenny. He collected folk stories and songs from old men and women for over 20 years, rewarding them with tobacco, snuff and drink.[8] John Davis White, also from Kilkenny, founded and edited the *Cashel Gazette* in 1862 and wrote a history and a number of guides to Cashel and its antiquities. In the 1870s, some writers extended this interest to the use of Gaelic fonts in their papers.

Secondly, there were proprietors who were engaged centrally or peripherally with the Fenian movement and whose papers were suffused with images of the past. William Kenealy, P.E. Gill and Martin Andrew O'Brennan were the most prominent members of this group, and all three had links with Young Ireland. William Kenealy wrote for Duffy's *Fireside Magazine* and *The Nation* in the 1850s as 'William of Munster', and he was probably the anonymous author of the preface to Hayes' *Ballads of Ireland*. Kenealy took over the *Tipperary Leader* on the death of the Young Irelander Maurice Leyne, and went on in 1856 to edit Cornelius Maxwell's *Kilkenny Journal*. P.E. Gill started the *Tipperary Advocate* in Nenagh in 1857, which was described by a hostile resident of Nenagh as the 'organ of the Young Ireland party'.[9] He was active in the many proto-Fenian organisations. Together with M.J. Sutton of the *Wexford People* and Patrick Dowdall of the *Newry Examiner*, he was a member of the William Smith O'Brien Monument committee. He was also president of the 'Tipperary Club', an organisation which associated itself with the Fenian front body, the National Brotherhood of St Patrick.[10] Martin O'Brennan, founder of the *Connaught Patriot*, who came into provincial journalism from semi-obscurity and disappeared from Ireland in the late 1860s, is dealt with below.

The Gaelic scholar, Father Ulick Bourke, President of St Jarlath's College, Tuam and one of the founders of the *Tuam News*, has been seen as one of those most

7 Hansard cc, 100.   8 NLI Ms 4251.   9 Dennis Carrol to R.R. Madden, 23 July 1864: Madden Papers Ms 276, Dublin City Library.   10 *Connaught Patriot*, 2 August 1864, 26 March 1864.

influential on the intellectual development of Fenians in the last quarter of the century because he had taught them in their youth. John Glynn, another product of St Jarlath's, edited a column in Irish in the *Tuam News* for over twenty years and later edited the *Tuam Herald*. Born in 1825 near Castlebar, Ulick Bourke knew the antiquarian James Hardiman, and was believed to have been taught Irish by him.[11] From Hardiman also he had learned his 'love for literature, for Ireland, her language, her history, her glories, [and] that desire which became the ruling passion of his mind to do something to revive the ancient language of our beloved land'. Bourke was educated at St Jarlath's and Maynooth and ordained in 1858. He returned to St Jarlath's as Professor of Classics, Logic and Irish. While still a student at Maynooth, he published the *College Irish Grammar*, which was designed for the students of both Maynooth and the Catholic University of Ireland. At A.M. Sullivan's suggestion he wrote a series of lessons in Irish which were serialised in *The Nation* and later printed as an elementary textbook, *Easy Lessons in Irish* (1867). Three years later, Bourke founded the *Tuam News* in order to provide 'a popular exponent of national and local opinion ...'[12] The *Tuam News* ran an Irish column which was edited for over twenty years by John Glynn. Bourke also started The *Keltic Journal and Educator*, a short-lived paper published in 1869, and he contributed to the publication of *An Gaodhal*, started in Brooklyn in 1881. In its early numbers, *An Gaodhal* was filled with extracts from the *Tuam News* and articles by Bourke and Archbishop MacHale. Bourke's *The Aryan Origin of the Gaelic Race and Language* (1875) was a scholarly attempt to dispel many of the myths about this subject that had accumulated over the years. As a teacher of young men preparing to enter a seminary, Bourke's influence went far wider than Tuam and County Galway. Among others, he taught Mark Ryan, the Fenian and founder member of the Gaelic League; a son of one of the Manchester Martyrs and O'Donovan Rossa's sons (whose education was paid for by the journalist Richard Pigott). According to Ryan, in the 1860s St Jarlath's was the only college in Ireland where the Irish language and history were taught and where the pupils hear 'the old Fenian tales'; and Ryan calculated that fifteen to twenty of his contemporaries at St Jarlath's became members of the Fenian movement. Ryan believed that Bourke, despite his essentially moderate political views, was 'a Fenian at heart'.[13] But Bourke was no extremist, and in later life he condemned violence outright.

Gaelic Ireland was presented in the provincial press with exhortations to 'cherish the name and memories of Ireland – her history and her heroes'.[14] For Bourke the Irish language was important because 'with it are interwoven a thousand national recollections which we fondly cherish, with it is bound up the history of our

11 Padraic Diskin, 'Irish Scholars and Language Workers in the West, 1800–1900', *Íarlair* (St Jarlath's College Past Pupils Union Magazine), 1961, pp 90–1. I am grateful to Dr J.A. Claffey for drawing my attention to this article. 12 Obituary of Fr Ulick Bourke, *Tuam News*, 25 November 1887. 13 Mark Ryan, *Fenian Memories* (Dublin, 1945), pp 27 and 29. 14 *Tipperary Leader*, 27 January 1855.

glory, of our triumphs, of our fame ... the language of a nation is the exponent of a people's antiquity; the index of their refinement; the mouthpiece of their history; the type of their freedom'.[15] Martin O'Brennan of the *Connaught Patriot* urged professors of Irish to engage in the direct teaching of Irish, rather than limiting themselves to 'reading old stories, however interesting'. He advocated 'they must be teachers rather than mere talkers, when a good national work is to be done ... work is necessary to uplift a fallen nation, "*res non verba*" [deeds not words]'. The *Connaught Patriot* lamented the 'great neglect of a knowledge of Irish History, in comparison with the histories of every other people on the globe'.[16]

The idea that Ireland's past was better than its present is familiar from the ideology of the repeal movement, and the provincial papers repeat this theme in moral as well as physical terms. Journalists and historians used the past as a tool to create the ideal of Ireland's present, and the publication of biographies and tales of the lives and deeds of past heroes made it possible for readers to be able instantly to recognise these men and women. Newspapermen themselves read the histories of Ireland produced by other newspapermen.[17]

The lives of saints and heroes were the subjects of potted biographies in the press, and long columns of newsprint were devoted to such topics as 'The Milesians in Ireland'; the association of the Glen of Maolughra in Wicklow with Fiagh Mac-Hugh O'Byrne and the tribe of Brann in the Flight of the Earls. In the mid-1850s, William Kenealy's *Tipperary Leader* devoted whole pages to Irish history before 1600. Unusually for a nationalist, Kenealy agreed with Thomas Davis who had dissented from the view that the preservation of the Irish language was as important as the preservation of Ireland's past history and customs. Kenealy thought it would be impractical to revive the Irish language. The true essence of nationality was to be found in the country's manners, customs, and superstitions, and these were constituted in 'the thoughts, feelings and idioms – the struggles, defeats, and the aspirations of a people', not in their language.[18]

Martin O'Brennan's interpretation of the origins of the Gaelic race and their settlement in Ireland was explored in detail over many editions of the *Connaught Patriot*. Here he continued work started by Thomas Davis in *The Nation*, when Davis advocated that a new 'national art' should be created through writing on the

---

15 Introduction, *The College Irish Grammar* (Dublin,1856), p. xi.   **16** Preface to *Ancient Ireland* (Dublin, 1855), pp xxi–xxii.   **17** Fr Ulick Bourke of the *Tuam News*, Alexander Bole, *Mayo Constitution*, Charles Cooper, *Hull Advertiser*, Patrick Donohoe, *Boston Pilot*, John Gray, *Freeman's Journal*, Jasper Kelly, *Tuam Herald*, J.F. Maguire, *Cork Examiner*, J. Mahon and Michael Winter, *Galway Mercury*, all subscribed to Martin O'Brennan's *Antiquities* when it was published in 1858: op. cit., pp vii–xvi.   **18** *Ballads of Ireland* (Dublin, 1856), p. xxxiv. Edmund Dwyer Gray gave Florence Arnold-Forster a copy of *Ballads of Ireland* in 1880 after they had discussed 'such safe subjects as Irish ballads, statues, etc., with only an occasional allusion on his part to subjects like Home Rule ... which I could hardly discuss with the Editor of the Freeman ...': cf. T.W. Moody and R.A.J. Hawkins (eds), *Florence Arnold-Forster's Irish Journal* (Oxford, 1988), pp 34 and 40–1.

early history of Ireland. His list of possible subjects headed by the landing of the Milesians. O'Brennan possibly relied on John O'Donovan's edition of Micheál O Cléirigh's *Annála Rioghachta Eireann: Annals of the Kingdom of Ireland by the Four Masters from the earliest period to 1616*, published in Dublin in 1851 or on Charles Vallancey's work on the origin of the Irish race and language.[19] Between 1855 and 1867 O'Brennan wrote five books dealing with Irish history and the Irish language, together with a translation of the catechism and a prayer book in Irish, later advertised in the *Connaught Patriot* but apparently never published. The main theme of his histories was that the Irish race originated in Scythia and travelled across south Europe, arriving in Ireland from Spain. The link between the teaching of history and the fostering of nationalism was claimed by O'Brennan in his preface to the second edition of his *Antiquities*. The sale of the first edition within two months had proved 'First – that there are at least one thousand nationalist readers to be had; Second – that there still exists an indestructible flame of nationality never to be wholly subdued'.[20] Ulick Bourke later rejected all O'Brennan's theses in the preface to his own *Pre-Christian Ireland*: 'The whole story ... regarding Fenius is entirely opposed to the truth in comparative philology, by chronology, geography, facts relating to eponymous heroes of the same social period'.[21]

Writing in 1883, Ulick Bourke placed the development of Ireland within the growth of European nationalism and saw the loss of the old rural society as the reason for the present collapse of order. His *Plea for the Evicted Tenants of Mayo*, written during the Land War and addressed to Gladstone, was couched in historical terms. Bourke described the former clan system where, before the Flight of the Earls, the idea of eviction was never entertained.[22] Patrick Francis Durkan (whose *National Poems* were printed by the *Connaught Patriot* in 1862) wrote in 1856 of the

> ... times as peasants say
> We plenty had, and we the rents could pay
> ... those good old days are gone
> ... But now, alas! the landlords, force prevails,
> And mocks the morals of the peasant tales
> And hence the dearth of olden legends dear.[23]

An election pamphlet for P.E. Gill in 1865 asked:

> Have you heard the Glorious News says the Shan Van Vocht
> P.E. Gill is going to stand

19 See Norman Vance, op. cit., pp 226–7.   20 Op. cit., (Dublin, 1858), p. 7.   21 Op. cit., p. 129.   22 Ulick J. Bourke, *A Plea for the Evicted Tenants of Mayo* (Dublin, 1883), p. 20.   23 Patrick Francis Durkan, 'Deal or the Peasant's Bride', *National Poems* (Tuam, 1862).

As Leader in the Land
Ireland's Freedom to demand
We'll have th' old times back again
Peace and Plenty both to reign
Each Farmer's house will be
A seat of hospitality
And Ireland will be great and free.[24]

And not just good times but good manners: Martin O'Brennan believed that the Scythians had deliberately decided to settle in Galicia on their way to Ireland because it was 'a country void of people'. This was 'proof incontestable of the innate love of justice of the Celts and their indisposition to usurpation and tyranny'.[25]

Propaganda on the use of Gaelic was a none too subtle means for the provincial press to urge independence from Britain. Together with Maurice Lenihan, Ulick Bourke was a member of the Society for the Promotion and Cultivation of the Irish Language. Founded in 1858, it was used by the Fenian movement as a recruiting base for isolated young shopworkers from the provinces who had come to work in Dublin.[26] In 1865 he had claimed that while 'ten years ago' written Irish had been a thing of the past, now it was being written and spoken 'by thousands of the growing youth ... in many parishes throughout Connaught'.[27] *The Nation* printed a column in Gaelic from the mid-1860s,[28] but before 1870 and the *Tuam News* column no provincial paper appears to have published material in Gaelic, and it is debatable whether it would have been profitable, even in those parts of Ireland where it was widely spoken. In 1859, the *Mayo Telegraph* had claimed that the 'Celtic tongue' was 'among the gems that a people should and do value most, after religion', but it did not print columns in Gaelic.[29] The following year, the *Connaught Patriot* forecast that they would soon have a Gaelic font to print and circulate national ballads, and announced that when they had 200 subscribers they hoped to publish an Irish prayer book, but there is no evidence that they did so by the time the newspaper ceased publication in 1869.[30] The only other provincial Irish newspaper which advertised an Irish column in the last quarter of the century was the *Cashel Gazette* edited by John Davis White.

In 1875 Ulick Bourke believed that while the professional classes were ignorant of and hostile to Irish, in contrast peasants buying and selling at fairs in the Tuam diocese spoke 'no language save Gaelic'.[31] In 1861, 61.4 per cent of the population of Mayo said they spoke Irish, 56.5 per cent in 1871 and 60.2 per cent in 1881. (These

---

24 *Lenihan Papers* NLI Ms 5159.   **25** *The Celtic Race* (London, n.d.), p. 12.   **26** Lenihan Papers NLI Mss 133; Comerford, op. cit. (1985) pp 66, 68–9.   **27** *The College Irish Grammar*, p. xi, and Preface to *Easy Lessons on Self-Instruction in Irish* (Dublin, 1867).   **28** *Connaught Patriot*, 4 February 1860.   **29** Op. cit., 3 August 1859.   **30** *Ancient Ireland*, p. xxi and 'The Milesians in Ireland', *Connaught Patriot*, 4 February 1860.   **31** Ulick Bourke, *The Aryan Origin of the Gaelic Race and Language* (London, 1875).

figures include those who spoke English as well.) Of the 409,482 people who spoke Irish in the whole of Connaught in 1861, only 77,818 said that Irish was their sole language, and by 1871 this had declined to 50,154 and by 1881 to 33,335. There are no figures on the numbers of people who read the Irish language, either alone or as well as English, and it is not surprising that there was no newspaper dealing in popular day-to-day affairs which was published in the Irish language alone.[32] This confirms Benedict Anderson's thesis that when print arrived, diverse spoken languages were curtailed. Print 'fixed a language', and in Ireland that language was English.[33] Arguments on the future of the Irish language focussed on whether it should be allowed to wither away as unsuited to a modern state, or preserved as part of the necessary foundation of a nation in the European concept of nationhood. For John MacHale and Ulick Bourke in Tuam there were no doubts: they believed that the English language of the National Schools was destroying the Irish language and Ireland's history. MacHale, himself a translator and writer of original stories in Gaelic, attacked the curriculum as 'mixed and dangerous'.[34] As well as the National Schools, Bourke condemned the convent schools and the Christian Brothers, when he recommended that there should be classes in Gaelic: 'If the people are in earnest, and if this desire for learning the language of our nation, and of teaching it, be not a passing fit of laudable fervor or of patriotism ...'[35] Various stratagems were advocated to ensure that the language continued in daily use. Sidney Godolphin Osborne believed that the Bible and literature published in Irish would have redemptive power and be of direct help to the social and political state of the people.[36] Both John Glynn and Ulick Bourke thought that it was imperative that judges and magistrates in Munster and Connaught should be 'perfect Celtic scholars'. They also urged priests to use Irish when they heard the confessions of Irish-speaking people.[37] Newspaper editors put pressure on the courts to use Irish when dealing with Irish-speaking defendants and witnesses. Describing a petty sessions hearing where a Resident Magistrate had bullied a peasant for giving evidence in Irish, Edward Byrne of the *Tuam News* attacked the R.M.'s attitude in strong language: 'The laws against speaking Irish are at this day just as intolerant as they were at the worst period of the penal code'.[38]

In the mid-1870s, pressure for spoken and written Gaelic united Irish and Scottish campaigns for Home Rule. A Scottish paper, *The Highlander*, had been founded by John Murdoch in 1873 to demonstrate to crofters that the Gaelic language was as important to them as their land. Like similar Irish newspapers, it included articles on the traditions, literature, ballads and pastimes of the Highlands. *The Nation* no-

---

32 Census of Ireland, Professions, Education and Occupation, HC 1863 [3204–III] lxi. 1; HC 1876 [Cl377] lxxxi.1; HC 1882 lxxvi.385.   33 Anderson, op. cit., p. 47.   34 MacHale to Palmerston, letter reprinted in *Connaught Patriot*, 4 February 1860.   35 Quoted by Daly, op. cit., p. 39 from Bourke's copy of Gallagher's *Sermons*.   36 Osborne, op. cit., pp95–6.   37 *Tuam News*, 21 July 1871.   38 *Tuam News*, 17 August 1874. A number of witnesses to the Special Commission hearing in 1888–9 spoke only Gaelic.

ticed an 'admirable article' in the paper which emphasised the unity of interest
between Scotland and Ireland. It expressed such 'sentiments of fair play, which
should make Highlanders above all men give *Cothrom na Feinne* [equality of oppor-
tunity] to the Irish ... We hail the article as an evidence that the Home Rule cause is
making friends among our Celtic brethren in the neighbouring island'.[39]

But there is no evidence that the main readers of Irish-language columns were
the Gaelic-speaking peasantry. The readers of such texts were Irish and English
revivalists, some of whom tended to be obsessive and pressing. In the 1890s, when
John Glynn was editing the *Tuam Herald*, he was urged by the Revd J.M. Shere
Brown of Bayswater, London that the 'use of the old square character ... will undoubtedly prevent any national return to a complete and familiar use of the noble
Gaelic.' Another Englishman repeatedly urged him to provide board and lodging
and lessons in Irish for 10s. a week.[40] It was clearly more effective for those intent on
raising nationalist consciousness to concentrate, not on printing in the Irish language, but on the dissemination of Irish history and recounting the lives of heroes.

The idea of being Irish was not confined to the revival of language. In the 1850s,
industrialisation had been encouraged to improve the virtue of the people. By the
1860s, some newspapers began to link the improvement Irish industry with Irish
nationalism and to advocate that Irish products were to be preferred because they
were identified with a past when Ireland was great and free. O'Brennan, in the first
and subsequent issues of the *Connaught Patriot*, appealed to this form of patriotic
protectionism and associated the modernisation of Galway with the use of Irish
produce. He acclaimed the completion of Tuam railway terminus in 1859, not just
on grounds of convenience but because the stones used came from a quarry at Kilroe,
nine miles from the town, and the bricks were made at Annadown. His newspaper
contrasted these examples of local patronage with the actions of Dublin Corporation who had bought English stone in preference to the products of Wicklow quarries.[41] When it was argued that a Dublin statue of Daniel O'Connell must be built in
Irish stone, the importance of protectionism as a form of patriotism was again highlighted. (Throughout the century, debates on proposals to construct monuments to
past leaders were a recurrent theme in the development of nationalism. In 1898
Alfred Webb, the Quaker printer, complained to J.F.X. O'Brien, 'The country appears *memorial mad*'.)[42] Martin O'Brennan advocated the use of peat, because cutting the bog would provide work for Irish boys and girls and stop their emigration to
England 'where their mortality [*sic*] would be in danger ...'[43] In the competitive
rush towards modernisation, he urged the Town Commissioners of Tuam to use

---

39 *The Nation*, 2 September 1876.   **40** Shere Brown to John Glynn n.d.: John McPhilpin Papers; W.E.
Stevenson to John Glynn, n.d.: NLI Ms 3254.   **41** But see R.F. Foster, *Charles Stewart Parnell: the man
and his family* (Brighton, 1979), pp 155–8 for an account of the use in 1883 by Dublin Corporation of
paving stones from the quarries on the Parnell estate in preference to Welsh stone.   **42** Webb to O'Brien,
21 September 1898. NLI Ms 13,431 (5).   **43** *Connaught Patriot*, 27 and 28 August 1860.

peat to light the streets, and rivalry between Tuam and Mullingar on the installation of gas street lighting was encouraged. 'When the time comes (and it shall come, please God if Irishmen be true to themselves) when our much-neglected bogs will be a source of social brightness and a credit to old Ireland'.[44] In his anxiety to promote the fuel's efficiency, O'Brennan managed to discover a locomotive in France fuelled by peat which ran faster than locomotives fuelled by coal.[45] (It is probable that local newspaper proprietors were paid for urging the use of peat. A testimonial thanking a Richard Locke Johnson who had advocated the use of peat to make gas was signed by J. Siggins of the *Westmeath Guardian* and Felix Byrne of the *Westmeath Patriot*.)[46] Another local product was flax. O'Brennan, a Mayo man, recalled a time when the linen trade was said to have brought prosperity to the homes of the farmers of Connaught, and his newspaper condemned the importation of cotton, the product of slave-labour. 'Before the famine ... the county of Mayo abounded in flax', and its re-introduction would introduce 'a powerful source into exhausted veins ... the fireside of the peasantry was then the scene of comfort and cheerfulness'.[47] This assertion of Ireland's ability to survive economically without England was in direct opposition to the policy of liberal governments to achieve European peace through free trade, and it could be interpreted by Westminster as a coded declaration of war.

Some nationalists questioned whether material of this kind was effective. The ancient history of Ireland was low in the priorities of the leaders of Fenianism. Many years later, describing the procession at the funeral of Terence Bellew McManus, T.C. Luby told John O'Leary that some Kingstown men had followed the coffin with 'some sort of vehicle with an Irish harper and a bag pipes performer twanging and skirling ... This feature ...was designed to bring back ancient Ireland to Imagination's eye'.[48] Despite their appearance on public occasions associated with Fenianism, nationalist newspaper proprietors such as William Kenealy, P.E. Gill and Martin O'Brennan were not close to the inner circle. Fenian leaders saw newspaper propaganda as of dubious value to their cause. James Stephens had judged newspapers to be just 'public instruction' and typically believed that he himself could mould public opinion in Ireland through the dissemination of propaganda to a limited and clandestine group. Luby told O'Leary that Stephens held that 'a newspaper was an abomination'. However in late 1863, Stephens told Luby that he was considering starting a joint stock company to publish a newspaper which he could himself control in order to make money and propagate Fenian principles, and the *Irish People* was founded. According to Luby, journalists were recruited from the south of Ireland, and certainly the printer of the *Irish People* was John Haltigan of

44 Op. cit., 10 March 1860. 45 28 January 1860. 46 *Connaught Patriot*, 10 March 1860. 47 *Connaught Patriot*,14 January 1860. These local touchstones of national pride coincide with Fenian martial images of nationalism. A Captain Beggs and the son of the Gaelic scholar John O'Donovan urged the use of the pike instead of the Enfield rifle. Charles Townshend, *Political Violence in Ireland* (Oxford, 1985), pp 33 and 46. 48 T.C. Luby to John O'Leary, 11 December 1890, NLI Mss 331.

Kenealy's *Kilkenny Journal*. When questioned by other Fenians at Stephens' apparent change of policy, Luby had to say that 'circumstances had changed and required new methods'.[49] In fact, the reason was that money had been supplied from America by John O'Mahony.

Martin O'Brennan's experience at the hands of Stephens and Luby was unhappy. Born in 1812, he was the ninth (or eleventh, the records disagree) son of Martin and Sara O'Brennan of Ballyhaunis, Co. Mayo, and was educated at St Jarlath's for six years, studying Greek, Latin, French, logic, metaphysics, science, the principles of canon law, rhetoric, *belles-lettres* and the practice and science of elocution.[50] In 1857 he was admitted to the King's Inns to study law and he qualified for call to the Bar, though in fact he was never called. In the next year, 1858, he was admitted to Gray's Inn, again for the purpose of call to the Bar, but here he never began study. He claimed later that he was a barrister, and he gave a clear impression that he practised law, but he never had any legal qualifications. He also claimed that he had been a student of Trinity College, Dublin[51] but he does not appear on their list of students. O'Brennan later wrote that he had come to Dublin in 1836, and his obituarist said that he had worked in the Repeal movement, served Father Mathew as 'Secretary for Ireland without pay', supported Young Ireland, and 'Laboured for Tenant Right with pen, votes and purse'. He was also said to have petitioned for a fair trial for William Smith O'Brien, and vetted the jury in Gavan Duffy's hearings.[52] By the 1850s, he was in Dublin running a seminary for young men studying to enter university, civil and military positions. Although it was not necessary for entry to these professions, O'Brennan advertised that he taught the Irish language.

O'Brennan founded the *Connaught Patriot* in 1859. His return to Tuam had coincided with the appointment of Father Patrick Lavelle to be administrator and parish priest at Partry. It is possible that this was not a coincidence and that their arrival may have been arranged by archbishop John MacHale.[53] Lavelle and O'Brennan worked hand in glove, Lavelle orchestrating local campaigns against Thomas Plunket, the Church of Ireland bishop of Tuam, who owned large estates in Partry. Lavelle and O'Brennan were jointly engaged in furthering the work of the National Brotherhood of St Patrick, of which Lavelle was vice-president and for which they both travelled all over Ireland and England. When Lavelle was sued by John Bole, the editor of the *Mayo Constitution*, O'Brennan defended him. When O'Brennan was insulted by T.C. Luby in the *Irish People*, Lavelle travelled to Dub-

49 Luby to O'Leary, 24 August 1891, NLI Ms 331.   50 I am grateful to the Librarians of the King's Inns, of Trinity College, Dublin and of the Honourable Society of Gray's Inn, London for these detaitls of Martin O'Brennan's education, and to Dr Claffey for help in tracing his obituary.   51 Title page of *Ancient Ireland* and *Antiquities* and obituary in the *Irish World*, 2 March 1878.   52 Letter from M.E. Murtagh, Birmingham, *Connaught Patriot*, 4 November 1865.   53 Father Lavelle's career has been covered in detail in Gerard Moran, *A Radical Priest in Mayo: Fr Patrick Lavelle: The Rise and Fall of an Irish Nationalist 1825–86* (Dublin, 1994).

lin to plead his cause. In support of Father Lavelle on the right of Catholics to rebel against the state, O'Brennan reprinted a long extract from the *Irish American* attacking Abraham Lincoln's imposition of an oath of allegiance on the states wanting to return to the Union, and he discussed at length the problems of obedience to the state.[54] Both men were well-read and adept in dealing with the authorities, whether it be Cardinal Cullen in Dublin or Propaganda in Rome or, in O'Brennan's case, Dublin Castle. Both O'Brennan and Lavelle scandalised the church authorities by denying that the National Brotherhood was a secret society, and the Papal Legate believed that the relationship between Lavelle and archbishop MacHale was sinister.[55] Both the Catholic church and Dublin Castle were angered by the unwillingness of both MacHale and Lavelle to condemn Fenianism.

O'Brennan endlessly involved himself in political activity, chairing a meeting in Tuam to support the O'Connell Monument, appearing in Dewsbury supporting the Polish insurrection, in Oldham for the National Brotherhood of St Patrick, and in Dublin at meetings in the Rotunda to arrange the funeral of Terence Bellew McManus. He believed himself to be of extraordinary energy and diversity: the variety of his work proved 'that an active politician, besides attending to his ordinary business, without losing a moment from it ... can think, write and produce a work as well as talk for his country'. Despite speaking for the National Brotherhood, O'Brennan was alive to its links with Fenianism and to the tensions in the relationship of the Brotherhood with the Catholic church. He urged the Society to 'be on their guard as among them might creep in mercenaries who would urge them to sever the tie between the Pastors and their flocks'.[56] He watched European nationalist movements with admiration: Ireland, to him, was 'the Poland of the seas'. He himself disclaimed being a revolutionary, but 'I am nothing of Mazzini. I anathematise the the *Carbonari*. But bless the sword and the scythe of the Pole, and I long for the freedom of my country'.[57]

O'Brennan's relationship with the Catholic church was uneasy. MacHale backed him in his attacks on Galway landlords and in his support for Father Lavelle against bishop Plunket. But O'Brennan's main target was Cardinal Cullen who, with the assistance of Propaganda in Rome, had attempted to discipline Lavelle. Cullen had been horrified by the events in Italy during the 1850s and 1860s, seeing the loss of the temporal power of the pope as the triumph of secret societies and the enemies of religion, and he had condemned Gavan Duffy as an Irish Mazzini. In 1865, Cullen denounced the Fenians as a 'compound of folly and wickedness'. While most Irish bishops followed Cullen's directive to have no dealings with Fenianism in any of its forms, MacHale of Tuam held out against him and contributed publicly to Fenian funds. O'Brennan described Cullen as 'the concurrent and efficacious cause of the spoliation of the pontifical states and of that complete ruination that has for the last

54 *Connaught Patriot*, 2 January 1864.   55 E.R. Norman, *The Catholic Church and Ireland in the Age of Rebellion* (1973), p. 101.   56 *Connaught Patriot*, 9 January 1861.   57 *Connaught Patriot*, 5 March 1864.

few years overtaken my unhappy country ... and shattered the tenant league ... Dr
Cullen has sown the whirlwind. Let him now reap the storm ... in the general wreck
his own would be the least of all'. He went on to attack Cullen as 'one of those
untold calamities which at this moment afflict my country', adding 'Your Holiness
may not agree with me in this'.[58] Over several months in 1863 and 1864, the church
authorities were enraged by the behaviour of both Lavelle and O'Brennan, the former
as an apologist for 'sedition' and the latter for publishing what bishop MacEvilly
described to Kirby in Rome as 'a malicious Garibaldian rag, which is sometimes
heretical, sometimes schismatical and at all times personally offensive to the Head
of the Church'.[59] MacEvilly claimed that when the paper was first published, the
Tuam clergy were expected to subscribe to it and that when it nearly failed MacHale
sent the newspaper money and a letter declaring it to be the 'true organ of Catholicity
in this part of the country'.[60] Cardinal Cullen had sent copies of the *Connaught
Patriot* and Richard Pigott's *Irishman* to Kirby, claiming that Lavelle's letters excited people to disobedience and weakened their faith. Cullen claimed darkly that
the newspaper leaders insulting the Holy See were 'manifestly written to order' and
calculated to do immense mischief. Clearly Cullen thought the *Connaught Patriot* to
be an instrument in the battle between himself on one side and Father Lavelle and
archbishop MacHale on the other. The disease of Mazzinianism, he said, had infected the press: 'the newspapers speak of him [Mazzini] as if he were some kind of
divinity or another redeemer of the world ... it is not surprising that the poor Catholics begin to think that secret societies are not so bad ...'[61]

Despite O'Brennan's support for the National Brotherhood of St Patrick and
his attacks on the government, it did him no good with the Fenian leadership. Luby
and Stephens thought him a fool (he was nicknamed 'Mary-Anne'), and he never
penetrated further than the periphery of their circle.[62] In 1864, Luby had reviewed
Ancient Ireland in the *Irish People*, headed 'Gems of Irish Literature: No. 1 Ancient
Ireland and St Patrick'. This was 'a sort of humorous ironicle [*sic*] review of a work
by the learned Dr O'Brennan ... the *Connaught Patriot* – a journal of which the sage
Doctor was editor and I believe, proprietor and of which ... I don't think I ever saw
a copy – had lately, most impudently asserted that the *Irish People* was in a mori-
bund condition'. Luby described the book as a 'literary Leviathan' with 'quaint old
title pages ... The reader never knows exactly where he is or in what age of the world;
so rapid and unceasing are the learned Doctor's changes of place and time'.
O'Brennan told Luby that the attack 'was the stroke of an assassin'. Father Lavelle
travelled to Dublin and remonstrated with the *Irish People* at the savagery of the

---

58 *Connaught Patriot* 5 and 26 March 1864.   59 Quoted in Norman, op. cit., p. 102.   60 Ibid.   61
Cullen to Cardinal Barnabó, 15 April 1864 quoted in Emmet Larkin, *The Consolidation of the Roman
Catholic Church in Ireland 1850–1870* (Dublin, 1987), p. 259.   62 *Connaught Patriot*, 18 April 1861, 9
January 1864.

review, but Luby later told O'Leary that 'the pathos of the reverend advocate was unable to soften our hard hearts ... the *soggarth* parted ... still baffled of his desire'.[63]

Dublin Castle eventually lost patience with O'Brennan and arrested him for an article on Fenianism which was couched, typically, in historical terms. In February 1865 he had published a letter from Lavelle which claimed that Propaganda in Rome had advised Monsignor Wood, the Bishop of Philadelphia, that '*Feniani non sunt inguietandi*' [The Fenians are not to be disturbed] and in the same paper an article declared that all Catholics were free to join the Fenian society.[64] In October 1865, O'Brennan and a clerk in the newspaper's office were arrested and charged with having published an article which was calculated to stir up foreigners and strangers to invade Ireland, levy war against the Queen and separate Ireland from the United Kingdom. O'Brennan had insinuated that Fenianism was widespread in the forces and in the police, and that Irishmen serving in the British Army had the right to disobey the orders of an unjust government.[65] The *Connaught Patriot* described O'Brennan's arrest as 'another Russian-like razzia ...'[66] The respectable Irish metropolitan press distanced itself swiftly from any possible association with the *Connaught Patriot*. The *Dublin Express* described the paper as 'one of a class of Irish papers, the spawn of disaffection that have their substance in ignorance and prejudice ... conjuring up imaginary injuries before the eyes of the poorest of people ...' The London *Times* reported 'tremendous excitement' in Tuam when O'Brennan was arrested and presses seized, and described the paper as notable for its violence pandered to anti-English prejudice.[67] O'Brennan pleaded guilty to the charge of sedition and was released on his own recognizances. He was arrested again in March 1866 for uttering seditious language but later released. O'Brennan suddenly reappeared in London a year later, editing a new paper, the *Irish News*, which ran for four issues between March and April 1867. This repeated the old themes on the origin of the American race, testimonials to Father Lavelle and included an attack on James Stephens for his intolerance. In its first edition it praised the Fenian rebellion in Canada as a blow struck for national redemption. The paper was seized on 13 April 1867 and O'Brennan disappeared from the scene. By attacking Cullen and the papacy, by supporting Lavelle and archbishop MacHale both implicitly and explicitly, and by speaking in public for the National Brotherhood, O'Brennan seems to have constructed a cats-cradle of allegiances, some of them internally contradictory.

Luby last saw him in Richmond Bridewell, where O'Brennan was exercising in the prison yard, reading 'some book (ancient classic, no doubt) with grand theatrical emphasis and gesture ... It is now many years since he departed this topsy turvy life in Chicago'. O'Brennan had gone to America after his last encounter with British justice. In 1878 he wrote to the Chicago *Irish World*, once again advertising his

63 Luby to O'Leary, 17 June 1892, NLI Ms 332.   64 Cullen to Barnabó, 24 February 1865, in Larkin, op. cit., p. 396.   65 John Savage, *Fenian Heroes and Martyrs* (Boston, 1868), p. 419.   66 *The Express*, 7 October 1865; *Irish Times* 7 October 1865.   67 *The Times*, 7 October 1865.

books, *Ancient Ireland* and *Irish Made Easy*. This work would have continued had not the 'tyrant Saxon through his minions in Ireland interfered with me', and he denied that his work was that of a 'thoughtless dreamer', it was the product of many years work in libraries. He believed that the decline of a nation's language resulted in the decline of the nation itself, and that Greece, Rome, Spain and France were examples of this peril. Only the Irish language was preserved 'unimpaired, unmixed, unadulterated ... More anon'.[68] He died in March 1878 as the result of an accident in the street, leaving a destitute widow and eight children.[69]

O'Brennan was a victim: repudiated by the Gaelic scholars he respected, ridiculed by the hard-line Fenian leaders who would have been unlikely to trust a man who had attempted to be called to the English Bar; with one exception he was repudiated by the Catholic hierarchy, and prosecuted by the authorities for association with Fenianism, an association which the *Connaught Patriot* indignantly denied on his behalf when he was in prison. 'The fact is the Fenians, at least the Editor and Proprietor of the *Irish People* have been his bitterest foes'.[70] Despite its excursions into local, national and international politics, the *Connaught Patriot* sold itself as a local Tuam paper. It conducted battles on the political alignments of the other local papers; it was Father Lavelle's main mouth-piece against bishop Lord Plunket in the 'War in Partry'; it bid unsuccessfully for local printing contracts, and it got embroiled in a libel case resulting from allegations that the Town Commissioners of Ballina were corrupt.[71] Yet one is driven to the conclusion that it was John MacHale and Father Lavelle's Catholic nationalist propaganda sheet. MacHale's hand remains hidden, and it is regrettable that his archives have been lost.

The messages behind the propaganda peddled by the *Connaught Patriot* were peculiarly difficult for the administration to decode. The hidden oath-bound nature of Fenianism itself was reinforced in the authorities' eyes by its relationship to the Catholic church and, as they saw it, Fenian organisations. The seizure of the *Connaught Patriot* and O'Brennan's prosecution may be interpreted a reaction against a threat embodied in an intangible mythic past. Difficulties were posed to the British government by the growing readership of papers that spoke in language and idioms that they could not interpret. In the 1870s, the British government's unease led to measures to limit the freedom of the press to claim to speak on behalf of a separate Irish people. While the appeal to the past to right present wrongs was described in the context of historical events and mores, there was a tension between the desire for modernisation and the longing for the return of a supposedly better world. But before 1890 the Irish language played a very small part in the struggle for national independence and certainly this was true of the growth in nationalism outside Dublin during the 1860s. Those newspapers that published articles urging the creation of an independent Ireland depended on the English language and used the history

68 *Irish World* (Chicago), 23 February 1878.   69 *Galway Vindicator*, 9 March 1878.   70 Op. cit., 7 October 1865.   71 27 April 1861, 24 March and 23 June 1860.

of Ireland to urge their cause. If Irish were to be the language of a newly independent nation, a change of heart had to halt its loss through emigration and the desire to rise in society by speaking English.

8

Anxiety and the beginning of suppression

The Fenian Press has been the fountain head of all sedition and treason in Ireland. I feel strongly that some measure for suppressing a Paper when proof of its treasonable character is established before one or two Judges would be desirable.[1]

The Peace Preservation Bill introduced in March 1870 included specific provision to control the press. Why did Gladstone, the man who ten years before had abolished taxes on knowledge, consider this to be necessary? During the debate on second reading in the house of Commons, he was criticised both by his supporters and the opposition for introducing such a provision, particularly because the newspapers he was attempting to control were advocating that Ireland should determine her own future. The press clause deeply offended two of the main tenets of mid-century liberalism, the right of freedom of expression and the self-determination of peoples. It also raised disturbing echoes of Napoleon III's repression of the press during the previous ten years. But Gladstone's 1870 decision on the Irish press must be considered in the context of mid-century anxiety about the condition of Ireland.

There is no doubt that Gladstone believed in the expression of strong opinions. Indeed, he described their utterance as the 'safety valve of passions' which was a 'sign we are safe'.[2] However, as is so often the case with Gladstone, his statements cannot be read in isolation from the rest of his political philosophy and his interpretation of events. Gladstone understood fears about giving power to people whose behaviour was unpredictable and who were not necessarily subject to the old forms of social control in the way that they exercised their vote. Of the new agricultural householder vote, he wrote that it exchanged 'a certain and well-disciplined support for a doubtful and many-sided chance'.[3] He was also aware of the effect of uncontrolled populism: describing it as the 'political electricity [that] flies from man to man', and he understood the effect of problems of arousing 'popular passions'. He speculated that 'when it does operate upon a mass of men, a very formidable case may conceivably arise. It is difficult to reason with the passions of an

---

1 Spencer to H.A. Bruce, Home Office, 19 December 1869, in Peter Gordon (ed.), *The Red Earl: The papers of the Fifth Earl Spencer* (Northampton 1981).   2 W.E. Gladstone, *Gleanings from Past Years* (London, 1879), p. 16.   3 *Gleanings*, i, p. 132.

individual or a few, with those of a multitude once aroused, it is impossible.' The utmost care was needed to control the threat posed to orderly society which was implicit within the masses. Gladstone was well aware of the dangers posed by their 'inferior information and capacity' which could only be controlled by the precepts and example of those who they believed to be better informed.[4]

Gladstone certainly did not support those who advocated revolution. He did not care for Mazzini and Kossuth, and was disturbed by the popular acclaim when Garibaldi visited London. Gladstone's fear of the masses and horror of revolution were accompanied by his deep concern about the condition of Ireland, a country where the people were believed to be ill-educated and imperfectly led.

Gladstone's belief in freedom of expression as a safety valve might be acceptable in Britain, where the press could not be said to threaten public order. However, this policy could not be so easily translated to Ireland, where the behaviour of both landlords and tenants was uncertain.

The four years after 1866 were notable for an increase in social unrest. Habeas corpus had been suspended between 1866 and 1869 and, after its restoration, an increasing number of landlords, agents, bailiffs and their servants had been attacked. The winter of 1869–1870 saw a rise in the number of agrarian disorders. Irish landlords, protesting at the decline of law and order, used their connections to bring influence to bear on politicians in Dublin and Westminster.

A clear relationship can be traced between the Irish press published in America and the press in Ireland. The *Connaught Patriot* reported Fenian congresses in America; the Fenian Irish-American newspapers which were seized on arrival in Ireland, such as the *Irish American*, reported the Congress of the Fenian Brotherhood in Chicago and also included extracts from the Irish provincial press with small town news. The *Fenian Spirit*, published in Boston in October 1864, included articles from the *Cork Herald*, the *Dundalk Democrat*, the *Wexford People*, and the *Belfast Northern Whig*.[5] Many Irish provincial papers claimed to circulate in America and Canada, and appeals for Irish causes were printed in both Irish and American papers.[6] It is worth noting that this link across the Atlantic could work both ways. Louis Schoenfeldt, a former reader on the *Irish Times*, introduced a 'Mr Smith' to the British Consul in New York. 'Smith' hoped to work for the British government as a paid informer. He told the Consul that he had lectured in Dublin about the Polish rising, and that immediately he had advertised the lectures, he was patronized, by the National Brotherhood of St Patrick, who had invited him to lecture in the provinces to promote the cause of Ireland through its supposed resemblance to Poland. Laudatory reviews of the lectures subsequently appeared in newspapers in the *Cork Southern Reporter*, the *Cork Examiner* and the *Kingstown Journal*. Smith,

---

4 Ibid., p. 158.   5 *Fenian Spirit*, 22 October 1864 and HM Consul, New York to Foreign Office, 3 May 1865, National Archives, Dublin, Fenian 'A' Files A2.   6 The *Irish American* printed an appeal for an Indemnity Fund for the *Connaught Patriot*: *Connaught Patriot*, 29 September 1860.

told the Consul that 'The active manager of the Fenian Clubs in Ireland – a kind of travelling secretary – is named Stevens, or Captain Stevens ... [who] has with him, as his secretary, a man named Mooney or Looney who is or was Editor of the *Galway American* newspaper, and had been an Editor of the *Irish American*'.[7] Officials in Dublin began to express increasing concern about the influence of the Irish American press on the population back home. The Irish post office was put under pressure to seize newspapers preaching treason and copies were sent to the government Law Officers, asking for their opinion on whether the editors could be prosecuted. Dublin Castle files on Fenianism during this period are full of heavily annotated cuttings from the *Fenian Spirit*, the *Boston Pilot*, and the *Irish World*, which were posted to Ireland and Britain from Canada and America and opened on arrival. In 1864 the Chief Secretary Sir Robert Peel sent an article from the *Irish World* to the Under Secretary, Major Thomas Larcom entitled 'Why should the Irish people lag behind in the glorious race of Nationalities?'[8] Inspectors of foreign papers arriving in Dublin in the last quarter of 1868 found that 'writing or unauthorised enclosures' had been higher than in any previous quarters.[9]

In early 1867, during the Fenian rebellion, Dublin Castle received reports and letters from local officials and private citizens urging the seizure and prosecution of particular newspapers. In April 1867, the commander of the Waterford Flying Column (shock troops sent by Dublin Castle to areas of disturbance) wrote to the Deputy Quartermaster General in Dublin Castle alleging that 'everyone, except the Gentry, Clergy and the Protestant party are more or less disaffected ... I am not at all surprised at the feeling of the people when they read nothing else except such newspapers as *The Irishman*, *The Shamrock* and the *Cork Weekly News* whose columns are filled with *open treason* and sedition.' The Deputy Quarter Master General sent this letter on to the Under Secretary, with a note asking whether there would be any means of 'putting the proper check on the most wicked and treasonable publications mentioned...'[10] An anonymous correspondent sent an extract from the *Belfast News-Letter* of 10 July 1867 to the Lord Lieutenant with a note: 'I call on you, and the Government, to control or put down such incendiary papers and pamphlets.'[11] Dublin Castle intelligence suffered from an understandable confusion in their interpretation of the motives and personalities involved in the various nationalist groupings. This combination of paranoia and pressure made press prosecution in Ireland almost inevitable. Policemen, anxious to identify those who were involved in nationalist movements, attended lectures on 'The influence of National poetry' at the Dublin Mechanics' Institute, listened to poems by Thomas Davis, Thomas Moore and Speranza (Lady Wilde) and recognised A.M. Sullivan in the audience.[12]

7 E. Archibald, HM Consul New York, to Foreign Secretary, 3 May 1864, National Archives Fenian A Files A2.   8 Peel to Larcom, 23 January 1864, Larcom Papers NLI Ms 7586.   9 Minute to Postmaster General, 11 January 1867, Larcom Papers NLI Ms 7586.   10 Major Bell to Deputy Quartermaster General, 3 April 1867; Deputy Quartermaster General to Under Secretary, 5 April 1867, National Archives CSORP 1867/6035.   11 National Archives CSORP 1867/12180.   12 Memorandum by

The absence of statute law to deal with the press was a recurrent irritation. Repeated attempts were made to get satisfactory legal opinions from the Law Officers as to whether newspapers sent through the post could be prosecuted. In March 1866 the Irish Law Officers thought that seizure of the American *Irish People* was justifiable under common law, but the English Law Officers were more cautious, believing that legislation would be necessary. Opinion was also sought as to whether it was legal to open and detain newspapers (as opposed to letters), and again the Irish Law Officers believed that the common law could be used, but that the statutory power of detaining letters could not be applied to newspapers. The English Law officers were again more cautious, and recommended that the Lord Lieutenant should make an order to the Dublin GPO instructing it to detain particular newspapers. Although the Post Office Acts did not authorise seizure, 'The treasonable nature of the paper would furnish a good defence to any proceeding' against the Post Office. However, this was not warranted by Act of Parliament, and it was once again recommended that legislation should be passed authorising the Lord Lieutenant to detain all papers or, alternatively, all printed papers from abroad.[13] The apparent lack of power to take action against papers, whether published in Ireland or America, made officials extremely restive.

The press was understandably sensitive about the prosecution of any one of their number. Writing about their own prosecution for libel by an Armagh JP in May 1861, an editorial in *The Irishman* referred to 'much discussion latterly ... on the liberty of the press; and English writers have pleasantly boasted how free the press was, in England, compared with the press in France ... the liberty of the press in Ireland is the liberty of the collared serf as compared with that of the newspapers of France'.[14] In November 1861, a committee called the 'Friends of a Free Press and Impartial Juries' was announced in Tuam, chaired by the O'Donoghue and with Ulick Bourke as honorary secretary.[15] Newspapers compared press prosecution with European totalitarianism: a leader in the *Connaught Patriot* paralleled the arrest of Martin O'Brennan and his printer in 1865 with the activities of the Tsarist police, when they were 'honoured with a visit from the Russian Myrmidons of Whig domination in Ireland'. When O'Brennan was committed for trial, his paper asked: 'Could Russia have done worse in Poland?'[16] Prosecution by the government on the one hand and restriction on freedom of speech by the Catholic hierarchy on the other,

Superintendent Daniel Ryan, DMP, 11 August 1868 National Archives 'F' Papers 3185R.   13 5 and 9 March 1866, Larcom Papers, NLI Ms 7694.   14 25 May 1861.   15 *Connaught Patriot*, 16 November 1861. The O'Donoghue, who had been a Member of Parliament since 1857, tried to keep one foot in the liberal camp and at the same time attempted to influence and lead various committees and movements formed in Dublin in the 1860s. He was a prominent member of the MacMahon Sword Committee and the National Brotherhood of St Patrick. He chaired meetings on the Trent affair and helped organise the National Petition of 1861. The O'Donoghue's attempts to assume prominence in the nationalist movement were doomed to failure because all these movements were manipulated by Fenians from behind the scenes.   16 Op. cit., 7 October 1865.

became confused in the internecine strife between O'Brennan, Lavelle and Cardinal Cullen. Defending the Irish priesthood, O'Brennan wrote that 'By the laws of the realm they are free to speak and free to write within the margin of treason, sedition or libel but by the laws of Dr Cullen, if they do, let them be prepared to meet the penalty.'[17]

Ministers were reluctant to prosecute, because it was recognised that prosecution would result in greater publicity for the newspaper and a probable increase in its circulation. The editor would be raised to a martyr's status at the hands of the Crown, and any interest in secret societies might be increased. Discussing the possibility of prosecuting A.M. Sullivan for an article in *The Nation*, Lord Derby wrote to Lord Naas that there was

> No question as to the seditious character of the article, but a prosecution even with the [clearest?] evidence does not necessarily imply a conviction – and even if we obtained one, it would as you observe, only have the effect of making a martyr of Mr Sullivan and increasing the circulation of his trashy paper. But it would have the further effect of raising to undue importance the members of the Phoenix Societies which the investigation, as far as it has gone, has proved to be very insignificant ... we shall do well to have Mr Sullivan and his balderdash unnoticed unless a string of articles should produce a strong and general feeling that in leaving him alone we are neglecting our duty.[18]

Gladstone, commenting on an article in the *Pall Mall Gazette*, wrote to General Grey that 'our purpose and duty is to endeavour to draw a line between the Fenians & the people of Ireland, & to make the people of Ireland indisposed to cross it. But ... the mere sense that their chances of proselytism are diminishing (if so it were) might increase their wrath', and wrote in similar terms to Lord Spencer, the Lord Lieutenant.[19] The *Times* identified another problem facing those who wished to prosecute the press in Ireland, namely they believed that it would be impossible to find reliable jurors. 'State prosecutions are precarious in their issue and when they fail they tend to produce a dangerous reaction and to perpetuate the evil they were intended to repress!'[20]

Thus, despite the anxiety to crush the expression of seditious opinion, it was well understood in Ireland that prosecuting the press was an issue to be handled with great care. This is clearly illustrated in Dublin Castle files in cases where local enthusiasm ran ahead of the executive's discretion. When the Under-Secretary replied to the complaint made by the Commander of the Waterford Flying Column in

17 *Connaught Patriot*, 5 March 1864. The police report on *The People of Ireland* added: 'Some of the articles ... have attracted the attention of His Eminence Cardinal Cullen': Chief Superintendent Daniel Ryan, 8 November 1869, National Archives Fenian Papers 3185R. 18 Derby to Naas, 19 January 1859, NLI Naas Papers Ms 11,059. 19 Diary, 28 March 1869; BL Add. Mss 44536 f.152. 20 Op. cit., 13 December 1869.

1867, he warned that 'a prosecution of the public press is a question of policy of very grave import, and is a matter which can only be considered by the responsible officers of the Crown'. Spencer was extremely annoyed in 1883 when a district officer in Galway prosecuted the proprietor of the *Western News* for inciting outrages; such prosecutions must always be approved by Dublin Castle.[21] With these caveats in mind, some ministers felt that action needed to be taken, and taken in the near future.

Between the end of 1869 and the beginning of March 1870 there was a change of policy on the feasibility of effectively controlling the Irish press. As late as 20 January, Gladstone was not contemplating 'exceptional legislation on the press'. However, on 2 February, Cabinet discussed a proposal to extend the 'exceptional legislation in Ireland to include the extension of the punishment for sedition to seizing printers' type'.[22] (One of the feared effects of the introduction of such legislation was that John Bright, the campaigner for the abolition of taxes on knowledge, would resign.)[23] But on 17 March, when the Chief Secretary for Ireland, Chichester Fortescue, introduced the Peace Preservation Bill, it included a clause giving the Lord Lieutenant the power to order the seizure of the printing presses, engines, machinery, types, implements and paper of any newspaper found to include seditious and treasonable material or incitements to commit crime. The *Times* referred to this as 'an enormous power, and every journalist must feel the deepest regret that it should be necessary, but it is too plainly indispensable'.[24]

In his speech on the introduction of the bill, Chichester Fortescue recurred to the old theme that that intimidation and terrorism which existed in Ireland had 'unsettled the minds of the poorer class'.[25] He was explicit in outlining the reasoning that had led to the introduction, for the first time in Britain, of legislation specifically to control the press. In the past, cases where newspapers had been prosecuted had resulted in mild punishment, as in the case of Sullivan and the *Irishman*, but meanwhile their papers continued as usual. Papers were able to evade prosecution with ingenuity; failure to get a conviction resulted in increased circulation for the press and, even if prosecution were successful, it dealt with only one paper at a time when many were offending. Up until then, it had only been possible to proceed against the proprietor or editor of the paper. Chichester Fortescue was able to quote a 'most respectable journal', the *Belfast Northern Whig*, which had repudiated the more extreme papers. The *Whig* felt that the liberty of the press as a whole was being abused by 'so-called Nationalist, but really Fenian newspapers' and had urged the government to take action.[26]

Those Members of Parliament who supported the government believed that the Fenian leaders had used the press to produce a 'more dangerous state of things than

21 Spencer to Jenkinson, 11 December 1883, National Archives Prevention of Crime (Ireland) Act 1882, Carton 6.   22 Diary, 2 February 1870.   23 Gladstone to Chichester Fortescue, 2 March 1870. *Diaries*, vii, p. 47.   24 18 March 1870.   25 Hansard, cc, 89–90.   26 Ibid., cc, 103.

even agrarian outrages ... Fenian writers had the lowest appreciation of the intelligence of their readers, where no falsehood too gross, no argument too ludicrous, no occurrence too trivial to use to instil disloyalty and disaffection'.[27] The liberal Solicitor-General for Ireland, Richard Dowse, described the press 'one of the chief curses of the country'.[28] Lord Claud John Hamilton, Conservative MP for King's Lynn claimed that 'As long as the Press of Ireland remained as it was' it was utterly impossible to establish loyalty, contentment, or prosperity. The press 'persistently stirred up bad feeling between the owners and occupiers of the Soil'.[29] Gladstone told the House that the present law on prosecution of the press was 'wholly inefficient'. The problem for the Irish executive was that it had very little influence and had no co-operation from any class of the people, high or low, to the same degree as in England. His description of the lower classes of Irish society encapsulates the British view of the Irish peasantry as 'a broad stratum of society ... a region of sentiment infinitely various ... all very different from that which is necessary to constitute loyal and healthy attachment to the law'.[30] The bill, he said, was aimed at articles in the newspapers 'written with a view to throw people into a treasonable attitude of mind, teaching them to expect rebellion, to prepare for it and to take part in it when it comes'. In his speech Gladstone drew on an article by W.R. Greg in the *Quarterly Review* which had welcomed the Bill, and especially the provisions to control the press. Greg believed that they went directly to the heart of the problem, 'steering clear alike of all dawdling over the mischief on the one hand and of all fetters of the true freedom of the press on the other'. The decision to confiscate the plant and type was right: 'the proprietor is the real malefactor, without him the writer would be ... a mere voice crying in the wilderness'.[31] H.A. Herbert, MP for County Kerry, compared the readers of the Irish press with the readers of similar papers in England. Echoing the views of bishop Moriarty quoted earlier, he claimed that in England the working class read all kinds of newspapers and 'heard and read both sides of the question', but in Ireland 'large classes of people only saw papers of one view'. If these newspapers preached sedition 'how could the country be expected to be quiet?'[32] A speaker who claimed that 'the agrarian population in Ireland do not read the newspapers' was answered with cries of 'Yes, yes'.[33]

Those who were against the bill varied in their opposition from personal experience to general prejudice. John Francis Maguire of the *Cork Examiner*, the veteran of tenant right, worried over the power that would be given to the executive in Dublin Castle, and pointed out that, were the bill made law, he would have come

---

27 Col. Wilson-Patten, a former conservative Chief Secretary for Ireland, Hansard, cc, 348. 28 Ibid., cc, 361. 29 Ibid., cc, 483. 30 Ibid., cc, 508. 31 W.R. Greg, 'The Irish Land Bill and the Peace Preservation Bill' in *Quarterly Review*, 128 (April 1870), pp 560–76. 32 Hansard, cc, 623. In 1881, Florence Arnold-Forster was told by Dr Lyons, the member for Dublin City between 1880 and 1885, that the 'great want' in Ireland was an independent newspaper. He believed that 'the people hear only one side, and can hear only one side, for the other side is never put before them': *Florence Arnold-Forster's Irish Journal*, 16 June 1881. 33 Hansard, cc, 406. Mr E. Horsman (Liskeard).

under its provisions if he had still been a journalist. Maguire thought the Fenian press was mere 'milk-and-water', compared with the *Rappel* and *La Marseillaise* which the even the French government had hesitated to prosecute. What redress was there, he enquired, when the Chief Secretary and other government officers could enter the newspaper's premises and scatter the type, smash the machinery and ruin everybody connected with the paper? Citing the case of Sullivan and *The Irishman*, Maguire believed that 'the bill would strike, not only at the liberty of the press but at the very life of a nation'.[34] The O'Donoghue's speech during the debate reflected his own tense and bruised relationship with Fenianism in the 1860s when he told the House that, 'All that the Bill would coerce was a small knot of scribblers, who had arrogated to themselves in the most unwarrantable manner that they alone were endowed with the attributes of nationality; a class of scribblers whose policy it was to efface the teaching of O'Connell, to vilify the priesthood and to change and pervert the confiding nature of the Irish people ...'[35]

The government was attacked from all sides for its apparent betrayal of liberalism, and examples of both liberalism and illiberalism in Europe were used to fuel these complaints. Irish members repeatedly cited the actions taken against the press over the last twenty years by foreign governments, and unkindly reminded Gladstone of his stand on Italy in the 1850s. The suppression of Herzen's *Kolokol* in Poland, and the actions against the editors of *Rappel* and *La Marseillaise* were cited as instances of European repression. Liberal MPs spoke of their sadness at the apparent death of their ideals at a time when comparatively new nations were courageously dispensing with the censorship of the press while at the same time maintaining law and order. In these circumstances, it was painful that a British government should contemplate arbitrary devices and oppressive powers. 'Was England to be asked to put on the cast-off clothes of French despotism?'[36]

Gladstone's policies, as they were interpreted by the House, were roundly exposed. One Member of Parliament observed acutely that 'Those who had so loudly proclaimed Italy for the Italians, Hungary for the Hungarians, Poland for the Poles, could ill afford to complain if unprincipled agitators at either side of the Atlantic raised the kindred cry of "Ireland for the Irish" '.[37] Even the *Times* took up this point, saying that Napoleon III must enjoy a grim satisfaction at the contrast between Press liberties under 'despotic' France and 'free' England.[38] Some of the Irish papers seized upon the proposal to control the press by specific legislation as 'not British'. P.J. Smyth addressed a demonstration in Dublin and spoke of the establishment of an autocratic system of espionage and police rule.[39] *The Irishman* compared the government's intentions to Turkish justice, and *The Nation* spoke of the government's 'Algerine press-code'. An Irish Press Brigade or National Guard was proposed, to be enrolled in London and ready in the event of an attack by the

34 Hansard, cc, 386.   35 Ibid. , cc, 610.   36 W.M. Torrens, ibid., cc, 630.   37 J. Lowther, ibid., cc, 380.   38 25 March 1870.   39 *The Times*, 28 March and 4 April 1870.

government on the liberty of the Irish press. Sixteen journalists, including Richard Pigott, undertook to provide the work of imprisoned journalists as a 'sacred work'.[40]

With the passing of the bill, the executive relaxed. Spencer wrote to Dufferin, Chancellor of the Duchy of Lancaster, that he was 'quite at leisure since the Peace Preservation Act has been announced. It is very remarkable how Irish difficulties collapse before a bold front ... I hope that the awful powers given to me by the Act will not require enforcement'.[41] He did not attribute the relative peace of the 1870s wholly to the legislation, but he hoped that the improvement in economic conditions 'as well as in opinion of the Agricultural Classes' was in part the cause for 'greater contentment'. But Spencer was a realist, and he judged that 'it will take many years to eradicate discontent from the Irish masses'; only 'firmness coupled with just measures' would win over the Irish to being governed from England.[42] In the event, the anguish in public and private over these new controls on freedom of expression was superfluous. During the whole period that the powers to prosecute the press under the Peace Preservation Act were available, they seem to have been rarely, if ever, used. Sections 30–34, which gave the executive power to seize newspapers, were renewed in 1871 and 1873, but were repealed by the Peace Preservation (Ireland) Act 1875.[43] The reasons why the powers had been thought to be necessary in 1870, and why there was reluctance to use them, can both be understood.

In the first place, the legislation was enacted during the first parliament after the second Reform Act. Two years later Bagehot, like Gladstone after him, drew together the strands of anxiety exposed by the 1870 debate. In the introduction to the second edition of his *English Constitution*, Bagehot dealt with the effect on the polity of the desires of the newly-enfranchised working class, and drew attention to elements that would inevitably bring about profound change. Comparing these changes in the country to the seeds waiting in the ground of a great forest, which would grow when light and air were brought in, he reminded politicians that the new Reform Act enfranchised, not only the skilled but also the unskilled – those ignorant and unled. He believed that 'continually agitated' questions would bring working men as a class together and that such a combination of the lower classes 'as such and for their own objects' would be an 'evil of the first magnitude ... their permanent combination ... would ... mean the supremacy of ignorance over instruction and of numbers over knowledge'.[44]

This could be applied to describe the Irish peasantry, whom the Irish executive believed to be both ignorant and at the same time cunning and dangerous.[45] The

---

40 Quoted in *The Times*, 21 March 1870.   41 16 April 1869: *The Red Earl*, p. 83.   42 Spencer to Queen Victoria, 23 February 1874: *The Red Earl*, pp 19–21.   43 Protection of Life and Property Act, 1871 and Peace Preservation Act Continuance Act, 1873.   44 Walter Bagehot, *The English Constitution* (London, 1878), pp xxii.   45 A Limerick RM, reporting on the state of the country in 1849 and the influence of the press, referred to the 'injury inflicted upon a mercurial People by these inflammatory and seditious essays': 18 January 1849 PRO CO 904/9.

influence of the press in stimulating violence added further concern. It was understood by successive governments that, without the powerful influence of responsible and balanced newspapers and moderately inclined readers in Ireland, and without the special relationship between landlord and tenant enjoining duty and rights on either side as it did in England, Irish public opinion was a volatile force, and the Irish propensity to take violent action unpredictable.

In the second place, as the debate in the House of Commons had made clear, press legislation was foreign in origin and spirit. A.V.Dicey, writing on 'The Right to Freedom of Discussion', particularly cited action against the Irish press in the context of European legislation. In his exposition of the 'supremacy of the law' as applied to the press, he pointed out that a liberty of the press is not specifically recognised in England. He compared this situation with Belgium, where there was a recognition of the special rights granted to those connected with the press. Freedom of discussion in England is 'little else than the right to write or say anything which a jury ... of shopkeepers think it expedient should be said or written'.[46]

The problem of drafting and enforcing legislation to control the press in the 1870s was bedevilled by a natural inhibition on the part of liberal governments, faced as they were with mounting evidence of nationalist activity and with pressure from sections of the population who believed that their assets, investments and peace were threatened by a force whose strength and influence they were unable to measure. The Peace Preservation Act controls on the press in 1870 were, in a sense, a gesture towards this pressure; the fact that the new powers were hardly ever used is evidence of the continuing power of Gladstonian liberalism.

46 A.V. Dicey, *Introduction to the Study of the Law of the Constitution*, fourth ed. (London, 1893), p. 234.

9

The militant nation, 1880–92

'It is not to what is written in Ireland, but to what is read in Ireland, that we must look' G.O. Trevelyan, 18 May 1882.[1]

There is a potent image in the autobiography of an Irish journalist, Andrew Dunlop, of Charles Stewart Parnell arriving at a railway station at night during an election campaign in the west of Ireland. People rush towards his carriage and mob him as he descends. How do they know in which carriage he would be seated? From the lighted candles stuck on to the window sills by the journalists with whom Parnell preferred to travel.[2] The picture of the charismatic leader arriving surrounded by lights in order to rouse the masses is one of enormous strength. Dunlop's portrait of Parnell arriving as a *deus ex machina* demonstrates the importance of visual and written propaganda in the 1880s. His description, and the memoir of Edward Byrne, then editor of the *Freeman's Journal*, contradict the general image of Parnell as cold and remote.[3]

In the 1860s, the press had been covert in its support of Fenianism; by the 1880s it performed a central and essential role in the spread of Land League activity. The first meeting of the Mayo Land League in Irishtown in April 1879 was conceived and assisted by James Daly of the *Connaught Telegraph*. What had been a source of 'political excitement and discontent'[4] in the mid-century now became a 'dangerous and formidable system of intimidation and terrorism.'[5] In 1880, the Land League flourished on a network of communications dependent on the press, and newspaper proprietors and editors were major Land League politicians. Ministers like G.O. Trevelyan, Chief Secretary in 1882, feared the new cohesive strength of the hitherto disparate elements of Irish nationalism. This unity had been achieved by Parnell. His power as the leader of Irish nationalism both in Parliament and out of doors was won by his own cool personality standing aloof from his followers and by his harnessing of the Irish political machine and of its propaganda. 'What lends effect to the speeches of Mr Parnell?' enquired T.P. O'Connor in 1889. 'No oratorical fire, no descriptive powers, mainly the strong personality.'[6] Parnell's status as a Protestant landowner gave him the ability to focus on the structure of rural society and to

1 Speaking as Chief Secretary: Hansard, cclxix, 1014.   2 Dunlop, p. 78.   3 Frank Callanan (ed.), Edward Byrne, *Parnell: A Memoir* (1898, reprinted Dublin, 1991), p. 13   4 PRO CO 904/9 Confidential report on the state of the lately disturbed districts 1849.   5 Chichester Fortescue, Hansard cc, 87.   6 T.P. O'Connor, 'The New Journalism', *New Review*, 1 (1889), p. 429.

perceive the influence of the Roman Catholic church. He and his party increasingly brought formerly liberal provincial newspapers in line behind them. Through Patrick Egan he bought up the insolvent Richard Pigott's struggling Dublin newspapers, *Flag of Ireland, Shamrock* and *The Irishman,* to found his own newspaper, *United Ireland.*[7] James Loughlin has pointed out that 'The public entity of "Parnell" ' itself was 'the creation of the leader, his lieutenants and the nationalist press.'[8] As Matthew has demonstrated and Loughlin emphasises, the press heightened the impact of public oratory and, like Gladstone, Parnell understood this process, and used it to the full.[9] He structured his speeches both in length, style and vocabulary in such a way that they should be readily understood on the printed page.[10] However, as has been seen this was not the first occasion that print played an important role in the life of the Catholic peasantry. The Galway County election petition hearing alone is evidence that, by the mid-1860s, the press was seen and read by the peasant farmers of Galway. Certainly the National League was organized, and Parnellism was operated, in forms that used the provincial press in new ways. The combination of the development of towns, the growth of literacy, the expansion of the railway system and, as Loughlin notes, the use of the electric telegraph, all worked together to establish Parnell as a national leader.[11] By using modern communications he made both Ireland and Westminster were his platform. He understood the forces now at his command. The relative unity of nationalism between 1880 and 1890, and the leadership of Parnell made the British government even more wary of the influence of the Irish press. A further ground for British fears of Parnell's leadership was in his work in making open links with Irish America. Already by the mid-1860s, the British government had been deeply concerned about the importation of Irish-American newspapers. This anxiety was now redoubled but their willingness to prosecute newspapers was still hampered by their concern about the freedom of the press.

Even while the population of Ireland declined, the numbers of people who could read and the numbers of newspapers in print rose steadily. An important feature of the 1880s was not just the increase in numbers of provincial newspapers, but the increase in the number of newspapers which claimed to have nationalist politics. Their readers were an increasingly literate populace who had moved away from rural labouring and into serving in shops and clerking in offices. When John Pope-Hennessy wrote in 1884 that the 'reading public in Ireland is comparatively large and larger than the reading public in any country in the world', he attributed its

7 Richard Pigott, *Personal Recollections of an Irish Nationalist Journalist* (Dublin, 1882). Joseph V. O'Brien gives the weakness of the nationalist press as one of the reasons for the founding of *United Ireland,* but in his analysis he misses the essential point of the transfer of the provincial press to nationalism, that the political objectives of the Land League were based in the country, not in Dublin: *William O'Brien and the Course of Irish Politics* (Berkeley, 1976), p. 15.   8 Loughlin, op. cit., p. 221.   9 Matthew, Introduction to *Diaries,* IX, p. viii.   10 Callanan, 'Postscript: Parnell and the Press' in Byrne, op. cit., p. 43.   11 Loughlin, op. cit., p. 6.

recent increase to the lower classes 'mainly the class who with an extension of the franchise will get a voting power that they do not now possess'.[12]

The connection that Pope-Hennessy made between the possession of literacy and of the power to vote is important if one is to comprehend the extent of British politicians' anxiety about the influence of newspapers. His analysis cannot have been of much comfort to Dublin Castle. He found that men and women read newspapers such as Richard Pigott's *Shamrock* and the *Cork Weekly Herald*, newspapers which Dublin Castle regarded as having a 'bad influence'.[13] The business records for the 1880s and 1890s of Wynne's, the Castlebar newsagents, also confirm some of Pope-Hennessy's observations. The Catholic priests in Castlebar had a pronounced taste for just the kind of reading he described. The constitution of the Irish National League reiterated the commitment of earlier nationalists to the spread of literacy and Irish literature.[14] Pope-Hennessy pointed out that the new Land League reading rooms had 'plenty of readers of pure, vigorous national literature ...', and the reading room of the Catholic Young Men's Society, he said, had taught the young clerks and well-to-do artisans 'ten times more about Irish history, poetry, and biography than was known to all the habitués of the fashionable clubs ... where the upper and middle-class Catholics may be seen ... Those working men of the country reading-rooms and these shop-boys and clerks of the city are no longer the lower classes'.[15] This new generation of readers identified by Pope-Hennessy corresponds with the social background of active members of the Land League, where shopworkers, clerks and artisans formed a significant proportion of those arrested under the Protection of Person and Property Act 1881.[16] The interest in Irish history and the Irish language noted in Pope-Hennessy's article, in the Castlebar newsagent's accounts, and in many provincial newspapers, was recognised by British politicians. Chichester Fortescue's reference to the newspapers 'rhetorical descriptions of other days'[17] was echoed by Florence Arnold-Forster, who kept a press cutting book for her father while he was Chief Secretary. In her diary she noted the '... historical disquisitions on the past wrongs and present grievances of Ireland [which] continue to fill the magazines and newspapers'.[18]

The messages behind the propaganda put out in the 1860s by newspapers like the *Connaught Patriot* were peculiarly difficult for the administration to decode. They were in language foreign to Westminster and, to an extent, to Dublin Castle. The hidden oath-bound nature of Fenianism had been reinforced in the authorities' eyes by its relationship to the Catholic Church, and Fenian front organisations such

---

12 John Pope-Hennessy, 'What do the Irish Read' in *Nineteenth Century*, 15 (June 1884), p. 920.   13 Pope-Hennessy, op. cit., pp 924 and 926; National Archives: Irish Crimes Records Register of Newspapers.   14 Article 5 (d) of the constitution of the National League resolved to encourage mechanics' institutes, working men's clubs and reading rooms. It is silent on the right to freedom of expression.   15 Pope-Hennessy, op. cit., pp. 920 and 926.   16 Samuel Clark, 'The Social Composition of the Land League' in *Irish Historical Studies*, 17, 68 (1971), p. 452.   17 Hansard, cc, 100.   18 *Florence Arnold-Forster's Irish Journal*, 22 January 1881.

as the National Brotherhood of St Patrick. The seizure of the *Connaught Patriot* and
O'Brennan's prosecution may be seen as the administration's reaction against a threat
embodied in an intangible, mythic past. In the 1880s, newspapers spread the news
of Land League activity by publishing information on branch meetings and resolutions. The reorganisation and refocussing of Irish nationalist bodies in the 1880s
brought with them a special need for propaganda; newspapers were essential to the
mobilization of the Land League across Ireland, and this particular activity was one
which the government found easier to grasp. The central direction of the National
League continued a development already believed to exist in the 1870s. Hartington
had been told in 1872 that the organisation of the Kerry County by-election had
been from Dublin 'through the instrumentality of itinerant orators, local and im-
ported Fenians, [and] the whole popular press ...'[19]

Thus, to the authorities in London and Dublin the use of the press to further
nationalist ends by whatever means in either the sectarian papers or the daily and
weekly press was of great concern; these campaigns influenced a population they
conceived of as ignorant and easily led. In the eyes of government ministers the
combination of a lack of dependable local leadership and the extension of the franchise was potentially incendiary.

Dublin and London continued to be under great pressure from many quarters
to take action against the press. Subscribers to the Irish provincial newspapers living in England included absentee landowners who became concerned at the apparent fomentation of treason and sedition in their own locality. For liberals, the ethical
question whether journalists should be prosecuted for opinions sincerely held was
extremely difficult. Writing at length on the problem of whether and when to prosecute, Leslie Stephen criticised those who advocated brute force against the expression of 'poisonous opinions'; they neglected to consider the secondary implications
of such an action. The real solution was to bring about the alteration of a whole
political and social organisation so that society could cure itself. He believed that
utilitarians might object to J.S. Mill's argument that persecution was the evil which
always resulted from prosecution; taking all in all, he said, each case should be judged
on its merits. Evilness of opinion should be measured by its corruption of a whole
social order, and it was possible for opinions themselves to be poisonous. That is,
the expression of evil could tip the delicate balance of society. Under certain conditions an opinion might be suppressed by prosecution and if so, that prosecution
must tip the balance in favour of good.[20] Stephen here articulates a solution to the
Irish question that is often found in Cabinet correspondence.

Unfortunately, in application to Ireland it was quite beyond their capabilities
because of the difficulty of penetrating a social order of which the government had

19 Kenmare to Hartington, 13 February 1872: Devonshire Papers, Chatsworth f.340–494.   20 Leslie
Stephen, 'On the Suppression of Poisonous Opinions' in *Nineteenth Century* 13 and 14 (March and
April 1883) p. 635.

little or no understanding. As Redvers Buller, then Special Commissioner in Kerry, pointed out to Hicks-Beach: 'You cannot govern the Irish ... by coercion alone'.[21] A further reason for liberal governments' failure to use coercion legislation against the press before 1880 can be found in the context of political thought at the time. This was explored by A.V. Dicey, who pointed out that legislation in Britain specific to the press was foreign, both in origin and spirit.[22]

Nonetheless, Gladstone believed in what he called the 'moral effect' of prosecuting the Land League: 'What we want is to enforce silence, abstention from guilty speech',[23] and with the excitable W.E. Forster as Chief Secretary from April 1880, it was almost inevitable that action would be taken against the press. In April 1881, Cabinet received a paper on the state of country which suggested that crimes which had been formerly confined to one district were now spreading through the medium of the press, and that new powers should be taken to seize newspapers. The form of further coercive legislation was being discussed in 1882 when the Phoenix Park murders reinforced the need for action. This came with the Prevention of Crime (Ireland) Act in July that year.

In March 1885, Spencer told Cabinet of the threat to order now posed by the National League, with branches all over Ireland holding meetings and publishing material calculated to inflame opinion and excite outrage: 'No antidote in the shape of counter meetings or opposing newspapers is found in any part of the south or west of Ireland.' Ministers' anger at the level of agrarian violence in Ireland was sharpened by evidence of the rising tide of intimidation in the form of threatening letters and boycotting encouraged by the publication of resolutions of the National League in some local newspapers which urged on these activities. Spencer was gloomy, feeling that public opinion in Britain would not allow an extension of coercion and he concluded that the government would have to come to terms with the nationalists, which he found an 'odious' prospect.[24] Only in 1887 with Salisbury's government did coercion once again seem possible and seem at last to be successful.

Balfour, the new Chief Secretary, tempered action with discretion. In response to privately-expressed concern, even by supporters of the Salisbury government, he said that unless they could 'drive ahead' with prosecuting the press for publicising suppressed branches of the League, their difficulties would be very great. He had a coercion bill drafted which did not mention the press by name at all but prohibited the promotion of the objects of any dangerous association in districts proclaimed by the Lord-Lieutenant. He described his new bill as primarily intended not to put down agitation, but to enforce the law. Printing the proceedings of suppressed branches was entirely to promote the League and to defy the authorities. Thus press

21 Redvers Buller to Hicks-Beach, 27 February 1887: St Aldwyn Papers D.2455 PCC/45.   22 Dicey, *Introduction*, pp 239, 251–2.   23 Gladstone to Forster, 25 October 1880: BL Add. Mss. 44308 ff.74–9.   24 Spencer to Lord Lansdowne, 2 February 1886: *The Red Earl*, pp 107–8.

prosecutions were 'a necessary element in the policy of suppressing the League ...'[25] The Land League was engaged in what W.T. Stead called 'Government by Journalism'. Stead believed that the House of Commons to be impotent, and functioned as 'a despotism tempered by the Press' a situation which was indicative of the extent to which, through the press, the nation was taking into its own hands the management and control of its own affairs.[26] In practice, however, on Salisbury's advice, Balfour preached caution; so as to avoid an appearance of tyranny he restrained others who wanted further action. Not surprisingly, the prosecution of journalists presented to men not backward in the skills of self-publicity, heaven-sent opportunities to exhibit themselves as constitutional leaders who were being pilloried by government. Editors were ready to become martyrs for their cause.

When Stead called the press 'the means by which the people give utterance to their will ...',[27] he described precisely the Irish condition most feared by Dublin Castle and London. They feared a transfer of power away from Westminster and Westminster's agents in Ireland and into the hands of those least fitted to lead others. This was their justification for their actions. In 1885, Dicey spoke of the special relationship that existed between the government and the press which was marked by the 'characteristics' of the rule of law.[28] It is a measure of the development of the concept of freedom of speech in the second half of the century that British governments realised that the options open to them in Ireland could not include arbitrary action, and that they were limited in their actions by their acknowledgment of the rule of the law.

25 Balfour to Salisbury, 22 December 1887 and 27 December 1887. Salisbury Papers Hatfield House 1887 f.228.   26 Stead, 'Government by Journalism', pp 654–5.   27 Ibid.   28 Dicey, Introduction, p. 247.

10

The newspaper business, 1880–92

Our People read more than formerly, but do they reason more or do they reason at all?[1]

NUMBERS, PRICES AND CIRCULATION

In 1886, a survey of the provincial newspaper scene during the previous fifty years over the whole of the British Isles looked back on what was seen as a period of steady growth.[2] In 1837, the Provincial Newspaper society had 23 members over the whole of Ireland; by 1885 it had 265. (Their membership would have included those working for Dublin newspapers.) The number of Irish provincial papers entered in the *Newspaper Press Directory* had grown to 128 by 1892.

Table 11: *Number of Irish provincial papers, 1880–92*

1880	125	1885	130	1890	129
1881	126	1886	128	1891	130
1882	128	1887	126	1892	128
1883	130	1888	124		
1884	132	1889	128		

Source: *Newspaper Press Directory*

About 31 papers were founded in Ireland between 1880 and 1892. These twelve years were remarkable for a sharp decline in the Ulster liberal press and a corresponding sharp rise in the numbers of nationalist newspapers in the rest of the country. Of the papers which began publication, four claimed to be conservative, or proto-conservative; and 20 claimed to be nationalist.[3] Three papers were liberal and three independent or neutral. There were regional differences in political allegiance.

---

1 P.J. Smyth to John Matthews, n.d.: NLI Ms 5762.   2 H. Whorlow, *The Provincial Newspaper Society 1836–1886* (London, 1886).   3 In this context 'national' did not mean that the paper circulated all over the Irish nation; the words 'national' and 'nationalist' seem to have been used interchangeably. The word 'nationalist' is used here to describe those papers which supported the Home Rule and land reform movements.

In all provinces, the new newspapers which claimed nationalist politics, and the existing papers which changed over to nationalism, took readers away from liberalism. They changed from conservatism in Munster and Connaught and from liberalism to conservatism in Ulster. This may seem to be a foregone conclusion given the political events of the period, but it is worth illustrating that newspapers were ever alive to their readers' interests and their own commercial health and, as has been shown already, worked closely with political movements out of doors. There is some evidence also that new nationalist papers founded in Connaught and Munster were short-lived, finding themselves unable to compete against the well-established press in the area, which itself was changing over to nationalist politics.

The apparent wasting away of the liberal Ulster papers and increasing polarisation towards Protestant Unionism continued with the death of the liberal *Down Independent* and the *Ulster Examiner* in 1882, and the disappearance of the independent *Larne Weekly Recorder* in 1885. This accelerating decline in the Ulster liberal press mirrors the collapse of liberal sympathy in the province analysed by Brian Walker.[4] In the general elections of 1874 and 1880, the liberal representation increased and the conservative party lost a little ground, mainly in the counties where the liberal party gained from its alliance with the resurgence of tenant right politics. The 1885 election saw the complete collapse of the liberal vote; lack of liberal organization and lack of a coherent agrarian policy handed their support in the counties to the nationalist candidates whose party organization was vastly superior.[5] The growth of the nationalist press in the west probably accounted for the end of the conservative *Roscommon and Leitrim Gazette* in 1882, and it is possible that when the *Clare Examiner* changed its politics from 'national' to 'constitutional' between 1880 and 1882, this proved its undoing. It ceased publication in 1887. The *Enniscorthy Watchman*, which ceased in 1886, included partly printed sheets sent from a central printing works (often in England) with local news added. By the 1880s this was an old-fashioned concept. The Sligo papers and the Ballina *Connaught People* faced heavy weight local nationalist competition. What is notable among these casualties of the 1880s and early 1890s is that none of the papers that died was involved in government prosecutions, thus putting the lie to the government's belief that prosecution would send nationalist papers to the wall.

Dublin Castle was alive to the content of the provincial press, and in the 1880s the Castle subscribed to an increasing number of newspapers.[6] In about 1892 Dublin Castle analysed the provincial press for intelligence purposes.[7] These records

4 Brian Walker, *Ulster Politics: the Formative Years 1868–1886* (London, 1989).   5 Ibid., pp 93, 94–5, 149, 151, 192–3, 219 and 223.   6 In July 1892 the Castle took the *Kerry Sentinel, Tipperary Nationalist, Kilkenny Journal, The People* [Wexford], *Tuam News, Dundalk Democrat, Clare Journal, Munster Express, Sligo Champion, Roscommon Herald, Roscommon Messenger, Connaught Telegraph, Midland Tribune, New Ross Standard, Western News, Cashel Sentinel, Donegal Vindicator, Limerick Leader, Derry Journal, Cork Daily Herald, Cork Examiner*: cf. National Archives, Irish Crimes Records Register of Newspapers.   7 National Archives, Irish Crimes Records Register of Newspapers.

cover the papers' circulation area and its size and readership. The Dublin Castle survey assessed the influence the newspaper was believed to have over its readers and noted whether the editor and proprietors had been prosecuted. Their circulation figures are very precise and in fact may not be circulation figures at all but the numbers of copies printed. On that footing, figures of this kind may be assumed to be close to reality. This would account for the extremely high figures quoted for the *Sligo Champion*, the *Nationalist and Leinster Times*, the *Limerick Leader*, the *Tipperary Nationalist* and Edmund Walsh's Wexford papers. The circulation of these papers may have been artificially swelled by printing extra copies for free distribution (as in the 1872 Galway County election). The Irish National League spent large sums annually on newspaper subscriptions.

Table 12: *Dublin Castle figures on the circulation of the provincial newspapers, c.1892*

Belfast Morning News	4,300	Cashel Sentinel	400
Belfast Weekly Examiner	11,500	Tipperary Advocate	20 or 30
Donegal Vindicator	2,000	Munster Express	1,000
Drogheda Independent	1,300	Waterford Mail	100
Dundalk Democrat	1,200	Waterford News	700
Derry Journal	13,980	The People (Wexford)	9,000
People's Advocate	240	Enniscorthy Guardian	1,500
Anglo-Celt	400	New Ross Standard	2,000
Leinster Leader	3,800	Wicklow People	2,500
Midland Tribune	12,300	Kerry Sentinel	480
Meath Reporter	200	Kerry Weekly Reporter	2,000
Sligo Champion	11,000	Clare Advertiser	500
Westmeath Examiner	600	Kilrush Herald	500
Westmeath Independent	150	(+100 subscription)	
Tuam News	332	Cork Examiner	2,000
Galway Observer	300	Cork Daily Herald (City)	2,000
Connaught Telegraph	312	Cork Daily Herald (County)	17,000
Roscommon Herald	773	West Cork Eagle (City)	500
Roscommon Messenger	696	West Cork Eagle (County)	2,000
Western News	960	Munster News	5,000
Western People	531	Limerick Reporter and	800
Nationalist & Leinster Times	1,900	Tipperary Vindicator	
Kilkenny Journal	454	Limerick Leader	7,000
Tipperary People	300	Fermanagh Mail	1,500
Tipperary Nationalist	3,000	Carlow Vindicator	600

Between 1878 and 1890, 24 papers changed their political allegiance to nationalism:

Table 13: *Existing newspapers who changed their political allegiance*
to nationalism, 1878–90

1878	Western News (Ballinasloe)		Wicklow People
1880	Clare Examiner	1885	Carlow Nationalist
	The People, Wexford		Cashel Sentinel
1881	The Watchman (Wexford)	1886	Sligo Champion
1882	Waterford Daily Mail	1888	Belfast Morning News
1883	Carlow Independent		Mayo Examiner
	Kerry Sentinel		Munster Express and The Celt
	Tuam Herald		Weekly Examiner (Belfast)
	Wexford and Kilkenny Express	1889	Cork Daily Herald
1884	Dundalk Democrat		Cork Weekly Herald
	Independent and Munster	1890	Roscommon Herald
	Advertiser		Waterford News
	Westmeath Independent		

To these must be added the twenty nationalist papers founded during this period. Only three of the newspapers that changed their political allegiance changed their proprietor or editor at the same time. The *Galway Observer* changed its proprietor and the *Wexford and Kilkenny Express* and the *Wicklow People* changed their editors. For this reason alone it can be deduced that these changes were a reflection of the trend towards overt nationalism and, as will be seen, to take advantage of the new and lucrative business to be gained from the Land League.

According to Dublin Castle, the readers of the newspapers were generally farmers, shopkeepers and labourers. Redvers Buller told Hicks-Beach, the Chief Secretary: 'It is the shopkeepers [in Kerry] who want Home Rule.'[8] The evidence collected by Dublin Castle on the readers of the provincial press in about 1892, probably provided by Resident Magistrates, is powerful evidence of the possible danger to order posed by the influence of the provincial press.

8 Buller to Hicks-Beach 4 September 1886: St Aldwyn Papers D.2455 PCC/45.

Table 14: *Dublin Castle on the readers of provincial newspapers*[9]

*indicates editor prosecuted for intimidation

Belfast Weekly Examiner	Nationalists and a good many farmers of opposite politics as it supplies a good deal of information re farming & etc. Great influence with its supporters.
Donegal Vindicator	All classes. Little or no influence.
Drogheda Independent	Shopkeepers and working classes. Little influence.
Dundalk Democrat	Chiefly amongst the farming class. Some little influence.
Derry Journal	Chiefly among the farming class. Considerable influence.
People's Advocate	Farmers, shopkeepers, artizans and Monaghan labourers. Very trifling influence.
Anglo-Celt	Roman Catholic Clergy and farmers. Very slight influence.
Leinster Leader	Nationalists of all denominations including farmers, shopkeepers and labourers. Considerable influence in sustaining agrarian agitation.
Midland Tribune	Nationalist farmers and shopkeepers. No influence with the respectable farming class, or generally speaking with the people.
Meath Reporter	Small farmers and artizans. Very little [influence]
Sligo Champion	Principally among officers of the Irish National League and tenant farmers. Of mischievous influence through the publication of resolutions of the National League. Otherwise of little influence.
Westmeath Examiner	Chiefly among nationalist farmers, labourers and artizans. Very little influence, the paper was condemned by Dr Nulty, Roman Catholic Bishop, and his clergy.
Westmeath Independent	Farmers, Labourers, artizans. Very little [influence].
Tuam News and Western Advertiser	Shopkeepers and farmers. This paper has but small influence.
Galway Observer	Shopkeepers and farmers. No influence.
Connaught Telegraph	Shopkeepers, farmers. No influence.
Roscommon Herald	Shopkeepers and farmers. Considerable local influence.
Roscommon Messenger	Shopkeepers and farmers. No influence.
Western News	Shopkeepers and farmers. Very little influence.
Western People	Shopkeepers and farmers. Has some local influence.

9 National Archives Irish Crimes Records Register of Newspapers (n.d.).

Nationalist and Leinster Times	Nationalists generally. R.C. Clergymen and a good many persons holding conservative views.
Kilkenny Journal	Farmers, Roman Catholic clergymen, shopkeepers. Little influence.
Cashel Sentinel	Farmers and shopkeepers. None.
Tipperary Advocate	Shopkeepers and farmers. None.
Munster Express	Farmers and shopkeepers, labourers and the labouring class. Fair influence.
Waterford Mail	Farmers, shopkeepers, artizans and the labouring classes. No influence.
Waterford News	Farmers, shopkeepers, artizans labouring classes. Fair influence.
The People [Wexford]	Farmers, shopkeepers, artizans, nationalists generally. Strong influence among nationalists.
Enniscorthy Guardian	Farmers, shopkeepers. Fair influence among nationalists.
New Ross Standard	Farmers and shopkeepers. Fair influence among nationalists.
Wicklow People	Farmers and shopkeepers. Fair influence among nationalists.
Kerry Sentinel	Nationalists and agitators. Its influence is for harm as it advocates agitation. It is against the Union.
Clare Advertiser	Superior classes. Nil.
Kilrush Herald	Higher classes, the price being 3*d*. Nil.
Cork Examiner	Nationalist farmers and shopkeepers. Considerable influence.
Cork Daily Herald	Advanced nationalist farmers. Bad influence.
West Cork Eagle	Farmers generally. Not much influence as a nationalist paper.
Munster News	All classes. No particular influence.
Limerick Reporter	Clergymen, teachers and farmers. Little or no influence.
Limerick Leader	Nationalist gentry, farmers and labourers. Bad, inciting to boycotting and intimidation.
Fermanagh Mail	Among the nationalists. Cannot be said to have much influence.

The League's activities were well-understood by government, and they were the foremost reason for the increased efforts of successive governments to control the press during the 1880s.

The fact that the readers of the local papers were, in the main, the farmers and farmworkers and the shopkeepers and clerks of the towns underlines the role of the increasingly nationalist provincial press in spreading the message of the Land League, and the work of its branches all over Ireland. In 1889, the *Midland Tribune*, published in Birr and Parsonstown, appealed to: 'TENANT FARMERS. In order to afford an extended sphere of usefulness to the MIDLAND TRIBUNE and thus make it a more powerful ally in your case, we ask for your extended support ... as a right that has been earned and Claim it as your Duty ... [to support the paper which] has made sacrifices for your interests and is devoted to your cause!'[10] The 'sacrifice' to which the paper referred was the jailing of John Powell, the proprietor, in January 1889 for attacking those farmers who, in opposition to the Plan of Campaign, had paid rent to the Broughal Estate.

Despite the continuing fall in population, the numbers of those who could read held firm, and the percentage of literacy as a proportion of the population declined.

Table 15: *Levels of illiteracy, 1881*

	Percentage illiterate	Percentage drop since 1851
Ulster	20	-15
Leinster	20	-19
Munster .	38	-32
Connaught	38	-28
Ireland	25	-22

Source: W.E. Vaughan and A.J. Fitzpatrick, *Irish Historical Statistics*

In 1851, the population of the whole of Ireland was 6,552,385 and 53 per cent of the population said they could read; by 1881, the population had fallen to 4,704,750, a decline of 28.2 per cent, and the level of literacy had risen to 75 per cent. Measured against the size of the population, the actual numbers of those who said they could read remained almost constant. In 1851, 3,734,868 people were literate. In 1881 this figure had fallen slightly (by 5.5 per cent) to 3,528,600. In the context of the press, what is of interest is that in 1851 there were 72 newspapers; by 1881 that figure had doubled to 142. On any calculation there must have been a substantial increase in the newspaper reading public. The National Schools and the reading rooms had done their work and literacy had spread through all classes. The provincial newspaper could encourage commerce through advertisements, publish the affairs of local institutions and publicise local politicians. It widened its readers' knowledge of literature. It could act as an important channel of information about politics,

10 Op. cit., 9 February 1889. John Powell was jailed on two further occasions, once in August 1889 for publishing an intimidatory article and once, in August 1890 for printing intimidatory notices.

both locally and nationally; local publicity about the meetings of National League branches were a model for imitative action. Much of this activity was based in the towns and, with the exception of news on sensational evictions, the remoter parts of the countryside were hardly touched.

The partial nature of Irish newspaper reading has been already noted. In 1851 the Select Committee on Newspaper Stamps had expressed concern about the need to ensure that the London newspapers were circulated in Ireland in order to spread 'national tone'. By the mid-1880s, readers had themselves become electors, and their guidance towards moderation was even more important. It was recognised that the further away the reading public were from the capital, the more influential the provincial press. In relation to Britain, this phenomenon has been discussed in detail by A.J. Lee.[11] In 1868, Edward Dicey noticed that the importance of provincial newspapers varied 'with the distance of their publishing places from the metropolis.'[12] In the more distant towns, London newspapers arrived late in the day and, as a result of the development of the electric telegraph, the provincial press had already been able to publish important news. Thus, 'the Belfast *Whig* under Mr. Finlay [has] exercised a most valuable and important political influence even beyond the area within which [it] circulates ...'[13]

Outside observers continued to comment favourably on the quality of the Irish press. An American academic, David Bennett King, travelling in Ireland in the early 1880s was surprised to find the newspapers 'as a rule, so ably edited ...'[14] He found they often contained much fuller accounts of debates in Parliament than American papers reported debates in Congress. The Irish press, he said, had 'done a great deal in the way of educating the people'. He too noticed that an Irishman learned English because it was 'infinitely more valuable to him', Irish having proved to be 'a serious barrier to the progress of knowledge and civilizing tendencies in the most remote and wretched parts of the country'.[15] King's assessment of the press of the 1880s contrasts with that of the journalist P.J. Smyth, a former Young Irelander who had returned to Ireland from America in the 1860s. Smyth complained to John Matthews, proprietor of the *Newry Examiner*, about what he perceived to have been a decline in the Irish press:

> In nothing is the decadence of Irish public life so noticeable as in the tone and spirit of the press of today. The papers which in my boyhood's days I remember handling – the *Freeman* of the time and the *Morning Register* & even old *Saunder's* were always interesting always instructive. See the *Freeman* of today. Look at the old *Nation* and look at the new. Where under the sun will be found any printed

---

11 Op. cit., infra.   12 Edward Dicey, op. cit., p 64.   13 Ibid. The 'Mr Finlay' to whom Dicey refers was Francis Dalzell Finlay, the son of the founder. He inherited the newspaper in 1857 on his father's death, and ran it personally until 1874.   14 David Bennett King, *The Irish Question* (London, 1882).   15 King, ibid., pp 284 and 295.

thing to surpass in coarseness & brutality *United Ireland* & *Weekly News* ... I rarely see provincial papers, and it was by accident that a copy of the [*Newry*] *Examiner* came into my hands.[16]

The increased number of newspapers and of those who read newspapers meant a larger audience for the greater numbers of nationalist newspapers during the 1880s. They brought together different groups in society; the rural society of small farmers and agricultural labourers learned more about the life of shopkeepers and clerks in the towns. Advertisements for the niceties of life: drapery, pianos, mineral water, watches, clocks and jewellery ran alongside advertisements for the basic necessities: horses, farm valuations, steam saws, floorboards and paraffin lamps. Leisure began to take some part. In 1887, the *People* in Wexford advertised 'Cheap footballs that will bear hard usage: the interest of Gaelic Pastimes are served immensely'. An advertisement for the Dublin Artesian Mineral Water Co. Ltd. in the same edition had Timothy Harrington as one of its directors, continuing evidence of the links between nationalism and Irish industry.[17]

However, reading the provincial press did not bring the gentry closer to the agricultural classes, whether in town or country. The gentry, whether major or minor landowners, and the professional classes read a different kind of press altogether.

PROPRIETORS, EDITORS AND JOURNALISTS

I am satisfied, from long and close observation, that the greatest difficulty in governing Ireland as a contented portion of the Kingdom follows from the tolerance of an unbridled and seditious press, which in the hands of wild and scheming knaves, corrupts and undermines the feelings of the country.[18]

The numbers of those involved in the newspaper industry increased sharply between 1881 and 1891. The censuses of 1881 and 1891 redistributed the occupations of those involved in newspaper production to separate groups. Once again, it is not possible to make true comparisons of the numbers of people employed in the newspaper industry over the previous period.

16 Smyth to John Matthews, n.d.: NLI Ms 5762.   17 26 October 1887.   18 Lord Chancellor Sullivan, Minute to Cabinet March 1885: PRO CAB 37/14/21. Sir Edward Sullivan (1822–85) Lord Chancellor of Ireland 1883–5. Law adviser and solicitor-general in 1865 when he dealt with the Fenian conspiracy. MP for Mallow 1866–70, attorney general 1868–70. In 1881, advised Gladstone on the arrest of Parnell.

Table 16: *Occupations, 1881 and 1891*

AUTHOR, EDITOR AND JOURNALIST

	1881		*1891*
Total	227	Total	409
Males	201	Males	36
Females	26	Females	45

Religion

R. Catholic	119	R. Catholic	223
Protestant Episcopalian	79	Prot. Episcopalian	79
Presbyterian	20	Presbyterian	37
Methodist	7	Methodist	15
All other persuasions	2	All other persuasions	24

REPORTER, SHORTHAND WRITER

	1881		*1891*
Total	187	Total	242
Males	187	Males	233
Females	0	Females	9

Religion

R. Catholic	102	R. Catholic	148
Prot. Episcopalian	50	Prot. Episcopalian	94
Presbyterian	22	Presbyterian	35
Methodist	5	Methodist	16
All other persuasions	8	All other persuasions	20

Source: Census of Ireland 1881, General Report HC 1882 [C.3365] lxxvi.385; Census of Ireland 1891, General Report HC 1892 (6780) xc, i

Journalists led a tough life. Mathias Bodkin, later editor of *United Ireland* and a County Court judge, worked unpaid on the *Freeman's Journal* while reading for the Bar. He noticed that while in England journalists specialised in particular subjects, in Ireland the reporter was a Jack of all trades, who covered everything. Andrew Dunlop, who worked successively on the *Wexford Constitution* and the *Limerick Chronicle* before going to the Dublin *Daily Express* was injured when a campaign platform built on porter barrels collapsed, and assaulted by a crowd in Cong, where he had been mistaken for a Dublin court official assisting at an eviction. While reporting a sermon by Monsignor Capel, Bodkin had his notebook forcibly confiscated by a 'formidable lady in black bombazine and mittens'.[19]

Journalists went on strike when they were given no food at official dinners, reported meetings of the Land League in snowstorms and had difficulties in protecting their notebooks in pouring rain. They had to practise writing shorthand with one hand while holding an umbrella with another. Pages of Dunlop's notes blew away from a jaunting car between Glencolumbkille and Killybegs, hats were left on railway trains and bags left on station platforms. (Irish journalists had an unrivalled knowledge of the developing railway system.) Dublin journalists with unfamiliar faces had special difficulties in the provinces. At Land League meetings journalists were frequently mistaken for Dublin Castle spies, mainly because for a while the Castle used newspaper reports as evidence in court, and called journalists as witnesses.[20] Dunlop was fired on in Derry in a mix-up between Orangemen and nationalists and others were cut by swords at Land League meetings. At the Glenbeigh evictions, he was thrown in a river with a cry of 'Down wid ye' by a man who had deviously offered to ferry him across.[21]

Journalists were mistrusted by local institutions who wanted to keep their proceedings secret. The *Dundalk Democrat* was asked by the principal of the Ballybay Male National School to send a reporter to a meeting of the Castleblayney Board of Guardians, all expenses paid, when it debated a motion to make the Union contributory under the National Teachers' Act. The presence of a reporter would 'deter those opposed to the motion from putting forward statements or remarks calculated to affect the division unfavourably for the teachers, and at the same time not bear the test of strict accuracy or truth'.[22] The Rathvilly branch of the Land League protested on behalf of the ratepayers of the Baltinglass Union against 'the despotic conduct of the Rossmore Guardians ... for refusing the *Leinster Leader* reporter admission to the board's room to publish their proceedings'.[23] On the other hand, Dunlop believed that his health, which had been broken by months of work in a Dublin newspaper office, was restored by an active out of door life, touring the country reporting meetings of the Home Rule League, the Land League and the National League. He shared poteen with the police in Galway, and in Longford the postmaster allowed him to use his drawing room to write a report of a meeting. The correspondent of the *New York World* lent him a 'broad pad' which made writing on mountain roads in a jaunting car much easier.[24] But journalists were never well paid. In 1864, *The Nation* had a regular staff of contributors who were paid fixed salaries of between £50 and £500 a year.[25] W.B. MacCall, later editor of the *Belfast Evening*

19 M.M'D. Bodkin, *Recollections of an Irish Judge: Press, Bar and Parliament* (London, 1914), p. 27. 20 Dunlop, op. cit., pp 31–2, 62 and 134. The Special Commission hearing had evidence that policemen took shorthand notes at Land League meetings: loc. cit., QQ 1051–1593. 21 Dunlop, op. cit., pp 73–5, 79 and 137–8. 22 William Rogan to Thomas Roe, 13 March 1889: National Archives Business Records of the *Dundalk Democrat* LOU 8/54. 23 Minute book of the Rathvilly branch of the Land League: NLI Ms 842. 24 Dunlop, op. cit., pp 46, 52–60 and 204. 25 Madden Papers Ms 276.

Telegraph told Maurice Lenihan in 1855 that he 'never did anything for less than a guinea', even for a quarter of an hour in the House of Commons Press Gallery.[26]

Newsagents and newsvendors, too, had a hard time. In the late 1880s they were at risk of arrest and prosecution for selling copies of newspapers which carried reports of suppressed branches of the National League. In 1887, the *Cork Daily Herald* advised newsagents not to sell copies of the paper to policemen or people whom they suspected of being 'tools or agents' of the police. Two newsvendors were prosecuted for selling the *Cork Weekly Herald* and *United Ireland* in November 1887 and were given a month's imprisonment. The *Cork Daily Herald* described this as an act of 'outrageous meanness'.[27] The constabulary visited Limerick newsagents and newsvendors in Limerick and warned them of the consequences if they continued to sell copies of *United Ireland*, the *Cork Daily Herald* and the Dublin *Weekly News*.[28] After the split in the Irish Parliamentary Party, a newsvendor in Cork was threatened by the Provincial of the Augustinian Order who told him to stop selling the *Cork Daily Herald* on the steps of the church. The newsvendor appealed to him not to interfere with his livelihood, and bystanders told the priest that no-one would tell them what to read and that he should remember that he was not in South Meath.[29]

Newspapers did not always work in competition with each other. They covered each others' stories and traded staff and stock. Richard Kelly of the *Tuam Herald* ran short of newsprint and appealed to the *Tuam News* in September 1884, asking John Glynn to lend him a ream.[30] John Glynn was asked by the *Freeman's Journal* to cover a 'government sermon' in Tuam, and Andrew Dunlop worked freelance for a number of other newspapers during his time on the *Dublin Daily Express*. William Johnston's experience with his drunken sub-editor was not unique. In 1901, Michael Davitt wrote to the Galway journalist, John Muldoon saying that Mrs Powell of the *Midland Tribune* had called to see him to know if he could

> recommend a competent – and *sober* – man to edit and manage the paper at a salary of £2 10s. 0d. per week. She led me to believe that who ever is recommended sh'd be qualified to conduct the paper on Dillon-cum-Freeman lines, but without any animus against the Knight of the Long Epistles. [William O'Brien] I am to see Dillon tonight & he may be in a position to help her to the kind of editor she wants. Possibly you may know someone in Dublin who might be qualified, but it must not be our whilom friend, Tim McCarthy, as I understand he would not be 'the man for Galway' otherwise Carlow or is it Tullamore?[31]

Actually it was Birr.

26 MacCall to Lenihan, 22 October 1855, Lenihan Papers NLI Ms 133.   27 *Cork Daily Herald*, 2 December and 30 November 1887.   28 *The Times*, 20 December 1887.   29 District Inspector's report, 12 December 1892: PRO CO 903/3.   30 Kelly to Glynn, 9 September 1884: McPhilpin Papers, LI Ms 3254.   31 Davitt to Muldoon, 3 August 1901: Muldoon Papers, NLI Ms 24,836.

Close contact between newspaper men gave them opportunities to buy into news-papers when they came up for sale. When the Ballinasloe *Western News* was sold in 1892, John Glynn (by then the editor of the *Tuam News*) was told that the paper had

> become defunct and Mr Walker is about selling the machinery and plant. When they came into his hands he got them for a little over £50 and I think it wd not take a great more to buy them now. The want of a paper of independent politics is much felt present in East Galway, and if a man like you took it in hand I am convinced it wd be a success. I have been in communication with some of the leading men in the towns around and I know they wd aid a man who wd have a small capital by forming a Co. with £ shares, which wd have an interest in push-ing its circulation and supporting it by advertisements. The job printing in con-nection with the paper was very good I am aware.[32]

This letter once again underlines the importance of the basis of a sound general printing business to ensure the commercial prosperity of a local newspaper. A suc-cessful paper could make a respectable profit. The *Waterford News* made a gross profit of £2,289 6s. 10d. in the ten months between January and the end of October 1899. They had £10,546 14s. 2d. invested in stock and copyrights and £7,766 14s. 9d. in print and paper.[33] Share issues became increasingly common. In 1880, the *Leinster Leader* was established as a limited liability company with a subscribed capital of £1500. In 1881, three Catholic curates in Birr promoted the *Midland Tribune* with a capital of £1,100, £600 borrowed from the National Bank in Ennis and the remainder raised in £10 shares. The 40 to 50 subscribers were all from Birr and included a Poor Law Guardian of the Birr Union and president of the Birr Land League, and a Birr town commissioner. These shares were paid off in adver-tising space and free newspapers.[34] The first manager was John Powell and the first editor was John St George Joyce, who had edited the *Galway Express* in 1872. In 1888 the newspaper was conveyed to John Powell under an agreement by which he was to pay £60 a year until he paid off the loan. The newspaper was lucky to survive, as the conveyance was made when the newspaper was threatened by a libel action for £1,000 and John Powell was jailed twice in 1889. Proprietors were jumpy about possible competitors. Immediately after the split in the Irish Parliamentary Party and during the North Sligo by-election, Parnellite supporters attempted to intimi-date anti-Parnellite newspapers. They wrote threatening letters to the secretary of the *Drogheda Independent* and put an advertisement for a newspaper office in the Sligo papers to frighten the *Sligo Champion*.[35]

In Britain, in the 1880s, provincial newspaper proprietors themselves became

32 W.O. Carroll to John Glynn, 4 December 1892: McPhilpin Papers, NLI Ms 3254.   33 *Waterford News* trading accounts, 1 January–31 October 1899: NLI Ms 10,064.   34 *Midland Tribune* Centenary Edition 1881–1981, p. 4.   35 T.M. Healy, *Letters and Leaders of my Day* (London, 1928) i, p. 356.

directly involved in parliamentary politics. Koss identified the 1880 general election as a watershed, when journalists elected to Parliament doubled in number.[36] It was the same in Ireland. Locally they became town councillors and were part of the nationalist take-over of the poor law boards, noted by William Feingold.[37] Before 1880, the journalist members of Parliament who stand out are John Francis Maguire and Edmund Dwyer Gray. Maguire, of the *Cork Examiner*, began political life as a repeal candidate and was elected as a Liberal for Dungarvan in 1852, and then for Cork City from 1865 to 1872. Edmund Dwyer Gray of the *Belfast Weekly Examiner* and the *Belfast Morning* News and the *Freeman's Journal* was Home Rule MP for Kilkenny City in 1875 and Tipperary County from 1877 to 1880, and Carlow County from 1880 to 1885. In the period between 1880 and 1910, fourteen proprietors/ editors stood for Parliament, all of them advocating varieties of nationalism. Twelve of them were elected. The 'Home Rulers' were C.J. Dempsey of the *Ulster Examiner*, an unsuccessful candidate for Belfast North in 1886, and E. Dwyer Gray. James Carew of the *Leinster Leader* stood first as a nationalist, was elected and remained a Parnellite until 1900, and then became an independent nationalist (Healyite). James Leahy, also of the *Leinster Leader*, was a Home Ruler Parnellite between 1880 and 1885 and subsequently a nationalist MP. Edward Harrington and Timothy Harrington of the *Kerry Sentinel* were both nationalist MPs. Edward Harrington was a nationalist MP from 1885–92 and was elected as a Parnellite nationalist in 1892 until 1900. Timothy Harrington, elected from 1885 to 1910, remained a Parnellite nationalist until his death in 1910. Luke P. Hayden of the *Roscommon Messenger* and the *Westmeath Examiner* was an MP between 1885 and 1897 and a Parnellite to the end. The anti-Parnellite nationalists were Daniel MacAleese of the *Ulster Examiner*, MP from 1895 to 1900; P.A. McHugh of the *Sligo Champion*, MP on and off from 1892 to 1906, and Jasper Tully of the *Roscommon Herald*, MP from 1892 to 1906. Two candidates entered politics as nationalists in the 1880s. Peter Gill of the *Tipperary Advocate* was a candidate, never elected, for Tipperary county, first as a Liberal and then as a nationalist; Thomas Patrick Gill of *Tipperary* was a nationalist MP between 1885 and 1892. Samuel Craig McElroy of the *Ballymoney Free Press* stood as a liberal candidate in Antrim North but was never elected. The only conservative politician/ journalist I have been able to trace was the former proprietor of the *Downshire Protestant*, William Johnston, who was conservative MP for Belfast 1868–78 and Belfast South 1885–1902.

The involvement of newspaperman in extra-parliamentary activities is shown by an analysis of the occupations of those suspected of involvement in Fenianism or arrested in 1881 under coercion legislation.[38] Between 1866 and 1871, newspaper editors and correspondents formed 2.1 per cent of Fenian suspects (the same proportion as teachers) when the total suspects classified by Clark as working in the

---

36 Koss, op. cit., p. 216.   37 William Feingold, *The Revolt of the Tenantry: the Transformation of Local Government in Ireland 1872–1886* (Boston, 1974).   38 Samuel Clark, op. cit., pp 203, 268.

professional sector totalled 6.4 per cent. Under the 1881 Protection of Person and Property Act, newspaper editors and correspondents were 1.6 per cent of those arrested when the professional sector formed 4.4 per cent of the total arrested.

During this period, there was an increase in what Clark calls the 'middle-status' social groups, particularly the lower professions.[39] In particular there was an increase in the number of Members of Parliament sympathetic towards the land movement. Journalists wanted to advance nationalism on three fronts: locally, nationally within Ireland, and at Westminster. Their rush to Westminster coincided with the heightened profile of local political issues and the founding of the Land League. However, there was a tension between local pressures for land reform and the centralizing tendencies of the Land League. James Daly, proprietor and editor of the *Connaught Telegraph* in Castlebar, confined his activities to the local scene alone, and with maximum effect. Michael Davitt had made proposals for the meeting in Irishtown in August 1879 which was the start of the Mayo Land League, but he never attended it, and the meeting was in fact part of a long campaign masterminded by Daly to bring attention to the grievances of a group of tenant farmers. Although Daly had worked with O'Connor Power in the late 1870s to further debate on the land question, Daly himself, not O'Connor Power, chaired the Irishtown meeting, which was said to have been attended by 13,000 people.[40]

Daly himself was a grazier. He was the son of a farmer and bailiff and himself became a tenant farmer and bailiff, with the tenancy of farms in both the Ballina and Castlebar union areas. He told the Bessborough Commission that he had become a newspaper editor by accident, buying into the *Connaught Telegraph* in 1876 with Alfred Hea.[41] In doing so, he said that his purpose was to 'advocate the cause of the poor struggling tenantry'.[42] Jordan calls him 'an enigma' and describes him as the voice of local revolt against centralization of political power in Ireland, a process initiated by the Land League. Although Daly defended the interests of the small farmers of Mayo he was not a Fenian. He was a difficult man, and difficult for the Land League to ignore as the proprietor of a major nationalist newspaper covering the whole of Connaught. The centre of political patronage, influence and power in Mayo was held by merchants and tradesmen.[43] Jordan describes the county as having a majority of small holders with good reason to be antagonistic to the larger farmer-shopkeeper coalition to whom they were indebted. The organisers of land agitation in Mayo in the late 1870s were Daly, John J. Louden, a barrister and extensive grazier and member of the Council of the Home Rule League, John O'Connor Power, MP for Mayo and former Fenian, Matthew Harris, member of the Supreme

39 0 in 1874 to 8 in 1880: Clark, p. 331.   40 Paul Bew, *Land and the National Question in Ireland 1858–1882* (Dublin, 1978) and Gerard Moran, 'James Daly and the Land Question 1876–1879' in *Retrospect: Journal of the Irish History Students' Association*, 1980, pp 33–9 and Donald Elmer Jordan Jnr, op. cit.   41 Bessborough Commission Report and Evidence, HC 1881 [C. 2779–I] xviii, 73 paras. 567 and 570; HC 1881 (C.2779–II] xix, 1 Appendix C p 1412.   42 Jordan, op. cit., p. 266.   43 Jordan, op. cit., p. 7.

Council of the IRB, Michael Davitt and Alfred Hea. The newspaper therefore played an important central role in voicing the policies of the Mayo Land League. One consequence was that the background and aspirations of the kind of men who became members of the local Land League branches led to a split between old-style romantic Fenianism and new-style, direct action Fenianism which tended towards centralization. Farmers in Mayo embraced the Fenian rhetoric on the threat to their livelihood through the consolidation of small farms by large graziers. In 1880 James Daly was approached by the tenants of Canon Geoffrey Bourke's estate in Quinaltagh, near Irishtown, asking for publicity for their landlord's alleged rack-renting and threats of eviction.[44] Daly declined to take part, fearing a libel action. Bourke's crops and wire were damaged because he had let land on conacre to a local convent. The moderates in the Mayo Land War in received backing from a slightly surprising source.

Father Lavelle, the thorn in the side of Galway landlords, who on the national stage had anathematised Cardinal Cullen, and on the international stage confronted the Holy See, survived still in the Galway and Mayo press. In the late 1850s, he had goaded bishop Plunket, a local landlord; in 1871 he had been prominent in the Galway County election, and he reappeared in the Mayo Land War, on the side of nonviolence and apparently in the pocket of Arthur Guinness of Ashford Castle.[45] Lavelle wrote to the *Connaught Telegraph* defending Guinness and his agent William Burke from accusations that they had ill-treated the Cong tenantry. Lavelle also defended Canon Bourke from accusations about conditions on his own estate.

Daly wanted to keep the direction of the Mayo Land War on his own territory because he distrusted the motives of those in Dublin who led the National League, believing that local leadership was the only guarantee that the interests of tenant farmers would not be compromised. Daly generally supported the arbitration provisions in the 1881 Land Act, which were used by the Mayo tenantry so enthusiastically that Castlebar ran out of official forms, and Daly aided the authorities by printing and distributing further copies. As Jordan says, Daly 'typified the tendency towards political parochialism and the growing distrust of moderate politicians towards the national administration'.[46]

The battles between the small farmers and the large graziers were weekly reflected in the resolutions of branches of the Land League which called for the boycotting of the large graziers, the so-called 'land-grabbers'. A leading article in the *Sligo Champion* in June 1888, named four men who took possession of a vacant farm in the county from which another tenant had been evicted. The article held them up to 'public odium' and asked 'Where is the Templeboy League? Where is the public opinion of the parish? If such deeds can be done without protest or condem-

44 The estate was administered by Canon Bourke as his sister-in-law's executor.   45 Evidence of Denis Feeling, RIC witness at Special Commission hearing examined by Sir Charles Russell: *Connaught Telegraph*, 5 July 1879; ibid., 12 July 1879.   46 Jordan, op. cit., p. 268.

nation we say:– "Hope no more for Templeboy". It behoves the people of the district to arise and stamp out the foul and desolating pest'.[47] The *Connaught Telegraph* had two notices displayed amongst the usual classified advertisements on the front page:

THE MAN WHO
TAKES THE LAND
OF AN EVICTED TENANT
IS THE ENEMY OF THE PEOPLE

LET NO MAN TAKE THE LAND
FROM WHICH
A TENANT IS EVICTED [48]

While the object in publishing such resolutions was to unite action against named people, they were not just for local consumption. There can be no doubt that the Land League used the press to make their activities more widely known throughout the country, and it is probable that the League paid for the insertion of branch resolutions in local newspapers, and paid for the defence of the newspapermen who were subsequently prosecuted. The newspaper industry received considerable financial support from the Irish National League. This kind of relationship between political organisations and the press was not new. In the 1820s, O'Connell's Catholic Association had a fund to pay for the advertisement of resolutions taken at country meetings.[49] The Special Commission hearing received evidence of the substantial sums spent by the Irish National League on advertising and newspaper subscriptions:

1883	Advertising and newspapers	£166 12s. 5d.
1884	Newspaper subscriptions	£554 9s.10d.
1885	Newspaper subscriptions	£631 0s.11d.
1886	Newspaper subscriptions	£723 0s. 2d.
1887	Newspaper subscriptions	£689 0s. 2d.[50]

The Rathvilly, Co. Carlow branch of the League paid the *Carlow Nationalist* £1 8s. 0d. in September 1885 for publishing a list of its members. These printed lists of members exercised public pressure on those who had not paid their subscriptions. The branch paid the *Leinster Leader* £1 11s. 6d. in September 1885 and the paper

47 From print intelligence notes for the Chief Secretary: PRO CO 903/1.   48 *Connaught Telegraph*, 12 July 1879.   49 A. Reynolds, *The Catholic Emancipation Crisis in Ireland 1823–1829* (New Haven, Conn. 1954), p. 78.   50 Irish National League Accounts NL Ms 8582 (1); Special Commission hearing Minutes of Evidence vol. 6, pp 326–33.

printed its proceedings on 13 September.[51] The cashbook of the *Dundalk Democrat* has entries for printing and advertisements billed to local branches of the League in Louth, Ardee, Faughart and Cooley and Carlingford in 1881–2.[52] It was this publicity given to branch resolutions which attracted the attention of government, who classified them as intimidation.

Landlords and members of the gentry called on the government to take action against the League and against the press. Spencer told the Cabinet that: '[t]here is no antidote to their doctrines to be found in other papers, and the classes who read them are most imperfectly educated. The result of allowing these writings to go on unchecked will be gradually to bring the peasantry of large districts and the humbler classes in large towns into a frame of mind which will prepare them for any step, possibly to the extent of a rising.'[53] As he had told Gladstone in 1882 'People in England forget that there is no antidote to a violent speech or Article'.[54] However, the Irish executive was aware that many of the reports of branch meetings and resolutions of the League were bogus; the meetings never took place and that the so-called resolutions were drafted by men in public houses. This was probably true, and once again it was nothing new. According to a letter forwarded by Sir Robert Peel to Wellington, the Catholic Association had worked in exactly this way.[55] The anxieties expressed in this letter about the activities of the Association and the consequences should the 'lower orders of society' read such statements are identical to feelings fifty years later. There were reports of bogus meetings passing bogus resolutions in the *Cork Examiner* in 1888, and the Crime Special Branch reported that *United Ireland* had admitted that there had been a bogus meeting in County Clare.[56]

The government intelligence service was quick to identify particular newspapers and their proprietors who were thought to be directly or indirectly involved in the commission of outrages.[57] T.S. Cleary of the *Clare Independent* in Ennis was, according to Dublin Castle, a paid secretary of the Clare Land League, and more: 'By the general tone of his paper and his speeches he excites the people to acts of violence'. The 'violent speeches' of James Daly were noted, and William Dorris, a reporter on the *Connaught Telegraph*, was described as his 'right hand man' and 'his active agent all over the country in carrying out the secret instructions of the Land League'. Luke P. Hayden, of the *Roscommon Messenger* was an 'Advanced Fenian and chief organizer of the various Land League meetings throughout the district'.

51 Minute Book, Rathvilly Branch NLI Ms 842. The list of members of the Rathvilly, Ticknock and Talbotstown branch appears in the *Carlow Nationalist*, 19 September 1885. 52 National Archives Business Records LOU 8/57. 53 23 March 1885, PRO CAB 37/14/20. 54 Spencer to Gladstone, 11 June 1882, Althorp Papers K5 f.35. 55 Letter written by 'A Friend', 3 November 1828. The Duke of Wellington (ed.) *Despatches, Correspondence and memoranda of Field Marshal Arthur, Duke of Wellington K.G.* (London 1873), v, p. 214. 56 *Cork Examiner*, 10 January 1888, quoted in PRO CO 903/2; Intelligence Notes 19 October 1889, PRO 30/60/1. 57 National Archives Crime Branches Special Registered papers 1880/34686; Reports of County Inspectors of the RIC. papers 1880/34686; Reports of County Inspectors of the RIC.

Timothy Harrington's paper the *Kerry Sentinel* carried 'Inflammatory and seditious teachings ... [and] has encouraged disobedience to the law and outrages'. Timothy Harrington was a particular *bête noir* of Dublin Castle. His arrest was actively
compassed to 'quiet the district'; 'Harrington is the class of man whose withdrawal
from public life would be of some service in the restoration of order'.[58]
    The Land League did not just agitate for the protection of tenants and the end
of landlordism; it believed itself to stand for a moral force which at local level extended to appropriating to itself the dispensation of justice to offenders against its
tenets. Land League courts arraigned 'land-grabbers' and punished them. These
'courts' were widespread in Connaught and west Munster and active in southeast
Clare.[59] Hicks-Beach told Salisbury of the 'tyranny' of the National League, which
in the worst places, was becoming 'an instrument of private malice'.[60] The Divisional Commander in Sligo in 1887 commented that 'no case is excluded from want
of jurisdiction, landlord, tenant, shopkeeper, artisan, the most private family dis-
putes are all heard and decided'.[61] The Cabinet was told in 1885 that the Land
League courts' judgments 'render more obedience than to the legally constituted
Courts of the land ...'[62] Of the operation of the National League courts, Balfour was
told in 1887, 'It is a matter of notoriety that these courts are held and they form a
very effective weapon for intimidation ... [their proceedings] are published in *United
Ireland* and other papers.'[63] Land League courts were sometimes held in the offices
of newspapers: the 'trial' of James White in March 1881 was held in the offices of
the *Roscommon Messenger*, presided over by Matthew Harris. The *Roscommon Journal* reported this as a 'somewhat singular proceeding', where White was summoned
to attend and threatened that if he did not give up the farm he had occupied, a Land
League meeting involving 7,000 people would take place on the land. The meeting
did take place and the house burned to the ground. In the *Roscommon Messenger* the
Land League court was reported simply as a 'hearing'.[64] The presence of newspapermen in ordinary courts was an additional form of intimidation. A County Court
judge in Tralee wrote of a hearing of appeals against rents in his court when the
editor of the *Kerry Sentinel* was present:

> The tenants nearly all came to me on Monday and so far as I was able I did for
> every man what he asked. The reason E. Harrington sat in Court all day and put
> himself in such a position [was] that every man coming up on the table was
> obliged to undergo his stare, notwithstanding which fact they all came up. One
> of them publicly thanked me for what I was doing for the Kerry tenants, all of

58 National Archives Crime Branch Special Peace Preservation Act 1881, Carton 2.   59 Clark, pp 313–
14.   60 Hicks-Beach to Salisbury, 20 October 1886: St Aldwyn Papers D.2455 PCC/31.   61 Irish
Office confidential memorandum, March 1887: PRO CAB30/60/12.   62 Memorandum on the State
of the Country, 31 October 1885: PRO CAB 37/15/57.   63 Irish Office confidential memorandum,
March 1887, loc. cit.   64 *Roscommon Messenger* and *Roscommon Journal*, 9 March 1881.

which Mr H. who was himself reporting, left out ... many of the best cases of reduction were left out in the reports – of course by mistake – by Harrington who sent up to Dublin the astounding news that I had issued over 700 decrees which was just about as true as the other reports of my doings in Kerry contained in the *Freeman*.[65]

The split in the Irish Parliamentary Party posed political problems and financial consequences for the provincial press. The North Kilkenny by-election held on 22 December 1890, came at a crucial moment for the Irish Parliamentary Party. The O'Shea divorce hearing, Parnell's manifesto to the People of Ireland, which denounced Gladstone and the Liberal Party for their role in undermining the Irish Party, and the meeting in Committee Room 15 which decided the future of Parnell's leadership, put the two Kilkenny papers into acute ideological and political difficulties. The Catholic nationalist *Kilkenny Journal* and the conservative *Kilkenny Moderator* each had particular problems in interpreting the motives of the parties involved.

The *Kilkenny Journal* announced the death of the sitting member, Edward Mulhallen Marum, on 10 October 1890. On 19 November it noted the 'anti-Irish' press reports of the O'Shea divorce case, describing them as 'brutal and indecent' and an 'unfortunate complication that has stained a glorious career'. The *Journal* did not claim to be Parnell's judge's or keepers, believing that 'with his private life it is not the province of the public to interfere'. However, and this was at the root of many difficulties in the next five weeks, at that moment the paper also believed that Parnell had become necessary for the success of the Irish cause. The first problem was the selection of a candidate agreeable both to the nationalist electors of North Kilkenny and to the members of the Irish Parliamentary Party. Had it not been for the crisis which came to a head when the party split in December, this would have been left in the hands of the leader after consultation with the constituency. This was to 'keep the Irish question to the front'. Even at that moment there were dissenting voices on the correct course to follow.[66] By 26 November, the *Journal* reported that Sir John Pope-Hennessy would be presented to the voters 'with the sanction of Mr Parnell and the Irish Party', and urged supporters to close ranks: 'We are beset with enemies ... it will be necessary for all to act at this crisis with no less prudence than patriotism'. Pope-Hennessy, a Catholic, had been a Tory member of parliament between 1859 and 1865, but had kept an independent mind on Irish questions. In January 1890, well ahead of his re-emergence in parliamentary politics, he had resigned from the Carlton Club, giving sympathy for Irish party as his reason.[67] On 30 November, the *Journal*'s leader, 'In Suspense' gloomily sur-

---

65 Judge Curran to Redvers Buller (n.d.) forwarded to Hicks-Beach: St Aldwyn Papers D.2455 PCC/ 45.   66 *Kilkenny Journal*, 19 November 1890. Letter from Edmond Walshe, secretary of the Tullaroan Branch of the Irish National League; N. Murphy, ibid., 22 November 1890.   67 *DNB*. He told Lord

veyed the crisis that was engulfing Parnell, the Irish Party and Ireland. 'Who can look back upon the history of the past ten years without feeling the old sentiment of enthusiasm and devotion at Mr Parnell's name? He was to her enslaved countrymen the same hero that the First NAPOLEON was to the OLD GUARD ...' Now, the clouds were beginning to gather around him. The debate of the meeting in Committee Room 15 was reported on 3 December, accompanied by a letter from Archbishop Croke, urging Parnell to retire. On 6 December, the paper reprinted the *United Ireland* article 'Parnell or Ireland' which ordered Parnell to retire. The *Journal* was squirming with difficulty when, on 10 December, it reported a meeting of the Kilkenny priests which approved the Irish Party's decision to abandon Parnell, condemned the *Freeman's Journal* for continuing to support him and endorsed John Pope-Hennessy's candidature, attacking the MP for Kilkenny City, Thomas Quinn for backing Parnell. The newspaper's leader demanded 'Our Bishops and Priests – away with them!'

When the writ for the by-election was moved in the House of Commons, Pope-Hennessy was reported to be a Parnell man and that the other side would run their own candidate. Pope-Hennessy's carefully drafted manifesto announced that he was bound by the resolutions of the Irish Party, and that he welcomed the advice of the bishops and clergy 'on questions affecting the welfare of Ireland'. Although Parnell had announced that he would be running another candidate, Pope-Hennessy felt that his duty was to safeguard the National Organization and keep the Irish cause above personal dispute. The next week, the *Kilkenny Journal* asked everyone to 'Be Consistent, Please'.[68] It had now switched tactics; Pope-Hennessy was the nominee, not of one man, but as 'champion of the Irish cause, as the soldier of Home Rule, as the selected one of the Bishops and Priests of Ireland'. The debate was on measures, not men and the issues raised recalled the tenant right campaign, when Ireland's needs had been abandoned for considerations of party and the pre-eminence of English affairs. Ireland was the issue, not men's fickle adherence to party. Davitt, addressing a Pope-Hennessy meeting, described the questions raised as not between Pope-Hennessy and his opponent, Vincent Scully, but 'between Ireland and AN INSULTING DICTATOR'.[69]

The other Kilkenny paper, the conservative *Kilkenny Moderator* was in equal difficulties. There was no conservative candidate, and to the newspaper the men standing for election were equally obnoxious. The paper resorted to attacking Parnell's behaviour and described the election context as pure theatre: 'The New Westminster Play'.[70] So extraordinary were the events which unfolded they eclipsed even the arrest of the Fenians on the *Irish People* and James Stephens on the run. Even the Pigott letters in the Times and subsequent exposure paled into insignificance at

Beauchamp, 'Though a conservative in principle, I am still in favour of the policy of the Irish party'. He had spent much of his life as a colonial governor, retiring in 1889. **68** *Kilkenny Journal*, 13 December 1890. **69** *Kilkenny Journal*, 13 December 1890. **70** Leader, *Kilkenny Moderator*, 6 December 1890.

present turn of affairs. In a leader, the paper outlined 'Our Position' which attempted to explain a situation in which a conservative paper was forced to reject a candidate who had formerly been a conservative, and to reject also his opponent (Vincent Scully) whose mentor, Parnell, had been supported by conservatives in his battle with the Irish Party, although Parnell's 'intrepidity, activity and resource' had to be admired. However, Pope-Hennessy was a former beneficiary of Tory fruits who was 'quite prepared to reap another golden harvest as the reward of services rendered to English liberalism', and the newspaper advised conservatives to record no vote.[71]

The North Kilkenny by-election was notable, even among Irish election campaigns, for its violence. Sticks and stones were thrown at candidates and their supporters, (Parnell had lime thrown in his face) and the language spoken was 'fierce and foul'.[72] Pope-Hennessy won comfortably, but the result was of no consequence to the *Moderator*, whose only hope was that the split in the Irish party would lead to the 'smashing of Home Rule'.[73] On New Year's Eve, the *Kilkenny Journal*, whose journalistic skills had been severely tested, understandably described the recent conflict as 'a political topsy-turvydom'.[74]

Intelligence sources noted with interest the financial difficulties caused to the press by the split in the Irish Party.[75] In Ulster, the *People's Advocate*, *Drogheda Independent*, *Donegal Vindicator* were all anti-Parnellite. The *Derry Journal* had at the beginning supported Parnell but claimed that 'finding that its circulation was falling off, it finally went on the opposite side in September [1891]'. A new Parnellite paper the *Wicklow and Wexford Leader* started in Naas: 'The Fenians believe it will serve their cause'. The new Tipperary newspaper, the *Tipperary Nationalist* which had been in financial trouble in early 1891, was purchased by Parnellites and a new editor, James Butler, appointed. The split was mixed up with the press campaigns during the Land War in Sligo, where the *Sligo Champion* ran articles against a landgrabber 'because he is a Parnellite'.[76] The Register of Papers in Dublin noted the allegiances of particular newspapers: the *Westmeath Nationalist*, *Cork Daily Herald*, *Waterford Star*, and the new Cork evening papers started in June 1892. The *Cork Evening Echo* and the *Cork Evening Star* were all anti-Parnellite, but it was believed that both the latter papers would scarcely survive.

Of those Members of Parliament who were also newspaper proprietors, four continued to support Parnell and four were against him:

71 17 December 1890. Even William Johnston of Ballykilbeg had written to the Dublin papers attacking John Pope-Hennessy: ibid., 17 December 1890.   72 *Kilkenny Moderator*, 20 December 1890. Stones were for 'women and girls', sticks were for men but lime was 'for devils'.   73 24 December 1890. The result was: Sir John Pope-Hennessy (Anti-Parnellite) 2527; Vincent Scully (Parnellite) 1362. Pope-Hennessy died on 7 October 1891, the day after Parnell himself.   74 31 December 1890.   75 National Archives Crime Branch Special: Annual Reports of Special Branch Officers 4641S attached to 4861S. 76 PRO 30/60/5 Report of R.B. Stokes, Divisional Commissioner, May 1891.

Parnellites
James Leahy, *Leinster Leader*
Edward and Timothy Harrington, *Kerry Sentinel*
Luke P. Hayden, *Roscommon Messenger*

Anti-Parnellites
James Carew, *Leinster Leader* (Healyite)
Daniel MacAleese, *Ulster Examiner*
P.A. McHugh, *Sligo Champion*
Jasper Tully, *Roscommon Herald*

Just as the Land War had reflected and intensified local battles, so the split refracted other localised antagonisms. In 1894, John P. Hayden's *Westmeath Examiner* was condemned as 'sinful' by the bishop of Meath in churches throughout his diocese. When Hayden appealed to Cardinal Logue and to Propaganda in Rome, they decided against him and their decision was read from the pulpits. However, Hayden told Logue that the bishop's hostility could be ascribed to Hayden's opposition to a water scheme six years before in Mullingar, which during the split in 1890 had intensified feeling already present.[77]

In the last two decades of-the nineteenth century the provincial press brought their readers increasingly into contact with the rest of Ireland, politically and economically. The business of the Land League and parliamentary politics were conducted locally as well as nationally and the size and importance of the provincial press grew accordingly.

---

77 PRO CO 903/4.

II

What did the Irish read?

'The spread of education has enabled people to read but what they do read is "poison"' Florence Arnold-Forster.[1]

Links between what the Irish read and what the Irish did have been frequently emphasised. But what did the Irish read in the 1880s? Were both liberal and conservative governments right in believing that the provincial press incited their readers to rebellion? They had some cause for concern when press was used by the National League to provide an organisational and propaganda framework across Ireland, and members of one branch of the League might adopt the actions of another. But the deeper motivation and the culture which might link theory and practice is harder to penetrate. Two observers, John Pope-Hennessy, a Catholic landlord and MP, and J.P. Mahaffy, the Protestant academic, wrote, one about the reading of the peasantry and the other on that of landlords. Their general observations can be examined in detail through the surviving order books of Wynne's, the newsagency in Castlebar, Co. Mayo. These records are extremely useful in decoding the reading of the different social classes in a town at the centre of the Mayo Land War.

John Pope-Hennessy thought that the great increase in readers had occurred, 'not in the upper or middle classes, but in the lower classes', and he quoted statistics which showed that the reading public in Ireland was comparatively large: 'larger than the reading public in any country in the world'. The new readers came mainly, he said, from the class who, with an extension of the franchise, will get a voting power that they do not now possess'.[2] Pope-Hennessy lists without emphasis the nationalist authors that were being read by these new voters. These included A.M. and T.D. Sullivan and the Young Irelander, Richard D'Alton Williams. A boy in a priest's house near Cork was seen reading *United Ireland* and the stories and poems of James Clarence Mangan, John Denvir's *Irish Penny Readings* and nationalist poetry. Pope-Hennessy quotes the priest, who said that the boy's literary tastes were 'like many others in the parish ... cultivated mainly in the Land League Reading rooms', which he called the 'true heirs-at-law' of Thomas Davis's repeal reading rooms of the 1840s.[3] The reading rooms of the Catholic Young Men's Societies, the priest believed, were 'civic academies of Nationality', and he quoted a long list of

1 *Florence Arnold-Forster's Journal.*   2 Pope-Hennessy, op. cit., p. 920.   3 Ibid., pp 920, 925.

books on Irish history which were kept there. The proprietors of the *Freeman's Jour-nal*, *The Nation* and *United Ireland* and other popular newspapers, said Pope-Hennessy, 'have very substantial reasons for knowing that the Irish reading public is a large and increasing one'.[4] Travelling in a third-class railway carriage, Professor David King had noticed that out of twenty-five farmers, 'more than one-half of the people read the morning papers, even those who looked the least intelligent, show-ing a great interest in the news. I discovered the man who sat opposite me, and who was a rather ragged looking individual, read the other side of my paper with evident interest'.[5] The walls of cabins in Galway were papered with illustrations from *United Ireland*, and the *Weekly Freeman* was 'the one luxury of those poor homes'.[6]

With growing apprehension about levels of agitation and the prevalence of in-timidation by threatening notices and letters, legislators increasingly turned to the press to find some explanation, and the lack of balance in reading material to correct extreme opinions was one of their greatest concerns. In January 1870, just before the debate on the Peace Preservation Bill, W.R. Greg had alleged that there were 'upwards of 80,000 ... articles a week circulated in Ireland, and that they are read to or by probably ten times that number of eager recipients at the forges and whisky shops of every village ... scarcely one man in a hundred reads any other paper or has access to any sounder means of information ...'[7] In 1881, Florence Arnold-Forster was told by Dr Lyons, the liberal MP for Dublin City, that the 'great want, in Ire-land was an independent newspaper: the people only hear one side and can hear only one side, for the other side is never put to them'.[8] Lord Spencer told the Cabi-net in 1885 at the Land War that 'no antidote in the shape of counter meetings or opposing newspapers is found in any part of the south or west of Ireland'.[9]

Through the business records of Wynne's of Castlebar it is possible to get some idea of the newspaper reading of one west of Ireland town during the height of the Land War. These show in detail the books, newspapers and magazines read by some of the population between 1879 and 1900.[10] In 1891 Castlebar had a population of 3,558 people, artificially enlarged by detachments of the army stationed in the bar-racks.[11] The army and the trade brought by tourism after the apparition at Knock in August 1879 made the town prosperous. The small farmers, 90–95 per cent of the farming community in Mayo, worked poor quality land and, in order to survive, depended on the trade of towns like Castlebar. Conversely, the traders in Castlebar were economically dependent on the prosperity of the small farmers. Together they

4 Ibid., p. 932.   5 King, op. cit., p. 293.   6 William Hughes, *Sophia Sturge, A Memoir* (London, 1940), p. 61. Sophia Sturge, daughter of the Quaker reformer, Joseph Sturge, founded a workshop making wicker baskets in Letterfrack, Co. Galway, in 1887 to give employment to the peasants. I am grateful to Margaret Legg for this reference.   7 W.R. Greg, 'The Irish Cauldron' in *Quarterly Review* (January 1870), p. 251.   8 *Florence Arnold-Forster's Irish Journal*, 16 June 1881.   9 Minute on legislation for Ireland, 23 March 1885, PRO CAB 37/14/19.   10 Order and account books of D. Wynne, Main Street, Castlebar, Co. Mayo: National Archives Business Records Mayo 7/1.   11 Population in 1851: 4,016; in 1891: 3,558: *Irish Historical Statistics*, Tables on Population of Towns 1813–1911.

formed a social elite which came into conflict with the landlords and clergy. Castlebar was a centre for those visiting the mountains and the seaside. It had a reading room which was also the home for visiting theatrical companies. In January 1881, one travelling company staged *The Shaughraun, East Lynne* and *The Colleen Bawn*.

Wynne's in Main Street, Castlebar, was founded by Thomas Wynne. Thought to have been born in America in 1838, Wynne settled in Castlebar and became an auctioneer, furniture salesman and newsagent.[12] He was also a photographer who travelled throughout Mayo. He advertised in the *Connaught Telegraph*, saying when he would be arriving in the smaller towns, and on Achill Island, and invited customers to make appointments with him for portraits and photographs of their land and their property.[13] The shop sold newspapers, magazines and books to private homes, offices and local institutions. Among their customers were James Daly of the *Connaught Telegraph* and A.H. and Martin Sheridan, proprietors of the *Mayo Examiner*. Wynne's also sold a mass of small items: office and domestic stationery, china, cosmetics such as brilliantine, religious objects, frames, photographs, dress material, toys and wallpaper, and they supplied the burgeoning souvenir industry at the new shrine at Knock. They also ran a small circulating library.

Three groups of customers had accounts with Wynne's: the gentry and professional classes, the army and the clergy. The gentry included doctors, solicitors, civil engineers, members of the Castlebar Board of Guardians, members of the bench of Petty Sessions, Town Councillors and local officials. These included the Senior Inspector of the Royal Irish Constabulary, the County Surveyor, the Union sanitary officer, the secretary of the Castlebar Gas Company and the secretary of the Mayo Grand Jury. Professional men of Castlebar, the doctors, the solicitor and the civil engineers, read the *Freeman's Journal*. One doctor also took *United Ireland* and the *Detroit Free Press*. Like the Senior Inspector of the RIC, the doctor at the Lunatic Asylum, one of the land agents, and the County Surveyor all took the *Irish Times*, as did the minor gentry. The *Irish Times* was also popular with the army: officers, non-commissioned officers, the library and officers' mess and the reading rooms and sergeants' mess all read it. James Daly read the *Freeman's Journal*, the *Irish Times* and the *Evening Telegraph*, but he does not seem to have taken the more extreme papers. Martin Sheridan of the *Mayo Examiner* took the *Freeman's Journal*. The *Freeman's Journal* was less popular with the army, and the London *Times* was read only by a handful of army officers and at one private home. Catholic priests read the *Freeman's Journal*; the Protestant clergy read the *Irish Times*. Catholic priests also read *United Ireland* and one priest read *The Nation*. The Castlebar Reading Room subscribed to *The Nation*, the *Freeman's Journal*, the *Irish Times* and the London *Times*, as well as *Shamrock* and *United Ireland*. The local papers, the *Connaught*

12 Introduction to Art Byrne and Sean McMahon, *Faces of the West* (Belfast, 1976), p. 9. Many of the photographs in *Faces of the West* come from the Wynne archives. Wynne also had branches of his photographic business in Loughrea, Tipperary and Portarlington.   13 *Connaught Telegraph*, 21 August 1880.

Telegraph, the *Mayo Examiner*, the *Western People* and the *Cork Constitution* seem to have been read mainly by the army and the priesthood. Three priests took *Insuppressible*, the anti-Parnellite paper, which was edited by William O'Brien after he had been evicted by C.S. Parnell from the offices of *United Ireland*.[14]

It should be borne in mind that the Wynne papers only deal with those clients who had monthly accounts. They do not reflect the day-to-day over the counter sales which would have included most of the copies of the local press sold in Castlebar. Nor do they include subscribers who dealt direct with the newspaper itself. These may have included the larger farmers living in outlying districts far from town and the Anglo-Irish gentry. This being so, one can conclude that, apart from the small numbers of copies sold on account, the local press was read mainly by those on lower incomes: small farmers, artisans and shopkeepers. This is confirmed by the Dublin Castle intelligence on the local press, which believed that the *Connaught Telegraph* sold about 300 copies weekly to shopkeepers and farmers.

If the evidence of the Mayo novelist George Birmingham is correct, landlords held that the local paper was below their notice. In *The Seething Pot*, set in Mayo during the Land War, Mr Godfrey, the land agent to the young landlord, Sir Gerald Geoghegan (who has lived abroad all his life) dismisses the local paper, the *Connaught News*, with scorn when his employer is distressed at an attack made on him:

> Writers for the daily press are entirely without responsibility ... The editor of the *Connaught News* ... poured forth his curses without the least idea that anyone would take them seriously ... No-one is more surprised ...when he is sent to prison. The sense of injustice rankles, for he knows he did not mean what he said, and that no-one except a Government official would suppose he did.[15]

Canon Johnston, the local Church of Ireland clergyman, tells Geoghegan that it was a 'hall-mark of respectability' to be abused by the *Connaught News*: 'Patriotism is all talk ... In Ireland the only thing to have or get is land ... That is the beginning and end of Irish politics. Everything else is high-falutin, talk thrown in for the sake of decency'.[16] This idea that the local paper is full of 'high-falutin' talk' not to be taken seriously, echoes the views of an English traveller who was in Ireland in 1872 and believed that the articles published in the press should not be measured by English newspaper standards. 'They are often mere sound and fury, and are taken in Ireland itself at their worth, for any political influence ... the real mischief ... is that they incite the poor ignorant Irishmen to crimes'.[17] Local newspapers were not all bad news. In hard times they frequently printed tributes to 'Good Landlords' who had reduced rents in times of hardship.

14 For an account of the founding of the *Insuppressible*, see Bodkin, op. cit., pp 175ff.   15 George A. Birmingham (Canon Hannay), *The Seething Pot* (London, 1905), pp 61–4. Canon Hannay was Rector of Westport, Co.. Mayo.   16 Ibid., pp 66–7.   17 J. Macaulay, *Ireland in 1872* (London, 1873), p. 342.

However the landlords risked paying a penalty for staying aloof from the local papers, and for their reliance on newspapers from Dublin and London. J.P. Mahaffy, in a typically coruscating examination of the Irish landlords, attacked them for their ignorance of local affairs.[18] One point in his article was that their reading was extremely limited, and that they only read newspapers from Dublin and London. Mahaffy ridiculed members of the Kildare Street Club in Dublin, who continued to read the *Pall Mall Gazette* without realising that the editor had changed from the Tory, Frederick Greenwood, to the radical, W.T. Stead. He warned that reading newspapers was an art that should be conducted with care and with one's faculties fully alert. 'These are men educated by reading newspapers only ... a man who reads newspapers only, not only remains perfectly ignorant; he labours under the ... delusion [that] when he sees his views strongly stated in his daily paper he fancies that is all that can be done'. He pointed out that, fatally, when the landlords appealed for aid during the Land War, they did not appeal through the Irish national or local press, they used the London papers. Thus when Captain Boycott screamed help, he 'screamed also, not in the *Tuam Herald* or the *Skibbereen Eagle*, but in the *Times* ... [and] he enlisted the sympathy of the whole English people',[19] but not the sympathy of the moderate Irish. Mahaffy also attacked their lack of education when, prefiguring Hubert Butler, he lamented the dispersal of the landlords' 'splendid libraries so common before the famine times ... it is now an exception to find a good library in any country house. They tell you it is no longer needed; have they not their daily papers and can they not get books down from a lending library in Dublin?'[20] In Castlebar, the newspaper reading of the gentry confirm Mahaffy's belief that the local large landowners did not read the local press. The members of a reading room of the same period, the County of Wexford Club, many of whom were Resident Magistrates, had the same diet of London papers and journals together with the conservative *Irish Times*.[21]

Pope-Hennessy's observations about what the Irish read is fully borne out by orders executed by Wynne's for books and magazines. The circulating library at Wynne's lent books at a 2*d.* a week.[22] There were cheaper rates for larger quantities

18 J.P. Mahaffy, 'The Irish Landlord', in *Contemporary Review* XLI (January 1881).   19 Ibid. pp. 167 and 172.   20 Mahaffy, op. cit., p. 171. Ten years later, J.M. Synge echoed Mahaffy's strictures when he lamented landlords' 'mouse-eaten libraries, that were designed and collected by men who voted with Grattan ... the descendants of these people ... do not equal their forebears ... nothing is read now but Longfellow and Hall Caine and Marie Corelli.' J.M. Synge, 'A Landlord's Garden in County Wicklow', *Collected Works* ii, *Prose* ed. Alan Price (London, 1966), p. 231. Hubert Butler explored both the dispersal of libraries and the limited reading matter of the Anglo-Irish in 'The Country House after the Union' and 'Portrait of a Minority' in *Escape from the Anthill* (Dublin, 1988), pp 48 and 117.   21 The Club took the London *Times*, *Daily Telegraph*, *Standard*, *Irish Times*, Dublin *Daily Express*, *Evening Mail*, as well as the *Pall Mall Gazette*, *Illustrated London News*, *Graphic* and *Punch*. County of Wexford Club Minute Book, 6 September 1875–25 September 1886. NLI Mss 19687.   22 Advertisement in the *Connaught Telegraph*, 8 January 1881.

of books borrowed over longer periods. Priests were voracious readers. They read Irish history and Irish language and were fond of biography and poetry. The Very Revd P. Lyons and the Revd P. Molloy read Father Ulick Bourke's *Pre-Christian Ireland*, and the Rev. Molloy studied an Irish grammar, possibly Ulick Bourke's *College Irish Grammar*, first published in 1856. He bought a book on 'Irish peasantry' (perhaps Carleton's *Traits and Stories*), a biography of the United Irishman, Michael Dwyer, and a *Story of Michael Davitt*. He had George Moore's *Parnell and His Island*, and a copy of Sir Charles Russell's speech to the Special Commission, ordered immediately after its delivery in April 1889. During the centenary year of the French Revolution, he read a guide to Paris and a copy of a history of the revolution. The poetry of Byron, Tennyson, and Longfellow, the *Pickwick Papers* and *Uncle Tom's Cabin* demonstrate that both English and American works remained popular. Copies ordered of Moore's *Melodies* and Hayes, *Ballads of Ireland*, the best-selling *Speeches from the Dock*, A.M. Sullivan's *New Ireland*, and T.P. O'Connor's *The Parnell Movement*, all testify to the construction of an Irish nationalist, Catholic mentality.

The other Ireland – the Ireland of Somerville and Ross, of Philippa Yeates and of *The Real Charlotte* – attempted to construct an up-country colonial culture through their reading. They faced an ever-present challenge to keep up standards and to keep out barbarity. Women needed to be *au fait* with the latest in hats and clothes and to be able to consult knowledgeably with local dressmakers, more necessary than ever the farther they were from Dublin and London. The wives of the gentry and of the officers stationed in the Castlebar barracks took *Myra's Journal* and the *Ladies Treasury*. *Myra's Journal* included cut out paper patterns.[23] The wife of Colonel Adams of the 45th Derby Regiment took the *Children's Dressmaker*, the *Portfolio of Fashion* and the *Queen*. Gossip about affairs back home was provided by *Belgravia*, the *Sporting and Dramatic* and *Vanity Fair*. Just as husbands and wives in homes all over Britain read Trollope during the Second World War, so Lady Lucan read *Mansfield Park* during the Land War. The *Illustrated London News*, with its large engravings of battles in other parts of the British Empire, was extremely popular in Castlebar, and subscribers included fourteen private households, two Church of Ireland clergymen and six of the regimental reading rooms and messes. (The second Zulu War was contemporary with the meeting at Irishtown in August 1879.) The Christmas supplements of the *Illustrated London News* and the *Graphic* once a year brought England a little closer. The County Surveyor subscribed to a large number of professional journals, *The Engineer* and *Engineering* and the *Electrician*. He also read the *Nineteenth Century* and (slightly surprisingly) he read Richard

---

23 In *The Old Wives' Tale*, Arnold Bennett, that acute observer of the nineteenth-century provincial town, noted that a supplement from *Myra's Journal*, 'Newest fashions from Paris. Gratis supplement' is pinned up in the Baines's drapery shop to aid customers in their decisions on fashionable dress: op. cit. (Penguin edition, London, 1983), p. 62.

Pigott's *Shamrock*. The content of some of the periodicals reinforced the stereotyped views of the Irish held by many of these leaders. The attitudes of *Punch* to Ireland have been extensively analysed by L.P. Curtis[24] and re-examined more recently by R.F. Foster, who points out that from late 1879, nearly every lead cartoon had an Irish reference, and that *Punch* contributed to the image of C.S. Parnell as an inscrutable, magnetic dictator conjuring up demons. More relevantly to the geographic isolation of Castlebar from Britain, and to the presence of the army in the Castlebar barracks, *Punch* also presented Ireland in colonial terms as a lesser, weaker mortal.[25] Thus, in Castlebar *Punch* was not taken by the Roman Catholic priests, but was taken by the army and professional men, a doctor and a civil engineer. *Judy*, which resembled *Punch* in format and content, waged a campaign against Fenianism and portrayed Gladstone as an incompetent and the Land Leaguers as murderous gorillas.[26] Like *Punch*, *Judy* performed a similar function in underlining prejudice, and was also taken by the army. The army read *Fun* which painted activists in the Land League as ape-like. One household took the nationalist journal *Zoz*, whose cartoonist, John O'Hea showed Ireland engaged in an heroic struggle against its Saxon rulers. Between 1879 and 1883, O'Hea worked for *Pat*, a cheap comic weekly which had Home Rule sympathies, and the Castlebar Reading Room took *Pat*. The Land War was depicted in more serious and less stereotypical terms in the *Illustrated London News* and the *Graphic*, read by the army.

Wynne's shop sold photographs ordered from Thomas Wynne. Residents bought photographs of themselves: Bandmaster A. Loughlin of the 76th Regiment ordered one of 'Self and Mrs'; Lady Lucan had her servants photographed. Pictures of groups of the Royal Irish Constabulary and of their houses reinforced their solidarity. Photographs were useful for keeping others in view: Lieutenant Colonel Allardice ordered a photograph of a 'Land Meeting' in 1881, together with a photograph of the Castlebar Barracks,[27] and of Parnell himself. The Sodality Reading Room had photographs of their heroes, Daniel O'Connell and their local Member of Parliament, O'Connor Power. Priests had photographs of each other.

The tourist industry was growing in the west of Ireland, with advertisements for sea-side lodgings and tours organised around the lakes and mountains.[28] After 1879, visitors to the shrine at Knock boosted business. The local press claimed a special responsibility for making the apparition known to the public. Wynne's sold copies of *The Apparitions and Miracles at Knock* by John McPhilpin, the proprietor of the *Tuam News*. McPhilpin had claimed that it was his duty to 'put the whole record of the varied events in a permanent form' and that it was only when the apparition had been described in the *Tuam News* that 'the faithful began to attach any credibility to

---

24 L.P. Curtis, *Apes and Angels: The Irishman in Victorian Cariacature* (Newton Abbot, 1971).   25 R.F. Foster, *Paddy and Mr Punch: Connections in Irish and English History* (London, 1993), p. 186.   26 Curtis, op. cit., pp 45–7.   27 Reproduced in *Faces of the West*, pp 88 and 83.   28 *Connaught Telegraph*, infra.

the facts before that time incorrectly narrated.[29] Hotels in Knock and Ballyhaunis were refurbished, and their proximity to the shrine emphasised in advertisements in the local press. In June 1880, a pilgrimage was made by 300 young men, members of the Sodality of the Angelic Warfare of St Thomas of Aquina, and 60 cars and waggonettes met the special train run by the Midland Great Western Railway to Ballyhaunis station.[30] On the first anniversary of the apparition, the roads around Knock were jammed with carts and cars when (the *Connaught Telegraph* alleged) 40–50,000 people visited the site, and hopes were expressed that, in piety as well as for their own safety, future pilgrims might make their way on foot.[31] Thomas Wynne was present to photograph the scene, and advertised 'A series of photographic views of the CHURCH OF KNOCK' and a picture of the parish priest, Father Cavanagh. Hundreds of copies of lithographs of Knock were sold by Wynne's. Cabins in Knock village set up stores selling souvenirs bought from Wynne's, who sold candles, crosses, rosaries and frames for photographs of the shrine. A stereoscope and slides of the site were sold to one Knock household. Lithographs of Knock were sold to people in Ballyhaunis and Claremorris and the governor of the gaol in Castlebar bought 200 copies. The commercialisation of the Knock shrine, and the spread of business to other towns in the area confirm similar commercialisation at other European shrines during the nineteenth century.[32]

Except for grammars, no-one ordered books in the Irish language. By 1891, the idea of a nationalist Ireland based on the Gaelic language and engaged with an heroic and romantic past was shifting away from the local press and towards Dublin. In 1890, John McPhilpin of the *Tuam News* had tried to interest the Tuam Town Commissioners in advertising job vacancies in the Irish as well as English language, but his efforts were unrewarded, even mocked by his fellow Commissioners: 'Anyone who can read Irish can read English. Suppose we send an advertisement to the *News*, who will translate it if Mr John Glynn be not there. Surely not the editor (McPhilpin) who doesn't know Irish.'[33] McPhilpin's friend the Revd Euseby Cleaver wrote to him, '... if the Tuam Town Commissioners represented the general feeling of Irishmen about their national language he must confess that after all Mr Balfour and his party are right in saying that there is no reality in the National movement and that if the land question were settled the people would be quite content to remain an English province'.[34]

The Dublin Castle analysis of the provincial press found that a few papers (the *Westmeath Nationalist and Midland Reporter, Limerick Reporter and Tipperary Vindi-*

29 John McPhilpin, *The Apparitions and Miracles at Knock* (Dublin, 1880), p. 1.   30 *Connaught Telegraph*, 12 June 1880.   31 Op. cit., 21 August 1880. Andrew Dunlop visited Knock in 1880 when he wrote four articles for the *Daily News*. He was told by the Chairman of the Midland Great Western Railway in 1882 that after these letters were published, traffic to the shrine had fallen away.   32 David Blackbourn, *Marpingen: Apparitions of the Virgin Mary in Bismarckian Germany* (Oxford, 1993).   33 *Tuam Herald*, 16 August 1890.   34 Cleaver to McPhilpin, 25 August 1890: McPhilpin Papers NLI Ms 3254.

cator, the *Nationalist and Leinster Times*, and the *Kilkenny Journal*) were read by the Roman Catholic clergy. The Belfast *Weekly Examiner* was read by 'a good many farmers of opposite politics as it supplies a good deal of information re farming & etc.' Contradicting the hysteria of local landlords and members of the Cabinet, Dublin Castle intelligence cited earlier thought that, with some notable exceptions, most newspapers were believed to have little or no influence on their readers. The exceptions were the *Derry Journal*, the *Leinster Leader*, the *Roscommon Herald*, *Nationalist and Leinster Times*, *The People* (Wexford), and the *Cork Examiner*. The old demon of Dublin Castle, the *Kerry Sentinel*, influenced 'for harm as it advocates agitation. It is against the Union'. The *Limerick Leader* incited to boycotting and intimidation and the *Sligo Champion* had 'mischievous influence through the publication of resolutions of the National League'. The *Westmeath Examiner*'s influence had been curtailed after it had been condemned by the local bishop and his clergy, and this condemnation had considerably curtailed its circulation.

The evidence of the Castlebar papers demonstrates that the Irish read, and read widely, but Mahaffy was right. The readers of the provincial papers were not those who believed their estates to be threatened by the Land League. They read papers from Dublin and London. The increasingly nationalist provincial press was read by those who really were threatened by agrarian violence, though they expressed it less vociferously: the local people who kept farms and shops and who were dependent on each other for survival.

'Journalistic terrorism' and the pressure to prosecute

'With the disappearance of the publicity of these Leagues would disappear the Leagues themselves. Publicity is their existence, and that is what the Government know, and that is why they wish to intimidate the journalists of Ireland' John Hooper, *Cork Daily Herald*, October 1887.[1]

Events between the start of the Land War in 1879 and the death of C.S. Parnell in October 1891 led to a series of confrontations between the authorities and the Irish press when demonstrations on the issue of land were opposed by successive governments in attempts to bring Ireland under control. Two of the three coercion acts passed during this period, the Prevention of Crime (Ireland)Act 1882 and the Criminal Law and Procedure Act 1887, included sections dealing with the press, which was increasingly perceived to be playing an important part in the spread of disorder. One writer described the role of the Irish press in the Land War as 'journalistic terrorism'.[2] Conservatives were clear on the concept of an ordered world based on the ownership of property, but, as in the earlier debates on the Peace Preservation Act 1870, liberals were troubled by attempts to curb the freedom of the press. Inside and outside parliament, both liberal and conservative governments were subject to outside pressures to take action to pacify Ireland.

The increasingly high political profile of some newspapers and some newspaper owners, and their involvement in the Irish National League, which was made an illegal organisation under the Criminal Law and Procedure (Ireland)Act 1887, could not for long be ignored. Government needed to act, and act effectively. Their problem was to decide which of the various methods of prosecution open to them would be most effective without disturbing liberal public opinion. The pressure on government to prosecute the press came partly from opinion out of doors, and partly from government's own assessment of the influence of particular papers. In 1880, when he was Chief Secretary, Forster circulated members of Cabinet with a letter from a clergyman, who referred to a 'reign of terror which is for some time past running riot through Kerry'. Speaking of 'desperadoes' in the National League

---

1 PRO CO 903/1 Ireland Confidential Print.   2 I.S. Leadam, *Coercive Measures in Ireland*, National Press Agency (London, 1880), p. 29.

who were demanding to inspect pass-books and threatening to cut off the ears of those violating their orders, the Revd O'Leary of Ballymacelligott alleged:

> For all the mischief being done in our county I hold the *Kerry Sentinel* newspaper responsible. Articles teeming with the most reckless abuse of landlords and agents, with the most pernicious advice and inflammatory utterances, appear in almost every number of that wretched journal ... our simple-minded people are brought to a state nearly bordering on insanity. I don't know what power the Executive possesses, but if it could suppress immediately the further publication of the *Kerry Sentinel* comparative tranquillity would shortly return to us.[3]

Dublin Castle received letters from Irish landlords living in England. Another clergyman who owned land in Cork and writing from Torquay, sent the Lord Lieutenant a report from the *Cork Eagle and County Advertiser* of a National League meeting which threatened evicting landlords.[4] In 1887, the *Times* urged Salisbury's government to take action against the Irish press, believing that

> The whole of the so-called national movement in Ireland is nurtured by a system of what the French called *blague* ...Those who have addressed themselves to the masses in Ireland have been obliged to exaggerate, to falsify, to invent, until the habit of looking for any sort of correspondence between speech and fact has been altogether lost.[5]

Cabinet received regular bulletins on the increasing amount of agrarian crime, and in the years between 1881 and 1889, incidents classified as 'intimidation' continued to form a considerable percentage of these crimes:

1881	35.5%	1887	43.6%
1882	54.1%	1888	47.8%
1885	54.2%	1889	43.4%[6]
1886	48.8%		

Liberal policy continued to believe that the extension of the franchise should go hand in hand with the extension of education. The death of Palmerston in 1865 – described by Bagehot as 'a rock removed' – made the achievement of such reforms more probable. James Bryce, one of the liberal intellectual reformers of the 1860s, was excited by the idea that the whole nation could take part in directing its affairs: that democracy had a special 'stimulating power'. The rich would lead, not through

3 The Revd O'Leary PP to W.E. Forster 26 October 1880, in Report on State of the Country, 9 November 1880: PRO CAB 37/3/67.   4 The Revd Hicks, 12 September 1885: Carnarvon Papers, PRO 30/6/57.   5 Loc. cit., 11 October 1887.   6 Cabinet Papers PRO CAB 37/4/72.

privilege but by energy and intellect, and the 'humbler classes' would be elevated by their sense of vision and their sense of responsibility.[7] In a democracy, the state would have unity and strength derived from this common interest and purpose. Not all liberals shared Bryce's optimism about the effect of democracy, and late nineteenth-century liberalism could still call up its inheritance from its landed Whig founders. The jurist, James Fitzjames Stephen, held that the most important liberty was the liberty to acquire property, and this right was threatened by reforms in the franchises.[8] Universal suffrage, although difficult to resist, was not necessarily welcome and the Home Rule Bill was an 'abject folly'.[9] As Stephen saw it, the problem was that under a democracy government by the wise and good could be manipulated and destroyed.

Bryce's arguments for democracy on the American model were couched in terms which were directly contrary to the Irish situation. Intellectual and moral leadership of the type envisaged by Bryce and his circle seemed absent in Ireland and the 'humbler classes' rejected the idea of a common purpose with Britain. Ireland's failure to fit into the liberal model of society was compounded by the British belief that the Irish were ignorant.[10] With Leslie Stephen and Goldwin Smith, Bryce explicitly attributed political corruption in America to the influence of ignorant emigrant Irish peasants 'utterly unaccustomed to any form of self-government'.[11] Writing in 1889 about the formation of American public opinion, he saw the average man as having little idea of how he reached decisions; he was told what to think and why: 'Although he supposes his view to be his own, he holds it rather because his acquaintances, his newspapers, his party leaders all hold it'.[12]

Perception grew of the harmful effect of American influence on Ireland. Geographically and socially, through letters and travel, American ideas and American institutions were powerful forces. The issues raised by importation of the Irish-American Fenian press recurred frequently in Cabinet papers and the same arguments about its restriction were frequently rehearsed. Moreover, as a paper to Cabinet noted in 1885, the Irish were 'familiar with American institutions and with the part the people take in the government of the United States and Canada. They devour the newspaper literature both of Ireland and America which now floods the country, of which the real or supposed wrongs of Ireland form so large a part ... an organic change is made by the recent enormous extension of the franchise to the masses ... The masses feel their power, and use it unsparingly'.[13]

7 James Bryce, 'The Historical Aspect of Democracy' in *Essays on Reform* (London, 1867); Christopher Harvie, *The Lights of Liberalism: University Liberalism and the Challenge of Democracy 1860–1886* (London, 1976), p. 4. 8 K.J.M. Smith, *James Fitzjames Stephen: Portrait of a Victorian Rationalist* (Cambridge, 1988), p. 2. 9 Smith, op. cit., pp 190–1 and 152. 10 Smith says that James Fitzjames Stephen had a 'severely limited faith in the general educability of the masses towards wholesome political judgements': op. cit., p. 191. 11 Harvie, op. cit., p. 221. 12 James Bryce, *The American Commonwealth* (London, 1889), p. 241. 13 Memorandum on the State of the Country [?Spencer] PRO CAB 37/15/57.

Liberal policies in the 1870s were thus composed of the earlier advocacy of free-dom of speech and the self-determination of peoples, together with the mid-1860s pressure for the extension of the franchise and the expansion of education. These were the contradictions that formed the background to Gladstone's Cabinet de-bates on coercion legislation for Ireland during the 1880s.

Given that the spread of democracy appeared inevitable, conservative politi-cians shared with Dicey the belief that the great political problem of the age was how to ensure stability and permanence by forming conservative democracies.[14] But the Irish gentry did not fit into the conservative mould of the paternalistic land-lord. Those who still believed that conservativism derived its greatest strength from the rural landlord and tenant relationship were puzzled and angered by the atti-tudes of the Irish, and Irish landlords were thought to have deserted their posts and abjured their duties. When landlords (with the aid of liberal governments) gave way to demands of tenants, it was not possible for legislators to act for the public good. Cabinet papers frequently bewailed the irresponsibility of Irish landlords, and the Marquess of Clanricarde was taken to task in his club and condemned by name before the Special Commission.[15] Salisbury's pessimistic view of the Irish situation after 1885 limited legislative action to coercion rather than to the gradual reform of institutions. In Ireland, the collapse of one tier of local government on which all governments had depended until the mid-century – the large landowners – made his Cabinet disposed to be ruthless, and Balfour as Chief Secretary was both tough and shrewd in drafting coercion legislation.

Unlike the situation on the continent, in Britain legislation specific to control-ling the press was not available (except in the case of libel). Writing during this period, Dicey described the legislation that existed to protect editors, printers and sellers of newspapers on the continent. These involved the recognition of special rights for those who worked with the press. This particular protection was incon-sistent with English law. Indeed, 'a liberty of the press is not recognised in England ...', and freedom of speech was in England 'little else than the right to write or say anything which a jury ... think it expedient should be said or written'.[16] The conti-nental practice of demanding caution money from a newspaper proprietor in ad-vance of publication was, Dicey pointed out, inconsistent with the 'pervading prin-ciple' of English law that men are punished only when they have committed some definite assignable legal offence. This was why in England there was no such thing as a licence to print or control by censorship.

14 Hugh Tulloch, 'A.V. Dicey and the Irish Question 1870–1922' in *Irish Jurist* xv Summer 1980.   15 By Chief Baron Christopher Palles, quoted by Sir Charles Russell. Cf. Special Commission Act 1888. Reprint of the shorthand notes of the Speeches, Proceedings and evidence taken before the Commis-sioners appointed by the above named Act (1890) vol. 6, pp 571–2.   16 Dicey, *Introduction*, p. 247. Chapter VI deals with the whole question of the right to freedom of discussion and compares the law in England with that of France.

Foreign governments who had different concepts of the idea of the freedom of expression put British governments under pressure to prosecute journalists who had attacked their governments from the safety of protection by British law. In 1870, the ambassador of the Ottoman Empire told Foreign Secretary Clarendon that *Hurriyet* (Liberty), a Turkish paper published in London, had advocated the assassination of the Grand Vizier and his ministers, and successfully persuaded him to have the editor prosecuted.[17] The prosecution in 1881 of Johann Most, the German refugee editor of *Die Freiheit*, also published in London, was said (wrongly) by the *Times* to be the first case where a newspaper editor was accused of incitement to crime.[18] Most had printed an article celebrating the assassination of Tsar Alexander II and was accused under the Offences Against the Person Act 1861, as well as the common law, for conspiring or soliciting to commit murder by printing an article which was alleged to incite the assassination of foreign rulers. Most's paper was unimportant and would have died for lack of subscribers had it not been brought into prominence by prosecution.[19] The effect of this prosecution was to arouse half the national press in Most's support, and Most himself believed that the charge was not so much an attack on him as an attack on the principle of the freedom of the press. Perhaps significantly in view of subsequent events in Ireland, Most's defence counsel was Alexander Martin Sullivan, the former editor of *The Nation*, who had himself been imprisoned in 1868 for publishing an article about the Manchester Martyrs. In his final speech for the defence, Sullivan pointed out that the prosecution of a newspaper set a dangerous precedent for the future security of the press.[20] However, the Home Secretary, William Harcourt, believed that the prosecution was justified by its success.[21]

There were numerous problems facing any government that wanted to prosecute the press. In Ireland they had the familiar difficulty of finding reliable jurors ready and willing themselves not to be intimidated. Then there was the question of whether it was legal to use the Post Office to seize newspapers, and the very real problem of how to suppress the press in a way that might be acceptable to the British public. They needed to stop the newspapers' publication immediately and not just bolt the stable door after the horse had gone, and needed also to prevent journalists parading themselves as the martyrs of a repressive regime. Between 1880 and 1887 various legislative possibilities were canvassed, tried and discarded by both political parties.

The traditional methods of control were by the suspension of habeas corpus; the

17 Ambassador to Lord Clarendon, 19 January 1870: PRO Ho45/9472/A38025. The writer of the article said that he was bound by a *fatwa* to call for the Grand Vizier's assassination.   18 *The Times*, 5–6 May 1881.   19 Bernard Porter, 'The Freiheit Prosecutions 1881–1882' in *Historical Journal* (1980), pp 833–56.   20 Reprinted in *The Freiheit Prosecution*, June 1881. Pamphlet in PRO HO 144/77/A3385.   21 Diary of Lewis Harcourt, 28 May 1881. Harcourt Mss B Bodleian Library, vol. 348, p. 74. John Bright remained consistent in his support for a free press; he was the only member of Cabinet to oppose Most's prosecution. Cf. Diary of Sir Charles Dilke, 26 March 1881, BL Add. Mss 43924 f.45.

exaction of caution money or recognizances for good behaviour or by use of the common law. The 1870 Peace Preservation Act, which lasted until 1875, had legislated for the seizure of type, plant and presses and of newspapers after publication. The 1882 Prevention of Crime (Ireland) Act had the more limited power to order the forfeiture of particular editions of a newspaper. This Act lasted until 1886. The Criminal Law and Procedure Act 1887 caught up the press in a sweeping power aimed at prosecuting those who promoted the objects of 'dangerous associations' in proclaimed districts.

All these measures had their different disabilities. The suspension of habeas corpus was felt to be too sweeping a power to control agrarian intimidation, although landlords were keen for such action to be taken. In 1880, Lord Donoughmore wrote W.E. Forster a letter which was circulated to Cabinet, asking for the suspension of habeas corpus on behalf of a deputation of landowners, in order to prevent meetings preaching conspiracy, sedition and communism.[22] E.W. O'Brien, Smith O'Brien's son, agreed that parliament should suspend habeas corpus: 'The simpler the measure of coercion the better. Leave the press alone – it can't do any harm that can't be prevented by coercion ... Govt. will have shown its teeth ...' Forster, however, believed that the suspension of habeas corpus would be a temptation 'to rely on despotic power, rather than on the law.'[23]

Edward Hamilton, Gladstone's private secretary, put his finger on one of the government's greatest difficulties if they prosecuted the Irish press, the creation of martyrs for the nationalist cause. In 1880, when Forster urged Cabinet to prosecute Parnell, Hamilton felt doubtful about the commonsense of such a move, believing that a state trial of that kind would lead to 'a disagreeable dilemma. If it succeeds, those prosecuted become martyrs. If it fails they become Heroes'. The only good effect of such prosecutions would that they would 'disabuse the minds of the Irish landlords' who believed that the government was countenancing the actions of the League.[24]

The Irish-American newspapers were simple to control, in theory, by seizure at the ports. The Law Officers' opinions on the legality of seizing the *Irish People* in 1866 were that if the paper were found to be treasonable it should not be distributed by the Post Office, and directions should be given to detain it.[25] But in order to find out whether a paper were treasonable the Post Office had to open the packet on arrival in Ireland, and tampering with the mail in this way was of dubious legality. In 1885 there were further consultations with the Law Officers on whether it would be legal to seize the *United Irishman* and the *Irish World*, were they published in Ireland rather than America. The Attorney-General advised that there were no statutory provisions justifying the seizure and detention of such publications. He pro-

22 BL Add. Mss 44617 ff.164–72.   23 O'Brien to W.E. Forster, 4 November 1880: BL Add. Mss 44617 ff.195–204; D.W.R. Bahlman (ed.), *Diary of Sir Edward Hamilton*, 2 vols (Oxford, 1972), 8 November 1880.   24 Ibid., 13 October 1880.   25 9 March 1866, Larcom Papers, NLI Ms 7694.

duced the rather uncertain observation: 'The common law right to effect such seizures is, in our opinion, doubtful, but we think it can be supported by strong argument'. If the courts found against the government the damages would probably be
light. Harcourt interpreted the Law Officers' opinion as giving the Irish executive
the right to seize the *Irish World* and enquired, rather surprisingly, whether it would
be possible to make an illegal seizure and see if they could get away with it. 'Let
them try an action if they please'.[26] In 1882 when *United Ireland* began publication
on the continent it was seized from ships landing at Queenstown and Cork.[27] In
1885 the police were said to have 'arrangements' with the Customs at Queenstown
to seize any newspapers, especially *Irish World* and *United Irishman*.[28] Patrick Ford,
editor of the Boston *Irish World*, who at that time published O'Donovan Rossa's
appeals for contributions to the 'Skirmishing Fund', called such seizures 'censorship', but Lewis Harcourt, Harcourt's nephew, said that his only evidence was made
up of resolutions of Land League branches and 'the editorials of unknown journals
published in insignificant villages'.[29] Sir William Harcourt was enraged at the advice he received that the American government would be unwilling to take action
against the Irish-American press. He asked the British Ambassador to the United
States, Lionel Sackville-West, to obtain counsel's opinion in the States, but the
answer was unhelpful. Sackville-West replied that the United States Secretary of
State could only recommend the Governor of a state to proceed against a paper by
indicting to a Grand Jury and the result could not be guaranteed, more especially in
New York where most of the Irish-American papers were published. He sensibly
advised the Foreign Secretary (Granville) of the adverse effect on public opinion
should the state prosecute *United Irishman*, and the consequent notoriety which
'would greatly benefit the funds of that infamous periodical'. This advice was ill-
received by Harcourt who responded by sending Sackville-West three copies of the
successful indictment against Johann Most and *Die Freiheit*.[30]

If the suspension of habeas corpus was unsuitable, the problem for government
was how to formulate legislation that was limited and yet effective. The Attorney-
General told Cabinet that intimidation of any kind to compel a person to do anything or abstain from doing anything contrary to his legal right of free action was
dealt with under the Conspiracy and Protection of Property Act 1875. Writers in
the press were, like everyone else, subject to the law of the land, and nothing else. A
difficulty with the power to exact caution money, as Spencer told Gladstone, was
that the government could not properly control the judges: '[Lord Chancellor] Law

---

26 PRO HO 144/102/A20387. 27 Examples reported in the *Times*, 2 January, 24 January, 23 February 1882. Anna Parnell and members of the Ladies, Land League organised its distribution around the
country: Dana Hearne (ed.), Anna Parnell, *The Tale of a Great Sham* (Dublin, 1982), pp 122–3. 28
Memorandum by Sir William Harcourt, 7 February 1885: PRO HO 144/102/A20487. 29 Article by
Patrick Ford in press cutting from *Pall Mall Gazette*: Lewis Harcourt, diary, 5 June 1881. 30 Correspondence between Harcourt and Sackville-West 17 July and 21 August 1882: PRO HO 144/104/
A21242.

is against giving to the judges anything to do with the newspapers or Caution Money
...'[31] Spencer considered hedging this power with special tribunals, or the Judicial
Committee of the Privy Council, but recognised the problems that these controls
would create in their turn. In the event he told Gladstone that the power should be
omitted from the Bill: 'This is a very strong & arbitrary power. It wd. simply shut
up a struggling Local paper the proprietor of which often lives from hand to mouth
and cd. not find £200'.[32] The government would have sufficient powers if they were
enabled to seize newspapers containing treasonable matter and to convict their proprietors of intimidation.

There was debate over the power, included in the 1882 Act, to exact recognizances
for good behaviour. This already existed under the Statute of Edward III. One difficulty was that the exaction of recognizances by the courts was an opportunity once
again for those prosecuted to be martyrs by their refusal to give an assurance of
future good behaviour. Balfour told the Attorney-General in late 1887 that although
they had prosecuted a large number of newspapers and newsvendors under the
1882 Act, the newspapers continued to offend. But, '... what to do next ... having
put our hand to this work it would be unwise to recede partly because retreat is in
itself an evil'. For this reason he suggested that editors and printers sd be bound
over in heavy recognizances for good behaviour, forfeited 'if they continue and then
if they still persevere let the operation be recommenced and on ad infinitum'.[33] By
1889 Balfour found that the Statute of Edward III 'rendered useless. Recognizances
could only be recovered by an elaborate and almost unworkable process ...'[34] The
seizure of a newspaper's type and presses and of the newspaper itself had disadvan-
tages. Seizure could take place after an offending newspaper had been printed and
circulated. As Spencer commented dryly 'If seized, the effect is not good'.

Lord Oranmore and Browne criticised the section of the 1882 Act which dealt
with the seizure of newspapers and type on the grounds that: 'no sooner was one
edition seized than another could be published and circulated. Under those circumstances, he thought the clause 'perfectly useless'.[35] It was impossible to seize
the entire print of one edition of the newspaper: it always had a head start.

In 1870 W.R. Greg had thought simplistically that if the publisher had a grievance he could sue the government but that no respectable newspaper would offend
'no government with such heavy penalties against them would take arbitrary action'.[36] Action was taken by the authorities against *United Ireland* for publishing a
No Rent manifesto in December 1881. The publishers of *United Ireland* issued a

---

31 Spencer to Gladstone, 23 May 1882: Althorp Papers K5 f. 23.   32 Spencer to Gladstone 29 May,
1882 Althorp Papers K5 f. 29.   33 Undated [December] memorandum Balfour to Under-Secretary
West Ridgeway and the Attorney General: Balfour Papers, BL Add.Mss. 49808.   34 27 June 1889
Balfour to West Ridgeway: Balfour Papers, BL Add. Mss 49828 f. 80.   35 Hansard cclxxi, 1890.   36
W.R. Greg, 'The Irish Cauldron' and 'Government dealing with Irish Crime', *Quarterly Review* 128,
January and April 1870, pp 567–70.

writ against Forster, the Chief Commissioner of the Dublin Metropolitan Police and various policemen for the wrongful entry into their offices and claimed £30,000 damages.[37] Forster was advised to try and get a Bill of Indemnity against prosecution. According to his daughter he was also advised that the Irish Law Officers believed that although there was no doubt that the paper was 'a violent No Rent placard ... a newspaper, it seems, is a difficult [matter] to deal with, and some of the lawyers ... are of the opinion that, by strict law, the seizure of the papers cannot be justified ... Father declares "that he would rather pay £200 out of his own pocket than have to carry a Bill of Indemnity for himself through the House" '.[38]

In 1885 Spencer had reviewed existing coercion legislation, and deemed the power to seize newspapers as 'practically useless'. While it had been helpful in preventing the circulation of the American papers, before an Irish paper could be seized its contents had to be considered and submitted to the Law Officers and while this was going on the paper was being circulated. 'As far as this section goes I should drop it ... its exercise will be sure to lead to an action [as it had with *United Ireland*] ... a succession of actions against the Executive is not to be lightly looked forward to'.[39]

There was one course of action where the newspapers were found to be vulnerable and where prosecutions were successful. In the Criminal Law and Procedure Act, Balfour, Chief Secretary from March 1887, had devised a method of control that went wider than just the newspapers themselves. He fully conceded that the press was responsible for much of the difficulties in Ireland but that 'a mischievous article is not therefore an article which ought to be prosecuted'. First, the Law Officers 'show much greater ingenuity in picking holes in their own act than they ever did in passing it', and 'in the second place interference with the freedom of the press is a cry which has more effect in England than almost any other'.[40] Balfour's intellectual grasp of the problem is striking. He was quite clear that only limited action could be successful, believing that it was 'undesirable on many grounds to fill the gaols with Editors, printers and newsvendors, however guilty they may be, for such action is sure to be seriously misrepresented'.[41] He therefore targetted the publication of the proceedings and resolutions of suppressed branches of the League believing that if these powers were 'vigorously exercised [they would be] sufficient

37 *The Times*, 24 January 1881.   38 *Florence Arnold-Forster's Irish Journal*, 16 April 1882.   39 Spencer: Notes on the Prevention of Crime Act 1882 23 March 1885: PRO Cabinet Papers CAB 37/14/20. Sir Henry James, the Attorney-General, made no comment on the press clause on his copy of Spencer's paper to Cabinet. On a proposal to make the Act applicable to England, he wrote that none of the clauses of the Act, with the exception of clause 16 (the power of justices to summon witnesses) was applicable to England. 'Any such suggestion would be opposed by Radicals'. On the clause on intimidation, he wrote 'No such offence is known in England. The Trades Unionists although not employing intimidation to any extent now ... would voluntarily oppose such a clause': BL Add. Mss 44219 ff 175–6.   40 Balfour to Salisbury, 16 October 1887: Salisbury Papers f.211. Balfour to Buller, 8 August 1887, Balfour Papers: BL Add. Mss 49826 f.149.   41 Balfour to West Ridgeway, December 1887: Balfour Papers BL. Add. Mss 49808.

either to root out or to render impotent and contemptible any branch against they were employed'.[42] Balfour's legislation enabled the executive, first to proclaim districts to prevent the commission of crime, and then prohibit or suppress any associations within these proclaimed districts and make unlawful any assembly connected with the associations and the publication of the objects and proceedings of the associations. On the introduction of the Act, Balfour told Buller: 'I hope we shall be able to hit the papers in our Bill sufficiently hard without introducing them *eo nomine*. Public opinion is sensitive about phrases though callous about things. I am afraid of the freedom of the press!'[43] Commenting on a letter from the Duke of Argyll who had apparently remonstrated against the terms of the Act, Balfour told Salisbury that 'our dealings with the press are the tenderest part of our policy. But ... no prosecutions have taken place for any expressions of opinion ... The difficulty of dealing with suppressed branches of the League unless we can stop these publications will be very great.'[44] To West Ridgeway, the Under Secretary at Dublin Castle, he wrote, 'We have now got our weapon and we must use it with vigour'.[45] Gladstone described the new Act as 'A savage law, savagely administered'.[46] When the Special Proclamation declaring the Irish National League a dangerous association was debated in the House in August 1887, Gladstone exposed Balfour's intentions behind the section of the Act under which the press could be prosecuted. Balfour had declared that there were no press clauses: 'No Press Clauses! Not for the world would this Government have the odium of Press Clauses; but it is a new and ingenious invention to avoid the odium of Press Clauses'.[47] In his reply, Balfour abandoned any pretence at dissimulation on the government's intention to prosecute the Irish press, pointing out that the Cowper Commission had drawn attention to the involvement of the press in boycotting. Resolutions were passed at National League meetings, reported in the press and named 'obnoxious men, and then Boycotting those named ... There is ample and overflowing material in the reports of the local newspapers in Ireland to justify the actions of the Government in this matter'.[48]

As has already been shown, Dublin Castle was well aware of those newspapers which had been most prominent in their association with the Land League, and which published the proceedings and resolutions of local branches on a weekly basis. Florence Arnold-Forster and her brother Oakeley kept a press cutting book for their father while he was Chief Secretary and which Oakeley drew on when writing a pamphlet on the 'No Rent' campaign. She refers to the 'rebel papers' and al-

---

42 Balfour to Salisbury, 21 September 1887: Salisbury Papers f.206.   43 13 March 1887, Balfour Papers, BL Add. Mss 49826.   44 22 December 1887: Salisbury Papers, Hatfield House f.228.   45 Balfour to West Ridgeway, 8 November 1887: Balfour Papers BL Add. Mss 49808.   46 Quoted by Balfour in an undated [December 1887] memorandum: Balfour Papers, BL Add. Mss 49808.   47 Hansard cccxix, 1842.   48 Hansard, cccxix, 1854–66. He quoted from seven papers: *Munster News*, *Dundalk Democrat*, *Kerry Sentinel*, *Tuam News*, *Midland Tribune*, *New Ross Standard*, *The People* (Wexford), *Weekly News*, *Leinster Leader* and *Kilkenny Journal*.

though the majority of cuttings may have been from *United Ireland* there is evidence that some were from the local press.[49]

The first proprietor prosecuted in 1887 under the new Act was Edmund Walsh, proprietor of the *Wexford People*, and a number of other Wexford and Wicklow papers. Walsh was accused of publishing a notice inciting people to take part in an unlawful assembly. T.M. Healy appeared for the defence and Edward Carson for the prosecution. Walsh was found guilty and sentenced to one month's imprisonment with hard labour. By chance, Wilfred Scawen Blunt and his wife were in the public gallery as part of their tour of Ireland. Travelling from Dublin to Gorey with Healy and Mrs Alfred Webb, Lady Anne Blunt hoped that they would 'have some fun at "suppressed" meetings'.[50] (Their 'fun' culminated with Blunt's arrest at a meeting in Woodford a week later.) Lady Anne called Walsh a 'cheerful little man who seems ready to face resident magistrates, crown counsel and if need be the 8 ft. by 4 ft. cell'.[51] After his sentence, Walsh and his papers made much of his experience: '... The jail is with us the retreat where the laurels are to be worn, and to a modest man such a sentence comes as astonishing proof that his life has been spent to some purpose ... in suffering he is not only advancing the national Cause but asserting for the press a freedom for which Wilkes was imprisoned ...'[52] Although Walsh had served his sentence, his conviction was overturned by the Court of Exchequer in February 1888. Baron Palles, a notably liberal appeal court judge, decided that the Act had 'created a new crime' and that before a defendant could be convicted of an offence of publishing the reports of suppressed branches, he must have notice beforehand of the suppression of that branch. Otherwise a defendant might commit a crime when he could not know it was a crime. Walsh was awarded costs. Jubilantly, the newspaper announced that 'The Crown received another roll in the mud by the Exchequer Division, Dublin'.[53]

The chief victims (or adversaries) of Balfour's policy were the *Kerry Sentinel* and the *Sligo Champion*. Edward Harrington was convicted in December 1887 and his brother Timothy (who had taken the over the paper) followed him in the same month. Again they were defended by Healy. There is some evidence that Healy did not find defending the press congenial. Healy described Edmund Walsh as 'a ... prosaic journalist'. Of Timothy Harrington he wrote 'I don't like the job, yet what can I do?' He was even more reluctant to appear for John Hooper, proprietor of the *Cork Daily Herald*: 'Still less should I like to defend Hooper, as he has no possible defence, whereas Harrington has nothing whatever to say to the offence with which he is charged, yet doubtless he also will follow his brother to jail'.[54] P.A. McHugh, proprietor of the *Sligo Champion*, was prosecuted in 1888 and 1889 for publishing intimidatory notices. McHugh was Mayor of Sligo, president of the County Com-

49 *Florence Arnold-Forster's Irish Journal*, 23 November 1881. **50** Diary of Lady Anne Blunt, 18–19 October 1887. Wentworth Bequest, BL Add. Mss 593960. **51** Ibid., 19 October 1887. **52** *The People*, 26 October 1887. **53** Ibid., 26 February 1888. **54** Healy, op. cit., pp 283 and 278.

mittee of the Gaelic Athletic Association, County Head Centre of the IRB and president of the local branch of the National League. He used the paper to the full to expose Balfour's policies in action and in so doing brought himself to local attention, receiving purses of money when he was released from gaol. The local Divisional Commissioner believed that prosecuting McHugh had a good effect 'The paper has not published any bad article or resolution since. The testimonial given to him was chiefly collected through the influence of secret societies with which he is deeply connected'.[55]

The National League had a Defence Fund 'towards State Trials' to pay the legal costs of those caught up in offences against coercion legislation.[56] This was drawn on to pay for the defence of newspaper editors. Some time later, when Jasper Tully of the *Roscommon Herald* was arrested in 1900 for a speech at a meeting in Sligo, he was refused financial help with his defence and complained to John Redmond, referring to his 'trials in the old days' when he had been helped by 'the Organisation'.[57]

By March 1890, there had been nineteen prosecutions of thirteen provincial newspapers. A very small number of sentences were reversed on appeal on legal or procedural technicalities.

Table 17: *Provincial newspaper prosecutions to 31 March 1890*
under the Criminal Law and Procedure Act 1887

Convictions for using evidence of the publication of proceedings of branches of the Irish National League

Cork Daily Herald	1887
Kerry Sentinel (Edward Harrington)	1887
Kerry Sentinel (Timothy Harrington)	1887
Cork Examiner	1887
Kerry Sentinel (Edward Harrington)	1888
Carlow Nationalist	1889
Munster Express	1889
Munster Express (H.D. Fisher)	1889 (reversed on appeal)
Leinster Leader	1889 (conviction quashed)
Wexford People	1889

55 Report of R.B. Stokes, DC Midland Division, June, 1890. Confidential Reports of Divisional Commissioners: PRO 30/60/5.   56 'December 31, 1887 Subscriptions from Defence Fund towards State Trials £1500': Special Commission hearing Minutes of Evidence, vol. 6, p. 330.   57 Jasper Tully to John Redmond, 26 December 1901: NLI Redmond Papers Ms 15,229.

Convictions for publishing articles other than reports of League branches

Sligo Champion	1888
Midland Tribune	1889
Tipperary Nationalist	1889
Tipperary Nationalist	1889
Tipperary Nationalist	1889
Waterford News	1889 (reversed on appeal)
Sligo Champion	1889
Limerick Leader	1889
Tipperary Sentinel	1889

Source: List of Press Prosecutions in Ireland from the passing of the Criminal Law and Procedure Act 1887 to 31 March 1890 PRO CO 903/1)

The same document notes the outcome of cases of persecution and intimidation 'successfully grappled with by the Government' between 1886 and 1892. As well as prosecuting for these two offences, editors and proprietors were caught by other charges. James Carew, editor of the *Leinster Leader*, was prosecuted for criminal conspiracy for a speech at Nurney in 1888; J.P. Hayden of the *Westmeath Examiner* was prosecuted for obstructing police at an eviction and again for a speech; Edmund Walsh was prosecuted in 1888, this time for making an intimidatory speech, and in 1890 for publishing intimidatory articles. James Daly of the *Connaught Telegraph* was prosecuted in February 1889 for publishing an intimidatory article. He pleaded guilty and 'expressed sorrow' and the prosecution was withdrawn, further evidence of Daly's wish to distance himself from the main activities of the National League. Jasper Tully was prosecuted with his mother in 1886 for publishing an intimidatory article, but the jury disagreed and the case was dismissed. In 1890 Tully was sentenced for six months for publishing an intimidatory article.[58] Occasionally the prosecutors had difficulty in identifying just who was the responsible person to charge. Timothy Harrington's appeal against his sentence was successful because Harrington was able to demonstrate that he was not the registered proprietor of the *Kerry Sentinel*. The usual sentence for offences under the 1887 Act was three months imprisonment, with or without hard labour.

In the late 1880s the relationship between the Land League and the press was highlighted by the Special Commission hearing on the alleged links between Parnellism and crime. One of the charges made by the *Times* articles was that the National League organisation was dependent on a 'system' of intimidation; that there was a 'system' of coercion and intimidation to promote agitation. The Land League described landlordism as a 'system'. The idea of classification, of systemisa-

58 National Archives Irish Crimes Record Register of Newspapers.

tion had been close to legislators' hearts since before Bentham. The development of a 'system of communication', whether of transport or the press is a very mid-century concept.[59] Judge Keogh told the Galway County election petition hearing that in his judgment the Roman Catholic church was responsible for an 'organised system of intimidation'. Rebutting the accusation that the League had created a secret network all over Ireland, Parnell said that there was nothing secret in connexion with the Land League; the Land League was not a revolutionary (implying secret) movement, even if it achieved revolutionary ends. In the eyes of the government, it was the League's use of modern communications and propaganda that furthered their ends. The modernism of the newspapermen who were called to give evidence to the Special Commission compares sharply with other witnesses, the small farmers and labourers from Mayo and Galway. The Commission report referred to a speech by John Dillon who had advised an audience in Ireland to use the press in publicising cases of hardship,[60] and to the press publicity which attacked landgrabbers and promoted boycotting. The opening speech of the Attorney-General at the hearing cited twelve newspapers with connections with the League, nine of which were published in Ireland, and three of which were local papers. He made a direct connexion between the United States, the press and the commission of crimes.[61] Referring to a speech made by Parnell in Kerry in June 1880 which was published in papers all over Ireland, he expressed his belief that the consequences of this speech were brought home by that very fact of their publication '... without this tyranny, without this intimidation, the Land League was powerless'. The *Kerry Sentinel* was once again cited as a means of enforcing the power of the Land League.[62] One peasant witness could not read but nevertheless had heard his neighbours say that resolutions had been published in the *Kerry Sentinel* and the *Kerry Reporter*.[63] Joseph Biggar MP dismissed the local press as unreliable evidence, as a great many of the local papers were read only by a small number of people and it was 'notorious' that some papers were bogus.[64] Parnell's counsel, Sir Charles Russell, attempted to defend the *Kerry Sentinel* against charges of incitement to violence by referring the court to the newspaper's 'apparently sincere, earnest, hearty denunciations of crime'. Citing two cases where the motive was simple murder, he pointed out that while the newspaper might not condemn Land League activities, it did condemn ordinary crimes.[65]

In 1889 Cabinet received a paper which set out to justify the prosecution of the Irish press. It said newspapers had been prosecuted not for reporting items of daily news or comments and criticisms 'however gross' of the government, or even attacks on landlords, but solely and entirely for 'enforcing the boycotting decrees of an irresponsible tribunal'. When papers published reports of bogus meetings which

59 'Parnellism' is a further example.   60 Special Commission Report, vol. I, p. 37.   61 Special Commission evidence, vol. 1, p. 43.   62 Ibid., pp 80, 235.   63 Evidence of John Conway, ibid., vol. 2, Q 11,124.   64 Ibid., vol. 12, p. 246.   65 Ibid., vol. 1, pp 554, 566 and 570.

never took place and illegal resolutions which emanated from 'the inventive genius of a village scribe', the plea of public duty fell to the ground. Editors and proprietors who had 'disgraced the press by allowing their journals to become the organ and engine of a criminal conspiracy' deserved to be prosecuted. There was no possible course open to the Irish executive but to prosecute and punish those journalists.[66]

Was press prosecution effective in achieving the aim of government to suppress the spread of agrarian crime and intimidation throughout Ireland? Although sporadic attempts were made to continue confrontation with the government, particularly by the *Sligo Champion*, on the face of it Balfour's legislation seems to have been successful in curtailing the publication of the resolutions of suppressed branches of the League. The effective coercion of the press came at a moment when the press itself was engaged in the chaotic aftermath of the split in the Irish Party, which took proprietors' attention away from battles with local landowners.[67] Membership of the National League then declined sharply. After 1891, individual editors carried on the old battles – P.A. McHugh of the *Sligo Champion* in particular – but with little effect. Only with the local government reforms at the end of the century was the nationalist provincial press given a new stage on which to perform.

66 Prosecution of Newspapers - necessity for, and distinction between what has been done and what has not been done 1889: PRO CO 903/2.   67 'The National League is too busily engaged ... in local quarrels to engage in any intimidation ...': Report of R.B. Stokes, Divisional Commander RIC March 1891, PRO CAB 30/60/5.

Conclusion

'The word in man is a great instrument of power' W.G. Gladstone.[1]

Newspapers are part of the theatre of the nation: the signal to the local residents, to tradesmen, to visitors, that their town and their county is of a distinct importance. A newspaper is conducted by the proprietor as a preacher in a pulpit in a church addresses the congregation. So the provincial press in nineteenth-century Ireland gradually realised its power to act as a lever on local affairs. The shape of this examination of the Irish provincial press in the second half of the nineteenth-century has been determined by themes that preoccupied it, and by the development of the relationship between proprietors and readers.

The abolition of taxes on newspapers after 1855 was the most important event that affected the growth of the provincial press both in Britain and Ireland. However, in Ireland the subsequent increase in numbers of newspapers and sharp reduction in their price gave a spur to the expression of nationalist ideas. To succeed as a separate nation, Ireland sought redemption through work and by changing its public image; it needed to recreate its past, and assert economic and political control over its future. These were the essential elements of the creation of a national identity. Other elements of nationhood – the development of domestic industry, the spread of the idea of the nation united by a common language, and the revival of that language from a past that could be claimed as wholly their own – all these were explored by the press. The newspapers used figures of the past to conjure up a new vision of the present. The heroes of Irish pre-history, and the politicians of the present, Daniel O'Connell and Robert Emmet; the Flight of the Earls, the Battle of Aughrim and the events of 1798 were cited as models of behaviour and of action. We have seen the newspapers' role in the tenant right movement and the assertion of

---

1 Matthew, *Diaries*, vol. IX, pp. lvii-lviii. This passage is quoted in a highly suggestive section referring to the conjunction of the publication of pamphlets and extra-parliamentary speeches as 'marking the way of the future' (p. viii). He points out that parliamentary speeches were not very popular with the provincial press, as being too long and dense in character. (In this he contradicts the evidence given by Edmund Dwyer Gray to the Select Committee on Parliamentary Reporting in 1878.) As the editor of the *Leeds Mercury*, Alex Ritchie, pointed out in 1870, there were two audiences for every political speech out-of-doors: those present at a meeting and the readers of the next day's newspapers. Gladstone had a very clear understanding of this modern process of propaganda, and of its strength.

the existence of an Ireland self-reliant, sober and hard-working. The growth of these ideals was paralleled by the expansion of towns and of the railway system which facilitated the circulation of the press and which in turn supported local economic developments.

The political polarisation of newspapers, which can be seen clearly in the early 1850s, accelerated through the 1860s until the Land War, which brought a sudden spurt of newspapers with nationalist politics. The papers with 'independent' or 'neutral' politics gradually declined.[2] Proprietors gave up serving behind the counters of drapers and grocery shops and recognised their new roles in the growing towns: their importance as leaders and interpreters of opinion and events, and the positions now open to them as town councillors and poor law guardians and, eventually, Members of Parliament. Their readers in turn gained status and respectability in being able to read and to be seen reading newspapers which informed their own growing political awareness and activity. The provincial press thus played a crucial role in the modernisation of the political movements and institutions of the country.

The character of the press, its policies and its position in the community underlines the importance of localism in the development of Irish nationalism. The issue of land dominates the decades between 1840 and 1910: again and again, land appears in the press in different guises. With the Tenant League, in the creation of a Gaelic past, and in the rise of Fenianism and the founding of the Land League, the interests of farmers in good times and bad are all-important. Land was the central plank in political platforms, and motor of the nationalist machine. Evidence of the great national issue made manifest in the locality is contained in newspaper reports of land sales, evictions, outrages, tributes to good landlords and attacks on bad landlords and publicity for branches of the National League. More, the scattered impact of local variations of national issues was re-integrated and reinforced by the messages broadcast by the local newspapers. To achieve maximum impact for its activities, the National League recognised the importance of bringing these far-flung local demonstrations together, so as to persuade the less militant counties to action; and they used the provincial press to spread their propaganda across Ireland. Parnellism brought nationalists together and the Land War provided the opportunity for action. Unifying the separate parts of Ireland convinced nationalist readers of the contribution that they could make towards the creation of a national identity.

The split in the Irish Parliamentary Party was reflected by newspapers who used the crisis to exercise control on events. With so many proprietors in active politics, newspapers had an intimate understanding of the working of politics in practice, and political parties gained a more subtle understanding of the way the press could be used.[3] The clarity and immediacy of the newspapers' reaction to

2 Papers describing themselves as 'independent' or 'neutral': 1850: 31 per cent; 1890: 24 per cent. 3 The crude blanket coverage conducted in the 1872 Galway County by-election disappeared with the reforms in the conduct of election campaigns.

public opinion was identified by W.T. Stead.[4] The shifts in newspapers' professed political adherence were a natural reflection of the shifts in allegiances throughout the period. The provincial press was another means by which Ireland could demonstrate to the outside world that the British government continued to treat the country as a colony which requiring legislation separate and different to that of England and Wales. In the national and provincial Irish papers read by the Irish diaspora in the United States, Canada and Australia, the message was that Ireland was a country where evictions and demonstrations were supported by the military stationed in barracks all over the country.

Coercion legislation demonstrated the concern felt in Dublin and London about the relationship between nationalists, the press and the public. Stephen Koss wrote of the British political press that that it was the job of politicians to keep the political press from going wrong: 'one man's "political prejudices" were another's political commitment. One man's "hysteria" was another's patriotism'.[5] It was correctly believed that the press played an important role in influencing the actions of nationalist groups. The increasing proportion of those who could and did read newspapers; the growing numbers of nationalist newspapers; the strong links between the Land League and the local press and the numbers of provincial journalists who had become members of the Irish Parliamentary Party, were evidence to the government that the power of the press to disturb the populace was great, and growing greater. But newspaper proprietors' political activities were not disinterested; they had a living to make. The observation of Stephen Koss once again is acute: it was the job of proprietors to keep the press from going bust.[6]

The Irish provincial press should not, therefore, be considered as subsidiary or inferior to the national press. It performed an essential role in the development of the idea of the nation and in understanding its parts and varieties. With the founding of the Gaelic League, the longing for past values and institutions which was embodied in so many mid-century papers, was reinvented in Dublin. This, and the creation of the Dublin-based Irish National League, were evidence of the increasing centralisation of institutions that characterised the period after 1880 and which, in the development of nationalism in the early twentieth century, nurtured the germ of a tension which came to a head in the Civil War.[7] As Vincent Comerford has pointed out, 'Political mobilization, the rise of popular nationalism, linguistic uniformity and increased ease of communication, all go hand in hand'.[8]

---

4 Stead claimed that an editor's mandate was 'renewed daily' op. cit., p. 655. Koss quotes William Thomas on the philosophic radicals who argued that newspapers' daily reflection of public opinion was better than stale election results. Koss, op. cit., p. 413.   5 Koss, pp 422, 424.   6 Ibid.   7 A section of the press of Roscommon, where Sinn Féin was active in the 1920s, persisted in supporting Parnell long after other newspapers had gone over to John Dillon.   8 R.V. Comerford, 'Nation, Nationalism, and the Irish Language' in Thomas E. Hachey and Lawrence J. McCaffrey (eds), *Perspectives on Irish Nationalism* (Kentucky 1989), p. 23.

By the 1890s, the habit of reading a newspaper was entering its golden age. To be able to read was no longer just a skill to keep a man from drink; it was an important passport to entry into the modern world. In towns, newspapers were read more at home and less in the public reading rooms. Newspaper proprietorship and journalism were recognised as professions in their own right, not adjuncts to other activities. Increasingly, the church saw the press as another means by which a Catholic nation could be consolidated. The issues of land ownership, the spread of literacy and mass communications, and the influence of the Roman Catholic Church, which was itself involved in founding newspapers, were cornerstones of the new Catholic Irish state.

So far, little or no work has been done on the place of the nineteenth-century Irish provincial press. This study aims to form the basis for further work, as it starts to identify the dramatis personae, the statistics of individual newspapers and the issues that they faced. The provincial press is not just a convenient source for citation by historians. It played a greater and far more important role, as a 'great instrument of power' which forcibly altered the vision of Ireland cherished by Gladstone and which helped create a new self-image of Ireland in the next century.

Irish provincial newspapers in print, 1850–92

The details of each paper are taken from entries in the *Newspaper Press Directory*. The *Newspaper Press Directory* was used by newspapers for advertisement, and they sent copy to the proprietors for insertion. These entries often remained without alteration for many years and anomalies can occur where a paper which has closed still appears in the *Directory*. The holdings of newspapers in reference libraries may be no guide to the continued survival of a paper and in most cases there is nowhere that shows a definite and final date of publication for any title.

With these caveats, the material here is intended to demonstrate the changes in price, publication politics and proprietors over the period. It does not claim to be an exhaustive record.

Each newspaper is presented in a standard form:

1 Name and date of first appearance and end of publication.
2 Place of publication if not clear from title
3 Publication day
4 Price with dates of changes
5 Political affiliation with dates of changes
6 Circulation area claimed
7 Policies advocated
8 Proprietors
9 Advertisement (if any) in *Newspaper Press Directory*

ANGLO-CELT [Cavan] (1846)
1851 Thursday; 1872 Saturday
1851 4*d*. and 5*d*.; 1866 5*d*. and 6*d*.; 1867 2*d*. and 3*d*.
1851 Neutral; 1866 Liberal
Circulates Belturbet, Clones, Cootehill, Monaghan, Killishandra, ... generally in Cavan, Meath, Westmeath, Monaghan, Leitrim, Longford and Fermanagh.
Advocates 1851 The social regeneration of Ireland and the abolition of distinctive names, contending that there is not now a pure Saxon hardly a pure Celt in the island. 1866 The *Anglo-Celt* is Liberal. It supplies the fullest local and general intelligence; is devoted to the agricultural and commercial interests of the country.
Proprietor 1857 Zechariah Wallace; 1858 Joseph Wallace; 1866 P. Brady; 1867 Philip Fitzpatrick; 1868 John F. O'Hanlon; 1888 Mrs O'Hanlon
Advertisement 1857 The tone of the Journal, so far as regards mere party matters is neutral, in other cases independent. It advocates the union of Irishmen of all creeds and politics for useful, practical and national purposes when the interests of their suffering down-trodden country are at stake. Advocates legalization of tenant-right, development of industrial resources, and in international matters, jealousy of and legitimate resistance to the centralizing policy of England ... pays particular attention to Poor Law matters. Established advertisement organ of Poor Law Boards. Special attention given to books sent for review.

ARGUS [Monaghan] (1875–7)
1877 Friday; 1885 Saturday
1875 1½d.; 1877 1d.
Conservative
Circulates Monaghan, Armagh, Cavan, Down, Fermanagh, and Tyrone and in the Irish metropolis.
Advocates General news of markets, proceedings of local institutions, railway and other public boards, reviews of new books, resumé of Church news.
Proprietor David Wood

ARMAGH GUARDIAN (1844–1982)
Friday
1851 5d.; 1857 6d.; 1865 3d. and 4d.; 1872 2d.
Conservative
Circulates 1851 Armagh and 10 mile radius; partially through other parts of Ireland; the Canadas; and the United States; 1865 Armagh and district
Advocates 1851 Agriculture and commerce. Its principles are genuine Conservative; rights of the farmer as identified with the manufacturing classes. [Omitted in 1864: Supports the Church Establishment. It freely concedes that toleration to others which is the glory of the Reformation.] The literary department occupies a prominent position. 1870 Supports the Church of Ireland.
Proprietor 1851 John Thompson, printer &c.[1851 only] Printer, stationer, perfumer, patent medicine vendor and agent for the Norwich Union Life and Fire Insurance Society; 1871 J. Thompson; 1881 W.C.B. Thompson
Advertisement 1857 The largest Newspaper in the Provinces. Central position of the City the nucleus of the Linen trade, and having Direct Railway Communication with the leading Commercial Towns renders the GUARDIAN a suitable medium for advertisements; 1885 Advocate of Conservative Progress.

ARMAGH STANDARD (1879–1909)
Friday
1d.
1885 Conservative; 1888 Constitutional; 1889 Conservative
Circulates Armagh and district
Advocates The *Standard* supports a Conservative policy. Local and district news, with correspondence, tales and miscellanies
Proprietor [1889 and editor]: John Young

ATHLONE SENTINEL (1834–61)
Friday
1851 5d.; 1857 3d.; 1864 3d. and 4d.
1851 Conservative; 1857 Liberal
Circulates Roscommon, Sligo, Mayo, Galway, Leitrim, King's county, Westmeath; Longford, Meath, Dublin, etc.
Advocates 1851 General Conservative principles, though a desire for the extension of commercial freedom is expressed, it aims at being a general newspaper and chronicle of local events rather than a strong partizan journal; 1857 The interests and views of the Roman Catholic body and contains the intelligence of the week, local and general; 1866 Advocates Liberal views and contains the intelligence of the week, local and general.
Proprietor John Daly
Advertisement 1857 The *Sentinel*, the oldest paper in the district, enjoys a large circulation particularly in Leinster and Connaught. Agents for advertisements W.H. Smith & Sons, Strand and Dublin, Eden Quay. Charles Mitchell, Fleet Street.

ATHLONE TIMES (1877–1902)
Saturday
2*d.*
Independent
Circulates Town and district
Advocates Local events, social, political and religious, and summaries of home and foreign intelligence.
Proprietor 1877 Henry McClenaghan; 1888 S.J. McClenaghan

BALLINA CHRONICLE (1849–51)
Wednesday
5*d.*
Independent
Circulates Mayo and local counties
Advocates 1851 measures of general utility for the general good; was opposed to repeal and rejoiced at the fall of the O'Connell dynasty.
Proprietor Thomas Ham, general printer.

BALLINA JOURNAL (1880–95)
Monday
1881 2*d.*; 1885 1*d.*
Liberal
Circulates Ballina, Mayo and the Province of Connaught
Advocates It is a thorough Liberal paper, and advocates the adoption of the Land Act. The *Journal* is a good local paper.
Proprietor 1881 W.R. Armstrong; 1888 J.T. Armstrong
Advertisement 1881 Started under most promising auspices at the special desire of a large number of the clergy, merchants and farmers ... with a guaranteed circulation of 1,000 ... that circulation has since doubled.

BALLINA NATIONAL TIMES (July 1866) Not in *Newsplan*
Wednesday
3½*d.* and 4½*d.*
Independent
Circulates Ballina and district
Advocate Entirely independent of party, and opposed with vigour a all tyranny and injustice. The local and general news is given with correspondence &c.
Proprietor John Bourns
Not entered in *Newspaper Press Directory* after 1867

BALLINROBE CHRONICLE (1866–1903)
Saturday
3*d.* and 4*d.*
Independent
Circulates Ballinrobe and county
Advocates Agriculture, commerce, politics and general literature.
Proprietor 1867 Gore Kelly; 1892 Miss Gore Kelly

BALLYMENA ADVERTISER (1866–92)
Saturday
1*d.*
Liberal

Circulates Ballymena and district
Advocates 1871 The *Advertiser* supports the Liberal party, and is anxious for a fair trial of their remedial measures.
Proprietor M. Edwin

BALLYMENA OBSERVER (1855–1985)
1857 Saturday; 1889 Friday
1857 1½d. and 2½d.; 1858 2d. and 3d.
Liberal-Conservative
Circulates Ballymena and the county generally
Advocates 1857: The principles of that section of the Conservatives which is most nearly allied to the Liberals. It inserts no matter not connected with the news of the day; 1888: Loyalty to the Throne and the maintenance of the Union, but its leading matter is characterised by firmness and independence.
Proprietor 1857: George White; 1877: John Weir

BALLYMENA WEEKLY TELEGRAPH (1867–1970)
Friday
1d.
Neutral
Circulates -
Advocates Copious local reports, markets, together with all the North of Ireland news carefully compiled. Original serial tales, joke columns, and competitions of various descriptions are a feature.
Proprietor J. Laughlin

BALLYMONEY FREE PRESS (1863–1934)
Thursday
1868 1d. and 2d.; 1889 ½d.
Liberal
Circulates Ballymoney and towns of the province
Advocates Contains copious reports of all the local news, meetings &c. The general news is also given.
Publisher S.C. McElroy

BALLYSHANNON HERALD AND NORTH WESTERN ADVERTISER/1884 DONEGAL INDEPENDENT (1831–84)
1851 Friday; 1868 Saturday
1857 3d. and 4d.; 1864 1d. and 2d.
1864 Conservative; 1884 Independent-Conservative; 1886 Independent
Circulates Extensively throughout Connaught and Ulster with a partial circulation throughout the United Kingdom.
Advocates 1851 The general interests of agriculture and commerce; is a political journal and attached to the principles of the Church of England. [1884: The general interests of society.]; 1858 Whilst being strictly Conservative in principle it attaches itself to no party; 1868: but advocates always the cause of truth and opposes that of wrong.
Proprietor 1857 David Carter; 1858 Andrew Green; 1884 Sam Delmege Trimble

BANBRIDGE CHRONICLE/1880 BANBRIDGE CHRONICLE AND DOWNSHIRE STANDARD (1870–1985)
1876 Saturday; 1888 Wednesday and Saturday;
1876 1½d.; 1880 1d.

Independent
Circulates Town and district
Advocates Independent of party and advocates Tenant Right
Proprietor J.E. Emerson

BANNER OF ULSTER [Belfast] (1842–69)
1851 Tuesday and Friday; 1857 Tuesday, Thursday and Saturday
1851 4*d*.; 1857 3*d*. and 4*d*.; 1858 2½*d*. and 3½*d*.; 1864 1*d*. and 2*d*.
Liberal
Circulates Generally to a large extent throughout Ulster, and especially all the counties of Down and Antrim. Its circulation in Dublin is also large.
Advocates 1851 No party but pursues in all subjects a strictly independent course. It is the organ of the General Assembly of the Presbyterian Church and in a great measure represents the opinions of all the Evangelical Protestant Dissenters of Ireland. Its agricultural and commercial intelligence respecting the produce ... of Ulster is extensive and it gives copious reviews of new books; 1865 It represents in a great measure the opinions of all the Evangelical Protestant Dissenters of Ireland.
Proprietor 1851 John Prenter; 1857 McCormick and Dunlop; 1866 Samuel E. McCormick
Advertisement Shown by Parliamentary returns to be with a single exception, the most widely circulated Newspaper in Belfast. Circulates in the best classes of society.

BELFAST DAILY POST / 1884 BELFAST WEEKLY POST (1882)
Daily ½*d*.; Saturday 1*d*.
Liberal
Circulates Belfast and the North of Ireland generally
Advocates The *Post* is unsectarian, and supports the Liberal party. It advocates the cause of the tenant farmer, but stoutly upholds the maintenance of the union with England, and the integrity of the Empire. All important matters that arise in Parliament affecting Ireland are specially reported and wired.
Proprietor 1882 P. Stirling; 1884 J. Clarence Newsome
Advertisement 1882 Possesses a circulation larger than any other Provincial Journal in Ireland.

BELFAST EVENING TELEGRAPH (1870)
Daily
½*d*.
Conservative
Circulates All classes in Belfast and Ulster
Advocates 1870 The interests of the Conservative Party; 1872. It advocates moderate political opinions, and devotes itself with spirit to questions affecting the moral and social condition of the working classes.
Proprietors W. and G. Baird

BELFAST MERCURY / 1854 BELFAST DAILY MERCURY (1851–61)
1851 Tues, Thurs and Sat; 1857 Daily
1851 4*d*.; 1857 2*d*. and 3*d*.
Liberal
Circulates Belfast and Ulster and generally throughout Ireland.
Advocates Every measure that may seem calculated to enlarge the true freedom, advance the intelligence, elevate the morals, and improve the social and physical conditions of the people. Proprietor and editor was for 20 years sole editor of the *Northern Whig*.
Proprietor 1851 James Simms ; 1857 James Simms and Frederick Farrer; 1860 Ulster Printing Co.

BELFAST MORNING NEWS/1880 ULSTER WEEKLY NEWS/1883 BELFAST MORNING NEWS
(1855–92)
1857 Monday, Wednesday and Friday; 1872 Daily; 1880 Weekly
1857 1*d*.
1857 Neutral; 1883 Independent; 1885 Home Rule; 1888 National
Circulates Belfast and the corporate and market towns in the North and North West of Ireland.
Advocates Free from party bias, but the chief attention (not neglecting literature) is devoted to
news, market intelligence etc. the object being to make it a full and complete family newspaper.
Proprietors 1851 R & D. Read, printers; 1884 Publisher F.W. Bell; 1888 Proprietor E. Dwyer
Gray; Publisher G.H. Page; 1889 Proprietor Mrs Dwyer Gray; 1892 The Morning News Co. Ltd.
Advertisement 1851 Non-sectarian and non political journal. Average Daily Circulation 7,080;
1885 The Organ of the Home Rule party in the North of Ireland.

BELFAST MORNING POST (1855–)
Tuesday, Thursday and Saturday
1*d*.
Liberal
Circulates Belfast and neighbourhood. A cheap vehicle of local news.
Proprietor None entered. Office 5 North Street

BELFAST NEWS-LETTER (1737–to date)
Daily
1857 2*d*. and 3*d*.; 1868 1*d*. and 2*d*.
Conservative
Circulates Every town in Antrim and Down. Generally throughout Ulster, partially in England
and Scotland. It is one of the county Advertisers for Antrim and Down.
Advocates 1851 Agriculture, commerce and manufacturing and is the leading Conservative Jour-
nal in Ulster. Literature and the Fine Arts receive especial attention in the columns of the *News-
Letter*.
Printer and Publisher 1851 James Alexander Henderson ; 1885 Henderson & Co.
Advertisement 1851 The oldest Paper in Ireland. Circulating among the Nobility, Gentry, Clergy,
and the leading Commercial men in the community. All books sent to the office are most impar-
tially and carefully reviewed. London Advertisers will find the *News-Letter* an invaluable medium;
1885 Advocates thoroughly Protestant and conservative principles.

BELFAST NORTHERN WHIG (1824–1963)
1857 Tues, Thurs, and Sat.; 1868 Daily
1857 3*d*. and 4*d*.; 1872 1*d*.
Liberal
Circulates 1851 Every Town in Ulster and generally to all other three provinces as well as Great
Britain, the Colonies, America and the Continent of Europe.
Advocates 1851 It may be considered a Whig journal belonging to that movement. Free trade ...
leading organ of the liberal and reform party in the North of Ireland. A political and literary paper,
not the advocate of any religious sect; 1871 Free trade, progress, and civil and religious equality,
and is the leading organ of the Liberal and Reform party in Ireland.
Proprietors 1851 Francis Dalzell Finlay and Sons; 1877 James Dickson
Advertisement Shown by the latest Government returns to be the most widely circulated Provincial Journal in Ireland. Circulation of Belfast Press from the latest House of Commons returns:
Belfast Northern Whig, 1,795; *Belfast News-Letter* 916; *Belfast Mercury* 864; *Ulsterman* 726; *Banner of Ulster* 654

BELFAST TIMES (1872)
Daily
1*d*.
Conservative
Circulates Belfast, Ulster, generally in Ireland and Scotland and also in England.
Advocates A liberal and enlightened Conservatism and sympathises with all measures calculated to advance the well-being of the community.
Proprietors D. and J. Allen [Editor: Nicholas Flood Davin]

BELFAST WEEKLY NEWS (1855–1942)
Saturday
2*d*. and 3*d*.
1857 Neutral; 1872 Protestant; 1885 Orange-Protestant
Circulates Belfast and district
Advocates 1857 Measures for the general good ... only weekly paper in Belfast which gives a compendium of the whole news of the week; 1885 The organ of the Orange Institution, and is most extensively circulated throughout Ireland.
Proprietors 1857 J.A. Henderson; 1885 Henderson & Co.

BELFAST WEEKLY PRESS (1858) Not in *Newsplan*
1864 Saturday; 1872 Friday
1*d*. and 2*d*.
Neutral
Circulates Belfast and North of Ireland
Advocates Not political; aims at being a family paper. Just attention given to agriculture and commerce and the staple trades of Ulster.
Proprietor 1864 McCormick and Dunlop; 1866 Samuel E. McCormick
Not entered in *Newspaper Press Directory* after 1885

BELFAST WEEKLY TELEGRAPH (1873–1964)
Saturday
1*d*.
Orange
Circulates –
Advocates Recognised organ of the Orange Society in the province of Ulster and abroad. It devotes itself to the development of sound Protestant and Constitutional opinions, to the advancement of religion among the masses of the community and to the cultivation of free and independent thought among its readers.
Proprietors W. and G. Baird

BRAY GAZETTE/1871 BRAY AND KINGSTON GAZETTE/1877 BRAY HERALD (1861–72)
Saturday
1864 1*d*. and 2*d*.; 1865 3*d*. and 4*d*.
Neutral
Circulates Bray and district
Advocates Local news and a list of visitors, advertisements [Omitted after 1865: are added to a partly printed sheet from London.]
Proprietor and editor 1864 G.R. Powell; 1879 Proprietor William McPhail

CARLOW NATIONALIST/1888 NATIONALIST AND LEINSTER TIMES (1883–to date)
Saturday
1½*d*.

National
Circulates Counties of Carlow, Kildare, Wicklow and Queen's
Advocates 1884 It contains full reports of National League meetings, agricultural and general. The local events are reported with fairness and accuracy; 1892 Contains full reports of all local Boards, political and social meetings, agricultural and general. Military news of the Curragh Camp and Newbridge a speciality.
Proprietor P.J. Conlan
Advertisement 1884 The recognised organ of the liberal-national party in the district ... wide circulation amongst the farming, trading and professional classes.

CARLOW POST (1853–78)
Saturday
4*d*. and 5*d*.
Liberal
Circulation Carlow, Kildare, Kilkenny, Wexford, Wicklow and Queens County.
Advocates Tenant right and the other measures of the liberal Roman Catholic party in Ireland. Takes the same ground which the *Carlow Morning Post* formerly occupied. Devotes columns to politics, news, not attending much to the claims of literature.
Proprietor 1857 Thomas Price; 1868 Louisa Price
Advertisement 1857 Edited by a gentleman of well-known abilities ... strenuously but temperately advocates an Equitable Adjustment of the Landlord and Tenant Question, the Extension of the Franchise, the Non-payment by the state of the Ministers of any religious denomination and Equality in Civil and Religious Rights ... also filed in the principal News Agency offices, Coffee-Houses and Hotels of Dublin.

CARLOW SENTINEL (1831–1920)
Saturday
1851 6*d*.; 1865 4*d*. and 5*d*.
Conservative
Circulates Carlow, Tallow, Bagnalstown, Goresbridge, Hacketstown, Leighlinbridge. Fenagh, Naas, Athy, Wicklow town and county, Dublin and county and Leinster generally.
Advocates 1851 Agricultural and commercial interests. Political and literary journal. Attached to Churches of England and Ireland. While it does not interfere with the interests [1868 opinions] of other Protestant sects. Circulates among professional and Commercial classes and is filed in most of the London hotels and coffee houses.
Proprietor 1851 T.A. Carroll; 1857 Mrs Sarah Carroll
Advertisement 1865 Mentions the abolition of the advertisement duty and competitively low advertisement prices.

CARLOW WEEKLY NEWS (1855–63)
Saturday
1*d*. and 2*d*.
Neutral
Circulates Carlow and District
Advocates Local interests
Proprietor T. Edwards, Bookseller

CARRICKFERGUS ADVERTISER AND COUNTY GAZETTE (1883–1946)
Friday
1*d*.
Neutral
Circulates Town of Carrickfergus and county of Antrim.

Advocates A thorough Protestant and Conservative paper, and gives all the local and county news at great length.
Publisher 1885 A.W. Wheeler; 1891 William Ritchie
Advertisement Advocates thorough conservative principles

CARRICKFERGUS FREEMAN (1865–6)
Saturday
1½*d*. and 2½*d*.
Independent
Circulates Carrickfergus and neighbourhood
Advocates Records news of Carrickfergus and concentrates public opinion on local topics.
Publisher John Henderson

CASHEL GAZETTE/1872 CASHEL GAZETTE, TIPPERARY REPORTER AND WEEKLY ADVERTISER (1864–93)
Saturday
2*d*. and 3*d*.
Neutral
Circulates Cashel, district and surrounding towns.
Advocates In politics and religion this paper is neutral. Contains original literature and antiquarian articles. [1883–6]: Has occasional articles in the Irish tongue.
Proprietor J.Davis White

CASHEL SENTINEL (1885–1914)
Saturday
2*d*.
National
Circulates Cashel and district
Advocates The *Sentinel* is thoroughly National and a staunch supporter of Home Rule. As a newspaper of general information it is very complete.
Proprietor T. Walsh

CASTLEBAR TELEGRAPH OR CONNAUGHT RANGER/1877 CONNAUGHT TELEGRAPH (1830– to date)
Wednesday
1851 5*d*.; 1872 3½*d*.; 1877 3*d*.
Liberal
Circulates Throughout Connaught, United Kingdom, France and America, India.
Advocates 1851 This Roman Catholic organ is conducted with much talent and energy. It is more political than polemical and is one of those journals so long remarkable for the patriotic lyrical effusions, which, like those of Tyrtaeus, find an echo in so many 'Irish Hearts'; 1857 Absence of coercion, free trade, employment for the industrious classes, and is a Roman Catholic organ. More political than polemical (and since the question of 'Repeal' has declined in estimation the *Telegraph* has taken up the question of 'Tenant-Right'). All the proceedings in parliament, and foreign and domestic news and reports of local meetings etc. are given.
Proprietor 1851 Published by the Proprietor Ellison Street, Castlebar; 186:4 Charlotte Macdonnell; 1877 O'Hea and Daly; 1880 James Daly
Advertisement 1857 Established on 17 March 1830 by the late Hon. Frederick Cavendish and now continued by his widow, Mrs Cavendish. Motto 'Be just and fear not' from which it has never deviated. Circulates extensively among all classes and respected for its honesty even by very many who are opposed to it in politics.

CAVAN OBSERVER (1857–64)
Saturday
5*d.*
Conservative
Circulates Armagh and Co. Cavan
Advocates The *Observer* is conservative ... devoted to agricultural and commercial interests of the
county.
Proprietor Charlotte Bourns

CAVAN WEEKLY NEWS (1864–1909)
Friday
1*d.* and 2*d.*
1868 independent; 1869 Protestant-Conservative; 1874 Protestant; 1888 Liberal-Conservative
Circulates Cavan and county.
Advocates Contains all local news, markets &c.
Proprietor John Fegan

THE CELT [Waterford] (1876–7)
Saturday
1*d.*
Advocates All news and articles are reported and written in a neutral spirit. Contains tales, miscellanies etc.
Proprietor M. Hayes
1879 Taken over by the MUNSTER NEWS

CHAMPION OR SLIGO NEWS / 1868 **SLIGO CHAMPION** (1836–to date)
1851 Saturday; 1857 Monday
1851 5*d.*; 1857 4*d.* and 5*d.*; 1868 3½*d.* and 4½*d.*; 1877 3*d.*; 1886 2*d.*
1851 Radical; 1857 Liberal
Circulates Sligo county and Leitrim, Mayo, Roscommon and Donegal
Advocates 1851 Liberal opinion. It is particularly distinguished in the locality in which it is
published for the fearless manner in which it exposes Grand Jury jobbing and other abuses; [1864
Grand Jury omitted] recognised political organ of the Roman Catholic clergy of Elphin and Achonry
... remarkable for the copiousness of its original matter; 1888 National opinions and the general
improvement of the country. It is particularly distinguished for ample and correct reports of all
local matters, including quarter and petty sessions and the public boards.
Proprietor 1851 Edward Howard Verdon, Town Councillor for the Borough of Sligo; 1864 Edward
O'Farrell; 1879 Edward Gayer; 1886 P.A. McHugh
Advertisement 1886: The recognised organ of the Nationalists of Sligo, Mayo, Roscommon,
Leitrim and Donegal. Most popular provincial newspaper in Ireland.

CITIZEN/1881 **CITIZEN AND COUNTY NEWS**/1886 **WATERFORD CITIZEN** [Waterford] (1859–
1906)
1864 Friday; 1870 Tuesday and Friday
1864 3*d.* and 4*d.*; 1870 2*d.* and 3*d.*
1864 Independent; 1881 Liberal
Circulates Waterford and District
Advocates Principles of the Roman Catholic church; 1868 Repeal of the Union 1870 Equal laws
with England 1891 A native parliament for purely Irish purposes subject to the control of the
Parliament of England.
Proprietor James Harnett McGrath

CLARE ADVERTISER [Kilrush] (1856) Not in *Newsplan*
Saturday
3*d*. and 4*d*.
Neutral
Circulates Limerick and Cork
Advocates Every improving measure
Proprietor John A Carroll

CLARE EXAMINER [Ennis] (1878–87)
Saturday
1*d*.
1880 National; 1882 Constitutional
Circulates Ennis and counties of Clare and Limerick
Advocates Gives all the usual local and county news, with full reports of the meetings in the district, and the progress of the 'land laws' question.
Proprietor Thomas Maguire

CLARE FREEMAN [Ennis] (1853–84)
1857 Saturday; 1877 Wednesday and Saturday
1857 3*d*. and 4*d*.; 1870 4*d*. and 5*d*.; 1877 2*d*.
Liberal
Circulates Clare, Limerick, Galway, and generally through south and west of Ireland
Advocates 1858 Principles of civil and religious liberty and gives a comprehensive record of the news of the week from all parts of the United Kingdom and abroad. Literature receives due attention; [1857 only]: Unity of feeling and a desire amongst all classes to promote the public good.
Publisher 1857 James Knox Walker; 1868 Mrs M Laing Walker; 1879 C.L. Nono

CLARE INDEPENDENT/1882 INDEPENDENT AND MUNSTER ADVERTISER [Ennis] (1875–85)
Saturday
2*d*.
1878 Catholic; 1881 Liberal; 1885 National
Circulates Ennis, Clare and Tipperary
Advocates The *Independent* is devoted to the Faith [1881 the Liberal-National party] and is in all respects an excellent local and county. paper.
Proprietor T.S. Cleary

CLARE JOURNAL/1879 CLARE JOURNAL AND ENNIS ADVERTISER [Ennis] (1776–1917)
Monday and Thursday
1851 4½*d*.; 1857 3*d*. and 4*d*.; 1873 2*d*.; 1874 3*d*.
1857 Conservative; 1864 Neutral; 1867 Liberal-Conservative
Circulates Ennis and the several towns in the county as well as through Ireland generally
Advocates Interests of agriculture and commerce. Attached to Church of England principles and though of Conservative principles is free from bias.
Proprietor 1857 John B. Knox; 1865 John B. Knox and son

CLARE SATURDAY RECORD [Ennis] (1885–1917)
Saturday
1*d*.
Neutral
Circulates Ennis and district
Advocates Local news of town and neighbourhood
Proprietor John B. Knox and Son

CLARE WEEKLY NEWS [Ennis] (1878–80)
Saturday
1*d.*
Liberal-Conservative
Circulates Ennis and the county
Proprietor J.B. Knox and Son

CLONMEL CHRONICLE/1888 **CLONMEL CHRONICLE AND WATERFORD ADVERTISER** (1848–1935)
Wednesday and Saturday
1851 4*d.* and 5*d.*; 1885 3*d.*
Conservative
Circulates Tipperary, Kings County, Antrim, Dublin, England, Scotland &c.
Advocates 1851 Commercial and agricultural interests of the Kingdom
Proprietor Edmond Woods

COLERAINE CHRONICLE (1844–1967)
Saturday
1851 4*d.*; 1857 3*d.* and 4*d.*; 1866 2*d.* and 3*d.*; 1883 1*d.*
1851 Conservative; 1864 Liberal
Circulation Antrim, Londonderry, Tyrone, Armagh, Down and other counties in Ulster and Great Britain and America.
Advocates 1851 Interests of agriculture, commerce, manufactures. A political, commercial and family newspaper. Theological controversy is altogether excluded and the interests of Protestant Evangelical Christianity and the advancement of Christian Union advocated. The paper is conducted on Presbyterian principles; 1864 The interests and extension of agriculture, commerce and manufactures and is a political, commercial and literary family newspaper. The paper is conducted on Presbyterian principles.
Publisher 1851 Robert Huey; 1857 John M'Combie
Proprietor 1851 H Boyde Mackey, solicitor ; 1868 John M'Combie
Advertisement 1857 *Coleraine Chronicle* headed the government returns for the provincial press of Ireland. Average number of readers for the last six months: 7,500.

COLERAINE CONSTITUTION (1875–1908)
Saturday
1*d.*
Conservative; 1888 Unionist
Circulates Derry and Antrim and through the provinces
Advocates Though advocating a Conservative [1888 Unionist] policy its articles have an independent tone and its reports are characterised by great impartiality.
Publisher J. Hamilton Simms; 1884 J.M. Russell
Advertisement Started by a company of shareholders more with the object of supplying the district with accurate and impartial news, and advancing the interests of the Constitutional party, than as a monetary speculation.

CONNAUGHT PATRIOT [Tuam] (1859–69)
Saturday
4*d.* and 5*d.*
Independent
Circulates Tuam and province
Advocates 1864 Popular rights but is the organ of no faction. Is strictly Catholic and thoroughly

national. Tenant right and every other Irish 'right' with the free exercise of religious worship by all Christians is also insisted upon.
Publisher Martin A. O'Brennan

CONNAUGHT PEOPLE [Ballina] (1883–86)
Saturday
2*d.*
National
Circulates Extensively in the lower part of county Galway, and in Roscommon, Mayo and the King's counties.
Advocates The interests of the National party, but pays great attention to agriculture and the commercial interests of the community at large. It is particularly distinguished for the ample and fair reports it gives of public boards all over the county, and is fast rising into a position of great influence.
Proprietor A.G. Scott

CONNAUGHT WATCHMAN [Ballina] (1851–63)
Wednesday
1857 6*d.*; 1858 5*d.*
Conservative
Circulates Mayo, Sligo, Leitrim, Galway, Roscommon
Advocates The Protestant cause, and measures of general utility for the general good. It gives the news of the week in condensed form with literary notices and extracts from new works.
Proprietor Thomas Ham, general printer.

CONNAUGHT WITNESS [Roscommon] (1870) Not in *Newsplan*
Saturday
1*d.*
Conservative
Circulates Roscommon and District
Advocates Conservative policy
Proprietor L.W. Lennon
Not entered after 1871 in *Newspaper Press Directory*

CORK CONSTITUTION (1822–1924)
Tuesday, Thursday, Saturday
1872 Daily
1851 6*d.*; 1857 3½*d.* and 4½*d.*; 1864 2*d.* and 3*d.*; 1869 1*d.* and 2*d.*
Conservative
Circulates Cork county and Towns and principal towns in Kerry, Limerick, Waterford and Tipperary and partially in rest of Ireland.
Advocates 1851 Interests of agriculture and commerce. A political and religious journal attached to Church of England principles. The tone of this journal is decidedly aristocratic and this has perhaps caused it to become a favorite in the messrooms of the Sister Isle, not less than the attention paid by it to the state and all prospects of military affairs. All general news and all the intelligence [of the] surrounding districts; 1883 Interests of agriculture and commerce ... is the only Conservative daily paper south of Dublin. All general news and all the intelligence which affects the surrounding districts, are carefully reported in the Constitution.
Proprietor 1851 Anthony Savage, George Edwards, George Savage; 1857 Messrs A. Savage and G.E. Savage; 1864 G.E. Savage; 1871 Proprietor: Cork Constitutional Co. Ltd
Publisher J. Atkins; 1874 J.B. Sandford; 1883 James Bleakley; 1890 News Co. Ltd.

CORK EXAMINER (1841–to date)
Monday, Wednesday and Friday; 1868 Daily
1851 6*d*.; 1857 3*d*. and 4*d*.; 1858 4*d*. and 5*d*.; 1864 2*d*. and 3*d*. 1868 1*d*. and 2*d*.
Liberal
Circulates Cork City and county, Kerry, Waterford, Tipperary and Limerick; in Dublin; in various reading rooms throughout Ireland and to some extent in Manchester and other English towns.
Advocates 1851 Strongly the Repeal of the Act of Union, is now the advocate of the 'Tenant Right League' and lends its warmest support to the advance of Irish agriculture, Irish commerce and manufactures. Though mainly a political organ, still its columns are much devoted to literature, and its reviews of books are very frequent; 1867 Reform and tenant-right. It has made the Irish industrial movement a speciality. To literary reviews it devotes a large space, and pays much attention to dramatic and musical criticism and to sporting events. 1872 It was the leading advocate of the tenant cause in the south of Ireland, and has adopted the Home Rule movement, but is most earnest in its endeavours for the promotion of industrial enterprise in the south.
Proprietors 1851 John Francis Maguire MP Barrister at Law; 1872 Executors of the late John Francis Maguire; 1877 B. Britton; 1888 P. Corcoran; 1889 George Crosbie; 1892 P. Corcoran
Advertisement 1865 it has taken the initiative in the recent industrial movement in the South and is the chief organ of all new undertakings which spring from it.

CORK EVENING ECHO (1872) Not in *Newsplan*
Daily
1*d*.
Independent
Circulates City and county of Cork; only daily evening published in the south of Ireland. Special edition for Queenstown where reporters permanently employed to collect the most reliable shipping intelligence.
Advocates All news of the day both foreign and domestic.
Proprietors D. Gillman and F.P.E. Potter
Not entered in *Newspaper Press Directory* after 1873

CORK DAILY SOUTHERN REPORTER/1871 **IRISH DAILY TELEGRAPH** (1807–73)
1851 Tuesday, Thursday, Saturday Daily
1851 4*d*.; 1857 3*d*.
1851 Liberal; 1872 Moderate-Liberal
Circulates City and county of Cork and Kerry, Tipperary Limerick and Waterford and province of Munster generally.
Advocates 1851 Interests of agriculture, commerce and manufactures. It strenuously urges enlarged education, especially in the practical sciences, and advocates united secular instruction, as afforded in the Queen's College and national schools. In agriculture, it is favourable to compensation for improvements made by the tenant and the abolition of the law of distress; but opposes the valuation principle. In commerce it is for complete free trade. It upholds the Roman Catholic interests; 1870 The ideas of the Liberal party and strongly discourages 'Irish Republics' and similar chimeras. It strenuously urges the redress of many grievances by strictly constitutional methods. It does not sympathise with the 'Nationalist' party and is devoted to both liberty and order. It is the sole organ in the south of Ireland of the moderate-Liberal party, the upper and middle class, viz. those who have something to lose; 1873 [as *Irish Daily Telegraph*] Contains copious supplies of news provided by editors, reporters and correspondents appointed in each county in the province of Munster. A speciality of the *Irish Daily Telegraph* is its devotion to agricultural interests, that department being edited by a practical agriculturalist. Its commercial intelligence is always fresh and reliable, while as a general newspaper it bears comparison with the very best of its metropolitan contemporaries. It has also a Dublin office, from which it receives special telegraphic dispatches. In politics, the *Telegraph* is the sole organ in the South of the Moderate-Liberal party.

Proprietors 1851 Patrick Dennehy; 1857 Felix Mullan; 1869 Bryan Hennessy; 1870 Daniel Gillman; 1872 D. Gillman and Frederick P.E. Potter

Advertisement 1870 This paper occupies a very remarkable position in Irish Journalism. It is the sole organ in the south of Ireland of Constitutional Liberalism and while strenuously urging the removal of every Irish grievance at the same time is devoted to the maintenance of law and order and to the integrity of the empire. It steadily resists the efforts of those who would lead the masses to pursue the phantom of an impossible nationalism instead of the blessings of constitutional reforms. The ideas which the REPORTER advocates were at one time very unpopular in Ireland but they have lately gained ground with extraordinary rapidity and to this fact as well as to a recent change in the proprietorship and consequent improvement in the management of this paper is to be attributed the fact that the circulation of the REPORTER has doubled. Read by prelates Catholic and Protestant, by a great number of clergymen and all denominations, MPs, magistrates and the middle and working classes.

1874 Taken over by *Waterford Mail*

CORK HERALD/1864 **DAILY HERALD** and **CORK WEEKLY HERALD** (1856–1901)
Saturday; 1864 Daily
1857 1½*d.* and 2½*d.*; 1858 2*d.* and 3*d.*; 1865 1*d.* and 2*d.*
1857 Liberal; 1858 Neutral; 1875 Independent; 1889 Nationalist
Circulates Cork, Queenstown, Youghal, &c.
Advocates 1857 In political measures independent ... gives local news more copiously than the general intelligence, has a tale of fiction continuing from week to week and devotes a considerable portion of its space to literature; the fashions with occasional explanatory woodcuts, domestic economy and general household matters; 1865 Gives local news very copiously with an extensive and carefully-prepared selection of all the general news both foreign and domestic.
Proprietor 1857 Samuel M. Peck [who also ran the freesheet *Cork Advertising Gazette*], 1868 Publisher Cornelius Murphy; 1875 Joseph E. Tracy and David A. Nagle; 1877 Cornelius Murphy; 1879 Charles O'Shea; 1886 P. Keegan; 1889 J. Geary
Advertisement 1857 Only weekly Newspaper published in the large and important Counties of Cork, Limerick and Waterford. Circulated very extensively among the wealthy and influential classes throughout the south of Ireland. Offensive Advertisements are excluded and no expense is spared to render it A FIRST-CLASS FAMILY NEWSPAPER.

COUNTY TIPPERARY INDEPENDENT [Nenagh] (June 1870) Not in *Newsplan*
Thursday
1*d.*
Independent
Circulates Nenagh, Tipperary
Advocates News of the county with tales
Proprietor J. Fisher
Not entered in *Newspaper Press Directory* after 1879

COUNTY WEXFORD EXPRESS/1881 **WEXFORD EXPRESS** (1875–1907)
1871 Wednesday; 1874 Wednesday and Saturday
1871 1*d.* and 2*d.*; 1885 2*d.*
Independent
Circulates Wexford, New Ross
Advocates Full supply of county news.
Proprietor 1871 J. Fisher; 1883 W.G. Fisher; 1891 H.D. Fisher

DONEGAL VINDICATOR [Ballyshannon] (1889–1956)
Friday

1*d.*
Nationalist
Circulates Ballyshannon and the counties of Donegal, Fermanagh, Leitrim and Sligo.
Advocates Thoroughly a Nationalist policy. Fully reports the local and district news.
Proprietor John McAdam
Advertisement Treble the circulation of any weekly newspaper published in the north west of Ireland.

DOWN INDEPENDENT [Downpatrick] (1878–82)
Saturday
1*d.*
Liberal
Circulates Downpatrick and district
Advocates Liberal measures, local intelligence and news of the county and district is given.
Publisher 1878: A.J. Matthews; 1881: Down Independent Co. Ltd.

DOWNPATRICK RECORDER/ 1879 **DOWN RECORDER** (1836–to date)
Saturday
1851 4*d.*; 1857 3*d* and 4*d.* 1877 2*d.*; 1879 1*d.*
Conservative
Circulates Through every town in county of Down, and in several towns in Antrim and Armagh
Advocates 1851 Interests of agriculture, commerce, and manufactures especially agriculture. A political, religious and literary journal, attached to the Church of England, but supports other Protestant denominations.
Proprietor 1851 Conway Pilson; 1877 J.S. Clarke

DOWNSHIRE PROTESTANT [Downpatrick] (1855–62)
Friday
2½*d.* and 3½*d.*
Protestant
Circulates In Downpatrick and the principal towns of Downshire and adjacent counties.
Advocates Protestantism in its widest sense. Gives reports of movements of Protestant societies in the United Kingdom, with the news of the week. Information on agriculture and manufactures and all local matters.
Proprietor William Johnston

DROGHEDA ARGUS (1835–to date)
Saturday
1851 4½*d.*; 1857 3½*d.* and 4½*d.* 1865 3*d.* and 4*d.*; 1885 2..
Liberal
Circulates Dublin, Navan, Kells, Carrickmacross, Ardee, Dundalk, Drogheda, etc.
Advocates The agricultural and commercial and manufacturing interests; is political, open to religious discussion and devotes some space to literature.
Proprietor 1851 Patrick Kelly, bookseller, stationer and patent medicine vendor; 1858 Anne Kennedy; 1868 John Hughes; 1888 A. Hughes

DROGHEDA CONSERVATIVE (1837–1908)
Saturday
1851 4½*d.*; 1857 3*d.* and 4*d.*; 1865 1*d.* and 2*d.*; 1868 2*d.* and 3*d.*; 1872 3½*d*; 1873 2*d.*
Conservative
Circulates Locally
Advocates 1857 Agricultural and commercial interests of the county ... portion always dedicated

to literature. Advocates the interests of Protestants on the common ground of truth.
Proprietor 1851 John Apperson, general printer; 1857 Alexander McDougall; 1870 James Willcock; 1874 John McDougall; 1888 A McDougall

DROGHEDA INDEPENDENT (1884–to date)
Saturday
2*d*.
Nationalist
Circulates Drogheda, Heath, Lough, Coleraine, Monaghan, Dublin and district
Advocates Is the recognised National organ. Advocates the interests of the large district in which it circulates and fully reports the local news.
Proprietor Drogheda Independent Co.

DUNDALK DEMOCRAT (1849–to date)
Saturday
1851 4½*d*.; 1857 4*d*. and 5*d*.; 1864 3½*d*. and 4½*d*.; 1877 2*d*.
1851 Ultra-Liberal; 1884 National
Circulates Dundalk, Drogheda, Newry, Louth, Meath, Cavan, Monaghan, Down, Armagh, Fermanagh
Advocates 1851 Advancement and progress of the democratic principle in government and tenant right, strongly opposes Whig measures. It is principally devoted to politics, general and local news; 1864 The advance of progress of the democratic principle in government and Ireland's right to a Domestic Legislative; self-government being the only remedy for her numerous wrongs; strongly opposed to Whig policy.
Proprietor 1851 Joseph Cartan; 1873 Thomas Roe

DUNDALK EXPRESS (1860–70)
Saturday
1864 1*d*. and 2*d*.; 1866 2*d*. and 3*d*.; 1870 1*d*. and 2*d*.
Independent
Circulates Dundalk and county of Louth
Advocates Just rights of the people and is uninfluenced by sectarian or political parties.
Proprietor Gerard McCarthy

DUNDALK HERALD (1868–1921)
Saturday
2*d*. and 3*d*.
Independent-Conservative
Circulates Dundalk, Louth, Monaghan
Advocates An Independent-Conservatism without reference to Party leaders.
Proprietor Edward Carlton
Advertisement Addressed to those of wealth and influence

ENNISCORTHY GUARDIAN (1889–1971)
Saturday
1*d*.
National
Circulates Wexford, Carlow and Wicklow.
Advocates The interests of the 'Peasant Proprietors' and is for 'Home Rule'. Fully reports all local news.
Proprietor E. Walsh

ENNISCORTHY NEWS (1856–1912)
Saturday
1857 2*d*.; 1868 1½*d*. and 2½*d*.; 1869 2*d*. and 3*d*.; 1878 1*d*.
Neutral
Circulates Enniscorthy and generally throughout county of Wexford &c.
Advocates The interests of the district free from party bias, gives local news fully, includes also reports of the proceedings of the Enniscorthy Union, corn markets, a brief account of parliamentary proceedings.
Proprietor 1857 John Pilkington; 1869 James Owens; 1884 R and W. Owens

ENNISCORTHY TIMES (1856) Not in *Newsplan*
Saturday
1864 1½*d*. and 2½*d*.
Neutral
Circulates Enniscorthy and district
Advocates To the news of Enniscorthy are added general news and biographies of eminent men.
Proprietor George Griffiths
Not entered in *Newspaper Press Directory* after 1868

ENNISKILLEN ADVERTISER (1864–77)
Thursday
1865 2*d*. and 3*d*.
1865 Neutral; 1867 Liberal but not partisan
Circulates Enniskillen and district
Advocates Takes no part in politics; but gives full reports of all local events, and a summary of general intelligence.
Proprietor J. Hamilton

FERMANAGH MAIL (1808–93)
Thursday; 1869 Monday
1851 5*d*.; 1857 5*d*. and 6*d*.; 1864 2*d*. and 3*d*.; 1867 1*d*. and 2*d*.; 1876 2*d*.
Independent
Circulates Through entire county and partially in Leitrim, Donegal, Cavan, Monaghan Tyrone fic.
Advocates 1851 Originally as the *Enniskillen Chronicle* a supporter of High Church principles and the Organisation of the Church in that district. As the *Mail* advocating the principle of civil and religious liberty it has adopted the motto 'The Crown and the people not a class'; 1858 Agricultural commercial and manufacturing interests particularly the first as this county is principally agricultural.
Proprietor T.R.J. Polson

FERMANAGH REPORTER/1874 IMPARTIAL REPORTER [Enniskillen] (1825–to date)
1851 Thursday; 1888 Wednesday and Saturday
1857 4*d*. and 5*d*.; 1865 3*d*. and 4*d*.; 1870 2*d*. and 3*d*.
Conservative
Circulates Enniskillen and the various towns of Fermanagh and the counties Cavan, Tyrone, Monaghan, Leitrim and Donegal. It is well known in the UK, America and the Colonies.
Advocates 1851 The common Protestantism of the Reformation, sincerely believing it the best, but is the organ of no sect. It is a political and agricultural journal. 1868 Editions published for Leitrim as the *Leitrim Journal*
Proprietor 1851 William Trimble, bookseller, stationer and patent medicine vendor; 1888 W. and W.C. Trimble; 1889 W. Trimble

Advertisement 1857 The *Fermanagh Reporter* is to the North West of Ireland what the *Times* is to London, read by all who read. Issue now 1,000 weekly and is increasing.

FERMANAGH TIMES [Enniskillen] (1880–1949)
Thursday
1*d*.
Conservative
Circulates Enniskillen and Co. Fermanagh
Advocates A thorough Protestant and Conservative paper, and gives all the local and county news at great length.
Publisher 1885 A.W. Wheeler; 1891 William Ritchie
Advertisement Advocates thorough conservative principles.

FREE PRESS [Wexford] (1890)
Saturday
1*d*.
Nationalist
Circulates Principal towns and villages of Wexford county
Advocates The *Free Press* is a nationalist organ and is entirely devoted to local and district news.
Proprietor W. Corcoran

GALWAY AMERICAN (1862–63)
Saturday
2*d*. and 3*d*.
Liberal
Circulates Galway and neighbouring counties
Advocates Liberal policy, is opposed to English rule in Ireland and with this view particular attention is given to all events likely to affect Ireland.
Publisher James Daly

GALWAY EXPRESS (1853–1920)
Saturday
1857 4*d*. and 5*d*.; 1864 3*d*. and 4*d*.; 1888 2*d*.
Conservative
Circulates Galway, Mayo, Roscommon, Clare, Limerick and partially throughout the United Kingdom
Advocates 1857 The integrity of the Protestant church, supports Protestant missionary efforts amongst the Roman Catholics of Ireland and the general interests of the country as connected with industrial occupations. Gives local and general news and has literary and miscellaneous departments; 1864 Advocates interests of the Protestant cause and is a firm supporter of conservative opinion... everything connected with the Galway packet station. Literary and miscellaneous departments.
Proprietor 1857 John and Alexander M'Dougall
Advertisement 1857 Journal the only Protestant organ in Galway ... extensive circulation among Nobility, Gentry and Clergy throughout the West of Ireland as well as partial circulation in all parts of the United Kingdom ... uses its influence locally in support of the Protestant cause in this locality and is a firm upholder of the church of the Reformation against all attacks made upon it by its assailants.

GALWAY MERCURY (1844–60)
Saturday
1851 6*d*.; 1858 4*d*. and 5*d*.

1851 Liberal
Circulates Connaught and Munster, Dublin and many important towns in England
Advocates The measures of the party which promoted repeal and is now contending for "Tenant Right". It is decidedly opposed to class legislation and pays particular attention to all matters affecting Ireland.
Proprietor 1851 James Davis, wholesale and retail stationer; 1857 J.C. O'Shaughnessy of Galway, solicitor and John Mahon printer; 1858 Michael Winter of Galway, solicitor and John Mahon printer

GALWAY OBSERVER (1881–1966)
Saturday
2*d*.
1881 National; 1883 Liberal; 1884 Independent; 1888 National
Circulates Galway and neighbourhood
Advocates 1881 Supports a national policy, and opposed to the Liberal Government. Contains local and general news; 1883 Supports a Liberal policy, but principally advocates commercial and trading interests; 1888 The OBSERVER is the recognised organ of the National party, advocates freedom for all classes but is principally devoted to the interests of the people of the district.
Proprietor A.G. Scott
Advertisement 1883 The GALWAY OBSERVER while holding its own as a political organ, rather seeks to avoid political and burning questions, and endeavours to direct the public of this large seaport of nearly 20,000 inhabitants into trade and business channels.

GALWAY VINDICATOR (1841–99)
Wednesday and Saturday
1857 4*d*. and 6*d*.; 1864 3*d*. and 4*d*.
1857 Liberal; 1868 Liberal-Independent
Circulates Galway, Mayo, Roscommon, Clare, Limerick and Cork and extensively in the English as well as Irish Metropolis.
Advocates 1857 Interests of agriculture, commerce, and manufactures. A political and literary journal, upholds the right of Ireland to a domestic legislature, is thoroughly independent in character; on politico-religious questions is Roman Catholic, but strictly tolerant; 1868 Is a political and literary journal and is thoroughly independent in character. It also advocates the industrial progress of Ireland and the establishment of perfect religious equality for all classes of Her Majesty's subjects.
Proprietor 1851: J.P. Blake, patent medicine vendor; 1857: John Francis Blake [Died March 1864]; 1865: Lewis L. Ferdinand.
Advertisement 1857: The *Galway Vindicator* is now the 'primal' and only two-day journal published in the West of Ireland. Legal and public advertisements at the rate fixed by the Commissioners of the Incumbered Estates Court

GOREY CORRESPONDENT/1878 **GOREY CORRESPONDENT AND ARKLOW STANDARD** (1855–92)
Saturday
2*d*. and 3*d*.
Neutral
Circulates In Gorey and Co. Wexford
Advocates A sheet of local and miscellaneous news.
Proprietor 1864 Samuel Clarke; 1877 Clarke and Son

KERRY EVENING POST [Tralee] (1774–1917)
Wednesday and Saturday

1851 6*d.*; 1857 5*d.* and 6*d.*; 1864 3*d.* and 4*d.*
Conservative
Circulates Local and south of Ireland
Advocates 1851 A liberal Reform of the Magistracy and the Poor Laws. This journal contains some spirited and even daring articles suggested no doubt by conscientious motives; 1866 Protestant interests and Conservative politics in particular, and all local improvements. The local information is always ample and well selected
Proprietor 1851 John and Jeffery Eagar; 1864 George Raymond; 1882 George and Alexander Raymond; 1884 George Raymond

KERRY EXAMINER [Tralee] (1840–56)
Tuesday and Friday
6*d.*
Liberal
Circulates Kerry, Cork, Limerick, Clare, Tipperary, Waterford and Wexford. Filed at principal clubs, Exchanges and coffee-houses in Dublin and London. Medium for public announcements.
Advocates Agricultural and Commercial interests. A religious political and literary journal and the special organ of the Roman Catholic clergy and people throughout the county.
Proprietor Patrick O'Loughlin Byrne

KERRY INDEPENDENT [Tralee] (1880–4)
Monday and Thursday
1880 2*d.*; 1885 3*d.*
National
Circulates Through all the towns of Kerry
Advocates Catholic, Home Rule and Tenant Right principles
Proprietor Henry Brassill
Advertisement 1884 The organ of the Roman Catholic clergy, gentry, merchants and farmers of the county generally.

KERRY SENTINEL [Tralee] (1878–1918)
1878 Friday; 1885 Friday and Tuesday
1878 3*d.*; 1888 2*d.*
Independent
Circulates Tralee and the county generally
Advocates The *Sentinel* is independent but advocates Home Rule. Its local news is full and complete, and the general intelligence is summarised.
Proprietor 1878 T. Harrington; 1888 E. Harrington
Advertisement The organ of the Catholic clergy. Advocates Home Rule, tenant rights, denominational education, grand jury reform &c. Has always ably written leaders on these and local subjects. circulates in Kerry, Cork, Limerick and the south of Ireland.

KERRY STAR (1861–63)
Tuesday and Friday
2½*d.* and 3½*d.*
Independent
Circulates Kerry and neighbouring counties
Advocates An independent course unfettered by party ties and desires to be considered 'Irish in tone as in heart and feeling'.
Proprietor T. J. O. Kane

KERRY VINDICATOR [Tralee] (1876) Not in *Newsplan*
Saturday
3*d.*
National
Circulates Tralee, Kerry and Munster
Advocates National in politics, the *Vindicator* supports all proposals for the benefit of Ireland, and all the news of the county and the province is fully reported.
Proprietor James Joseph Long
Not entered in *Newspaper Press Directory* after 1878

KERRY WEEKLY REPORTER [Tralee] (1883–1936)
Saturday
1½*d.*
1885 National; 1888 Liberal
Circulates Tralee and county of Kerry
Advocates National [1888 and Liberal] principles. The *Reporter* gives all the news fully, with tales, sketches and miscellanies.
Proprietor J. Quinnell

KILDARE OBSERVER [Naas] (1879–1935)
Saturday
2*d.*
Independent
Circulates Naas, and the Eastern Counties
Advocates The *Observer* gives full reports of the local news including sessions and union meetings.
Proprietor William S. Gray
Advertisement 1880 Being entirely devoid of political or religious bias, it circulates among all classes, the object of the Proprietor being to furnish a respectable local newspaper at the most moderate charge ... a large *bona fide* circulation.

KILKENNY JOURNAL (1767 as *Finn's Leinster Journal*. Under present title 1830–1935)
Wednesday and Saturday
1851 5*d.*; 1857 4*d.* and 5*d.*; 1864 3*d.* and 4*d.*
1851 Liberal; 1892 National
Circulates County and City of Kilkenny. Sent to subscribers in various other parts of England and Ireland
Advocates 1851 Ireland for the Irish, a national legislature and the interests of Irish agriculture, commerce, manufactures and literature. In religion it is rather the defender of Roman Catholic principles than the impugner of other men's creeds. It is not bigoted but firm in the expression of its opinions.
Proprietor 1851 Cornelius Maxwell, general printer, bookseller and stationer; 1858 Mary Anne Maxwell; 1882 Representatives of Mary Anne Maxwell

KILKENNY MODERATOR (1814–1925)
Wednesday and Saturday
1851 4*d.*; 1857 3*d.* and 4*d.*
Conservative
Circulates Kilkenny, Carlow, Waterford, Wexford, Clonmel, Cork
Advocates 1851 Agriculture, commercial and manufacturing interests. Is a political and literary journal attached to the Church of England.
Proprietor 1851 Abraham Denroche, general printer and stationer; 1857 John G.A. Prim, gen-

eral printer and stationer; 1877 M.W. Lalor
Advertisement 1857 The *Kilkenny Moderator* circulation double that of any other journal published in Kilkenny

KILRUSH HERALD (1877–1922)
1878 Thursday; 1885 Saturday
1878 1*d*.; 1881 2*d*.
1879 Independent; 1880 Liberal and Independent
Circulates County, Limerick, Kerry, Galway, Tipperary, Dublin, England, America and the Colonies
Advocates 1878 Contains ample and impartial reports of all local and county meetings [1888: is a fearless advocate of civil and religious liberty] with spirited leaders on all subjects of importance engaging public attention.
Proprietor P.J. Boyle

KING'S COUNTY CHRONICLE [Parsonstown] (1845–1963)
Wednesday; 1873 Thursday
1851 4½*d*.; 1857 5*d*. and 6*d*.; 1871 4*d*.; 1875 1*d*.; 1877 4*d*.; 1888 3*d*.; Conservative
Circulates 1851 Local and Tipperary, Galway and Westmeath; 1867 Editions are published for Roscrea and Tullamore under the titles of *Midland Counties Advertiser* and *Leinster Reporter*
Advocates 1851 Interests of trade, manufactures and agriculture. Interests embraced by political economy are supported with discrimination and tact ... the portion more especially devoted to politics being characterised by Judgment and vigour; 1873 Attached to the Church of Ireland; 1879 All those interests which are embraced by political economy are supported in this journal.
Proprietor 1851 Francis H. Shields; 1873 John Wright

KINGSTOWN AND BRAY OBSERVER (1870–1)
Saturday
1*d*.
Independent
Circulates Local to Kingstown
Advocates Domestic legislation for Ireland
Publisher W. Reid

KINGSTOWN COURIER (1856) Not in *Newsplan*
Saturday
3*d*. and 4*d*.
Neutral
Circulates Dublin, Kingstown and county
Advocates Measures independent of party, and just spirit to men of all parties. Opposed to everything which it considers contrary to the true interests of Ireland and the Irish people. As a newspaper it has the general features of a respectable weekly journal.
Proprietor Resident
Publisher Robert Chamney
Not entered in *Newspaper Press Directory* after 1857

KINGSTOWN JOURNAL (1863)
Neutral
1*d*. and 2*d*.
Neutral
Circulates Kingstown and district
Advocates News of watering place with list of visitors

Publisher P. Kelly
Advertisement Claims a circulation of 10,000

LARNE WEEKLY RECORDER (1881–5)
Saturday 1*d*.
Independent
Circulates Larne and District
Advocates Local and general news, with selections, varieties &c.
Publisher 1881 John H. McLean; 1885 P.O'C. Patman

LARNE [WEEKLY] REPORTER (1865–1904)
Saturday
1½*d*. and 2½*d*.
Liberal
Circulates Larne and district
Advocates Local news and advertisements with tales and varieties.
Proprietor: 1867 J. Read and Son; 1877 S.A. Read and Sons; 1882 John S. McAlmont

LEINSTER EXPRESS [Maryborough] (1831–to date)
Saturday
1851 6*d*.; 1857 4*d*. and 5*d*.
Independent
Circulates Local and Midland counties
Advocates 1851 General interests, treating public questions solely upon their own merits, without party bias and regardless of sectarian prejudices. It is principally devoted to the development of the industrial resources of Ireland.
Proprietor 1857 Henry W. Talbot, Kingston, Co. Dublin; 1868 J.W. Talbot; 1874 Geo. W. Talbot; 1889 Michael Carey

LEINSTER INDEPENDENT [Maryborough] (1869–75)
Saturday
3*d*.
Independent
Circulates Throughout Province
Advocates A special letter from Rome is made a feature.
Proprietor J.T. Quigley
Publisher W.M. Galbraith

LEINSTER LEADER [Naas] (1880–to date)
Saturday
2*d*.
National
Circulates Naas, Kildare, Carlow and the Queen's county
Advocates Home Rule and tenant right principles
1884 Nationalist principles The leading Nationalist Provincial Paper in Ireland.
Publisher S.J. Fletcher
Advertisement 1883 Circulates largely amongst clergy, professional men, traders, graziers and farmers.

LEINSTER REPORTER AND CENTRAL WEEKLY TIMES [Tullamore] (1858–1930)
1864 Wednesday 1874 Thursday
4*d*. and 5*d*.

Neutral
Circulates Tullamore and District
Advocates Gives news of the town a family paper
Proprietor 1864 Francis H. Shields; 1873 John Wright

LEINSTER REPORTER AND COUNTY KILDARE HERALD [Naas] (1859) Not in *Newsplan*
Friday for Saturday
2*d*.
Progressive-Conservative
Circulates Kildare and generally in the province of Munster
Advocates Mutual forbearance and toleration amongst Irishmen, the development of the various branches of manufacture and agriculture. Aims, as its name denotes, at giving copious supplies of local and provincial news independent of party or politics. Also devoted to literature and sporting topics.
Proprietor Richard Bull
Not entered in *Newspaper Press Directory* after 1879

LEITRIM GAZETTE/1868 LEITRIM AND LONGFORD ADVERTISER/1870 LEITRIM ADVERTISER** [Mohill] (1856–1924)
1857 Saturday; 1872 Thursday
1858 2*d*. and 3*d*.; 1865 2½*d*. and 3½*d*.; 1873 2*d*.
1858 Liberal; 1864 Liberal-Conservative; 1865 Conservative; 1869 Independent
Circulates Leitrim and Connaught
Advocates Irish interests, is unsectarian and contains the news of Ireland as well as that from England and abroad, with tales and varieties.
Proprietor 1857 Robert J. Turner; 1880 E. Turner; 1881
Representatives of late R. Turner

LEITRIM JOURNAL [Carrick on Shannon] (1850–72)
Saturday
3*d*. and 4*d*.
Independent
Circulates Carrick-on-Shannon
Advocates Political freedom 'independent of party, fearless, vigilant and impartial'. It promises to be a good local paper.
Proprietor William Trimble

LEITRIM OBSERVER [Carrick-on-Shannon] (1890-to date)
Saturday
2*d*.
National
Circulates Leitrim, Roscommon, Longford, Sligo &c.
Advocates 1891 Supports the National party. It is a thorough local and district paper.
Proprietor F. Mulvey

LIMERICK AND CLARE EXAMINER (1846–55)
Wednesday and Saturday
5*d*.
Liberal
Circulates Generally more especially in those districts most favourable to repeal
Advocates The principles of the party which calls itself 'National' in all their various bearings ... It devotes much space to the reports of public meetings and all makers of radical reform.
Proprietor R. Goggin

LIMERICK CHRONICLE (1766–to date)
1851 Wednesday and Saturday; 1864 Tuesday, Thursday and Saturday
1851 6*d.*; 1857 4*d.* and 5*d.*; 1864 3*d.* and 4*d.*; 1872 2½*d.*; 1880 2*d.*
1857 Neutral; 1867 Moderate-Conservative
Circulates Ireland, England, Scotland, and partially in the Colonies, France, India &c.
Advocates 1851: General interests, it is not the organ of any individual or sect; always supports the constitution as by law established and is a literary newspaper
Proprietor 1857 Henry Watson; 1864 William Hosford and Sarah Bassett; 1875 William Hosford
Publisher 1857 J. Connell
Advertisement 1884 Always been moderate in politics, has always ranged itself on the side of order.

LIMERICK LEADER (1888)
Monday, Wednesday, and Friday
1*d.*
Nationalist
Circulates Limerick, Clare and Tipperary
Advocates Gives an unqualified support to the principles of the Irish National League, and all combinations formed to promote the welfare of the people.
Proprietor John McEnery

LIMERICK OBSERVER (1856–7)
Tuesday, Thursday, and Saturday
3*d.* and 4*d.*
Neutral
Circulates Local, Dublin and Cork
Proprietor Patrick Lynch

LIMERICK REPORTER/1850 **AND TIPPERARY VINDICATOR** (1839–96)
1851 Tuesday and Friday; 1857 Wednesday and Saturday
1851 5*d.*; 1857 4*d.* and 5*d.*; 1864 3*d.* and 4*d.*
Liberal
Circulates Tipperary, Limerick, King's County, Queen's County, Kerry, Clare, Galway, Cork, etc.
Advocates 1851 The right of the people of Ireland to an independent parliament ... the interests of the great bulk of the people generally. The abatement of those evils in Church and State without which it supposes national contentment cannot exist; the adjustment of the land question by the legal recognition of Tenant Right. Its original translations from the foreign journals are a novel feature. Its reviews elaborate. It is a political, literary and family newspaper and is generally replete with matter of the deepest interest to all classes in Ireland; 1864 Advocates continuously and stead-ily the industrial interests of the population; the abatement of those alleged evils in church and State without which, it contends, national contentment cannot exist; Parliamentary Reform, and the adjustment of the land question by the local recognition of Tenant Right. It is a political, literary and family newspaper; 1870 The industrial interests of the population, parliamentary re-form, religious equality in church and state, home rule and the land question; 1874 A domestic legislature; the settlement of the land question in relation to agricultural labour; 1888 Advocates the industrial interests of the population, religious equality in church and State; a domestic legis-lature; the settlement of the land question on the broad basis of justice and right.
Proprietor Maurice Lenihan M.R.I.A.

LIMERICK WEEKLY NEWS (1888) Not in *Newsplan*
Saturday

1*d*.
National
Circulates Limerick and district
Advocates National cause, fully reports the National League meetings. The general news is given in a partly-printed sheet.
Publisher E. Asbie
Not entered in *Newspaper Press Directory* after 1890

LISBURN STANDARD (1876–1959)
Saturday
1*d*.
1885 Neutral; 1888 Conservative
Circulates Lisburn and neighbourhood
Advocates Local and district news are added to a partly-printed sheet of general intelligence.
Proprietor 1885 W. Johnston; 1888 J.E. Reilly

LONDONDERRY GUARDIAN (1857–71)
Wednesday
1864 2*d*. and 3*d*.; 1870 1*d*. and 2*d*.
Conservative
Circulates Londonderry and Ulster
Advocates 1858 Church principles and harmony amongst orthodox Protestants of all denominations. Is Conservative in politics, adhering to principles, not men. It has an extensive and well-arranged department of general news, with poetry, nouvellettes, and a miscellany of literary and scientific extracts and notices.
Proprietor George Alleyn O'Driscoll
Advertisement 1858 The Proprietor is from the *Londonderry Sentinel*. Supported by the landed gentry, clergy and mercantile and agricultural classes ... desire of the Proprietor is to render the *Guardian* a trustworthy and effective exponent of the opinions and feelings of the enlightened, influential, industrious and loyal inhabitants of the north-west of Ulster ... its Protestantism is of an enlarged type befitting the 'maiden City' which owes its world-wide renown to the endurance and heroism of Protestants of different denominations ... wealth and respectability of its readers ... The *Guardian* cannot be surpassed as an advertising medium.

LONDONDERRY JOURNAL/ 1877 DERRY JOURNAL (1772–to date)
1857 Wednesday; 1865 Wednesday and Saturday; 1872 Monday, Wednesday and Friday
1851 1*d*.; 1857 4½*d*.; 1851 3½*d*. and 4½*d*.; 1864 1*d*. and 2*d*.
1851 Liberal; 1868 Independent-liberal; 1888 Independent; 1892 Nationalist
Circulates Province of Ulster
Advocates 1851 Agricultural and commercial interests. Political journal and non-sectarian; 1878 Leading articles, copious telegraphic supply, a careful selection of general news, a full market note with a summary of the current important events, while the local news has every prominence. By means of special correspondents in the principal cities of England and Scotland, as well as in the chief towns of the Irish provinces, everything of national public interest is presented.
Proprietor 1857 Arthur M'Corkell; 1864 Thomas M'Carter
Advertisement 1857 Owing to the recent extension of the Telegraphic wires to Derry, the Proprietor of this JOURNAL has also been able to insert a complete resumé of all Foreign and Parliamentary intelligence a few hours after the announcement of such in London.

LONDONDERRY SENTINEL (1829–to date)
Tuesday and Friday; 1873 Tuesday, Thursday and Friday; 1880 Tuesday, Thursday and Saturday
1851 5*d*.; 1857 4*d*. and 5*d*.; 1864 1*d*. and 2*d*.

Conservative
Circulates Derry, Donegal, Tyrone, Fermanagh
Advocates 1851 Necessity for protection for the agriculturalist. Takes a high moral and religious tone in dealing with public matters. Is not attached to any one religious denomination, but advocates the cause of Protestantism generally. Medium through which the clergy of the Church of England usually bring their announcements before the public; 1865 Agricultural and commercial interests, and is the recognised organ of these classes. 1866 It is especially a non-sectarian journal; 1869 Regard to the interests of the agriculturalist but not to such an extent as to interfere prejudicially with the interests of commerce and manufactures, it takes a high moral and religious tone in dealing with public matters ... advocates the cause of Protestantism generally.
Proprietor 1851 Mrs Barbara Hamilton Wallen (Mrs William Wallen);1858 Proprietor John Montgomery Johnston, James Calhoun printer and publisher; 1864 Thomas Chambers and James Calhoun proprietors; James Calhoun printer and publisher; 1879 Proprietor James Calhoun

LONDONDERRY STANDARD/1889 **DERRY STANDARD** (1836-1964)
1851 Thursday; 1869 Wednesday and Saturday; 1888 Monday, Wednesday and Friday
1851 5*d.*; 1857 5*d.*; 1864 2½*d.* and 3½*d.*; 1865 1*d.* and 2*d.*
1851 Conservative; 1858 Liberal-Conservative; 1880 Liberal; 1889 Liberal-Unionist
Circulates Locally Dublin, towns in Scotland and England
Advocates 1851 Interests of the merchants and manufacturers of the district itself for a number of years by its strenuous support of the tenantry of Ireland. Advocates the interests of the Orthodox Presbyterians of Ireland who constitute the great bulk of the Protestant population of Ulster it adheres to the principle of religious establishment upon a proper basis. 1857 Always proved itself the farmer's friend; 1872 Support of the just rights of the tenantry; 1880 Organ of Ulster Tenant Right, it is specially distinguished for its support of the just rights of the tenantry of Ireland; 1888 The recognised organ of the Liberal party in the important influential and wealthy division of the North-West of Ulster. It has secured a wide reputation for its bold and trenchant leaders, and has made its mark on the politics of the North-west by the return of the gentlemen it advocated at recent elections. It advocates reform of the land laws, grand jury reform, and generally follows the politics of the Liberal party. It is known as the organ of "Ulster Tenant Right"; 1889 It supports the Unionist policy as a whole, and its political principles are identical with those upheld by Lord Hartington, Mr Bright, Mr Chamberlain and others of the old Constitutional Liberal party.
Proprietor 1851 James Macpherson and Thomas McCarter, general printers; 1868 James Macpherson; 1879 William Glendinning

LONGFORD CHRONICLE (1855) Not in *Newsplan*
Saturday
2*d.*
Neutral
Circulates local
Advocates This is one of the London compendiums of news, exported to Ireland, and the news of Longford with late telegraphic despatches, are added.
Proprietor M.G. Parker
Not entered in *Newspaper Press Directory* after 1857

LONGFORD INDEPENDENT (1868–1925)
Saturday
2*d.* and 3*d.*; 1871 1*d.*; 1877 1½*d.*; 1878 2*d.*
Liberal; 1872 Liberal-Independent; 1877 Independent
Circulates Longford and Midland counties
Advocates Useful Irish measures are strongly advocated
Proprietor 1869 R Turner; 1880 E. Turner; 1888 Representatives of the late R. Turner

LONGFORD JOURNAL (1839–1937)

Saturday
1851 4½*d*.; 1857 3*d*. and 4*d*.; 1864 2*d*. and 3*d*.
Conservative
Circulates Co. Longford
Advocates Interests of the Church of England and all sects of Protestantism. Agriculture and commerce receive especial attention.
Proprietor 1851 John Dwyer, bookseller and stationer; 1869 W.T. Dann; 1871 Edward Dann; 1877 W.T. Dann

LURGAN GAZETTE/1871 **LURGAN WATCHMAN AND GAZETTE**/1878 **LURGAN WATCHMAN** (1856–74)
Saturday
1*d*. and 2*d*.
Conservative
Circulates Lurgan and Ulster
Advocates 1857 Conservative and Protestant policy; 1877 Progressive Conservative policy and local news
Proprietor G.W. McCutcheon

LURGAN TIMES (1877–1915)
Saturday
1*d*.
Independent
Circulates Lurgan, surrounding towns, and counties of Armagh, Antrim, Down, Londonderry, Tyrone and Louth
Advocates Local news and miscellanies
Proprietor [1889 and Editor] William White

MAYO CONSTITUTION [Castlebar] (1805–72)
1851 Tuesday; 1872 Saturday
1851 5*d*. and 6*d*.; 1872 3*d*.
Conservative
Circulates Throughout Mayo, Sligo, and Galway and in Dublin, London &c.
Advocates The general interests of the county, is chiefly political; is not the organ of any particular section of the Protestant Church. [1872: is the organ of the Church of Ireland.]
Proprietor 1851 Alexander Bole, general stationer; 1864 John Bole; 1870 Norman Bole;

MAYO EXAMINER [Castlebar] (1868–1903)
Monday
3*d*. and 4*d*.
1868 Liberal; 1888 National Catholic
Circulates Castlebar, the county and the West of Ireland.
Advocates Tenant right and the interests of Roman Catholics
Proprietor 1868 A.H. Sheridan; 1877 M. and A.H. Sheridan; 1882 Martin Sheridan

MEATH HERALD [Kells] (1845–1936)
Saturday
1851 4*d*.; 1857 2*d*. and 3*d*.
Independent
Circulates Kells, Meath, Westmeath, Louth, Cavan and Kildare
Advocates 1851 Advancement of agriculture and especially commercial interests of the country,

and also the diffusion of useful general knowledge at the same time strenuously avoiding and discountenancing all polemical and political disputations.
Proprietor 1857 Thomas Kelly Henderson, bookseller, printer and stationer; 1866 George and John Henderson, printers, booksellers and stationers; 1880 James B. Henderson; 1892 John G. Henderson.

MEATH PEOPLE [Naas] (1857–63)
Saturday
5*d*.
1858 Liberal; 1864 Anti-Whig
Circulates Cavan, Meath and Westmeath
Advocates In a fair and liberal spirit, [advocates] the principles of the Roman Catholic church, tenant right and an independent opposition with a view to obtaining what the conductor calls 'Justice' and to ward off what he regards as oppressive ... tales, poetry and reviews.
Proprietor James O'Reilly
Advertisement Circulates among clergy, merchants and farmers of Leinster

MEATH REPORTER [Trim] (1870–1901)
Saturday
2*d*.
Neutral
Circulates Trim
Advocates News of the town and county
Proprietor T.K. Henderson

MID-ULSTER MAIL [Cookstown, Co. Tyrone] (1891–to date)
Saturday
1*d*.
Conservative
Circulates South Derry, East and South Tyrone, and Mid-Ulster generally
Advocates The *Mail* supports the Constitutional party and is a good local and district paper.
Proprietor H.L. Glasgow

MIDLAND COUNTIES ADVERTISER [Roscrea] (1854–1948)
1857 Saturday; 1864 Thursday
1857 4*d*. and 5*d*.
Independent
Circulates Roscrea
Advocates Cause of law and government and of public order and leaving questions of general politics to the 'leaders of the metropolitan press'.
Proprietor 1857 Francis H Shields; 1873 John Wright

MIDLAND COUNTIES GAZETTE [Longford] (1852–63)
Saturday
4*d*. and 5*d*.
Liberal
Circulates Longford, Westmeath, Leitrim, Roscommon and King's county
Advocates The measures of the Irish Liberal and tenant right party.
Publisher B. Casserly, Longford

MIDLAND NEWS [Roscrea] (1880) Not in *Newsplan*
Circulates Tipperary, King's, Queens and Kilkenny counties. Neutral

Advocates Non-political it is supported by all classes in the community. It is a good local paper.
Proprietor and Publisher James Gray Jun.
Not entered in *Newspaper Press Directory* after 1884

MIDLAND TRIBUNE [Parsonstown] (1881–to date)
Thursday
2½d.
National
Circulates King's and Queen's Counties, and the counties of Tipperary, Galway, Roscommon, Clare and Westmeath.
Advocates Thoroughly National in tone, and is conducted altogether irrespective of political parties. It aims to be the reflex and exponent of popular feeling throughout a wide-spread district in the Midland Counties of Ireland.
Proprietor 1881 The Midland Tribune Joint Stock Co.; 1889 John Powell
Advertisement Its promoters – a Joint Stock Company – have invested a considerable capital in a project they conceive must be an undoubted financial success. Its opening circulation they guarantee as large as any other weekly in Ireland, and anticipate – from an extensive connection and a decided expression of public feeling and sympathy in consonance with the paper – that this circulation will, within a short period, be largely increased.

MUNSTER EXPRESS/1879 MUNSTER EXPRESS AND THE CELT [Waterford] (1860–to date)
Saturday
1864 3d. and 4d.; 1869 2d. and 3d.
1864 Neutral; 1889 National
Circulates Waterford and Munster
Advocates 1864 General news; 1881 The creation of a class of owner occupiers in Ireland
Proprietor 1864 Joseph Fisher; 1883 W.G. Fisher; 1891 H.D. Fisher

MUNSTER NEWS [Limerick] (1851–1935)
Wednesday and Saturday
1857 4d. and 5d.; 1870 3d. and 4d.
Liberal
Circulates Limerick and Munster generally
Advocates 1857 Measures of the Tenant-League party; 1865 Measures of the Tenant Right in Ireland, and measures of utility to all parties in Ireland, and is a general and local newspaper.
Proprietor Francis Counihan [1869 and son]

NENAGH GUARDIAN (1838–to date)
Wednesday and Saturday
1851 4½d.; 1857 3½d. and 4½d.
Conservative
Circulates locally
Advocates 1851 Interests of agriculture, literary and political journal of considerable reputation and attached to the Church of England, the *Guardian* has gained much celebrity as a 'state of the country' newspaper justly exposing crime, and fearlessly holding up the perpetrators to public reprobation ... Patronised by the aristocracy, merchants and shopkeepers; 1870 attached to the Protestant Episcopal Church of Ireland
Proprietor 1851 Charles W. Kempston; 1858 George Prior; 1866 Adam Prior; 1892 Margaret Prior

NEW ROSS EXPRESS/1883 WEXFORD AND KILKENNY EXPRESS (1800) Not in *Newsplan*
Wednesday

1*d*.
National
Advocates The creation of a class of occupying owners in Ireland
Proprietor J. Fisher

NEW ROSS REPORTER (1871–1910)
Wednesday and Saturday; 1877 Saturday
1*d*.
Neutral
Circulates New Ross and counties of Wexford, Waterford, Kilkenny and Carlow
Proprietor 1871 Ward and Longmire; 1877 W.R. Ward

NEW ROSS STANDARD (1879–99)
Saturday
1*d*.
Catholic and National
Circulates New Ross, Wexford, Kilkenny, Carlow and district
Advocates 1880 The best interests of Ireland. Though Catholic and National will be liberal. The local and district news is well given; 1881 self-government for Ireland, and the establishment of a peasant proprietary, by purchase of the landowners' interest.
Proprietor 1880 W. Corcoran; 1881 E. Walsh

NEWRY COMMERCIAL TELEGRAPH/NEWRY TELEGRAPH (1812–1970)
Tuesday, Thursday and Saturday
1851 4½*d*.; 1857 3*d*. and 4*d*.; 1865 1*d*. and 2*d*.
Conservative
Circulates Locally. Recognised as official and grand Jury organ of Down, Armagh, Tyrone, Londonderry
Advocates 1851 Commercial and agricultural interests and is a political and literary paper. Supports the Established Churches of Ireland, and England and of Scotland;1858 Churches of the Reformation;1888 Constitutional principles
Proprietor 1851 James Henderson; 1864 Henry G. Henderson; 1877 J. Henderson & Co.

NEWRY EXAMINER AND LOUTH ADVERTISER/1880 **DUNDALK EXAMINER AND LOUTH ADVERTISER** (1830–1960)
1851 Wednesday, Saturday; 1880 Saturday
1851 4½*d*.; 1857 3½*d*. and 4*d*.; 1865 3*d*. and 4*d*.; 1871 2*d*.
1851 Liberal; 1880 National
Circulates Louth, Meath, Dublin, Westmeath, Sligo, Donegal, Fermanagh, Tyrone, Armagh, Antrim, Down, Leitrim and Derry and (1889) America
Advocates 1851 Tenant right, free trade and the agricultural interest generally. It is thoroughly independent of political parties, but its tone is decidedly Liberal; 1880 The agricultural [1886: and mercantile] interest generally. It is thoroughly independent of political parties but the tone is decidedly national.
Proprietor 1851 P. Dowdall, patent medicine vendor; 1857 Patrick Dowdall; 1865 P. Dowdall; and son; 1866 P. Dowdall; 1880 John Matthews [died 1883]
Advertisement 1883 A weekly paper of national politics, circulates extensively through Ireland, also through England, Scotland and the United States.

NEWRY HERALD (1858–64)
Tuesday, Thursday and Saturday
1858 3*d*. and 4*d*.; 1865 1*d*. and 2*d*.

1858 Liberal; 1864 Liberal and Independent
Circulates Newry and the North of Ireland
Advocates The advancement of civil and religious liberty and other measures of the Liberal party ... supports all measures likely to promote commercial and agricultural prosperity of the district and the town of Newry.
Proprietor 1858 Walter Burns; 1864 Proprietor and publisher: William Hutchison

NEWRY REPORTER (1867–to date)
1868 Wednesday and Saturday 1872 Thursday and Saturday 1873 Tuesday and Saturday
1*d*. and 2*d*.
1868 Independent; 1873 Liberal
Circulates Newry
Advocates Contains all the news of the county
Proprietor James Burns

NEWRY STANDARD/1883 BELFAST AND NEWRY STANDARD (1879–99)
Independent
Circulates Newry and district
Advocates Fully reports the local news while general intelligence is given in a partly-printed sheet from London.
Published Bank Parade, Newry.

NEWTOWNARDS CHRONICLE (1873–to date)
Saturday
1*d*.
1873 Liberal Conservative and [1879] Independent Tenant Right; 1883 Liberal-Conservative
Circulates local and county
Advocates 1873 Local and district intelligence with general news; 1882 Non-political journal
Publisher William Henry

NORTH DOWN HERALD/1884: NORTH DOWN HERALD AND BANGOR GAZETTE [Bangor] (1880–1952)
1880 Saturday; 1888 Friday
1*d*.
1880 Independent; 1892 Liberal
Circulates North Down and district
Advocates Non-political journal devoted to the interests of agricultural, manufacturing and mercantile life.
Proprietor W.G. Lyttle

NORTHERN HERALD [Ballymoney] (1860–3)
Thursday
1864 2*d*. and 3*d*.
Independent
Circulates Antrim, Londonderry, Donegal, and Tyrone
Advocates The *Herald* is conducted on the most Independent principles and devotes a large part of its columns to local reports, sessions meetings etc.
Proprietor James W. Lithgow

NORTHERN HERALD [Londonderry] (1879) Not in *Newsplan*
Tuesday, Thursday and Saturday
1*d*.

Liberal
Circulates Londonderry and throughout the north-west of Ireland
Advocates Catholic and Home Rule principles, and is also in favour of Tenant Right.
Publisher J. Coghlan
Not entered in *Newspaper Press Directory* after 1881

NORTHERN STANDARD [Monaghan] (1839–to date)
1851 Saturday; 1877 Friday; 1891 Saturday
1851 5*d*.; 1857 4*d*. and 5*d*.; 1864 6*d*.; 1867 3*d*. and 4*d*.; 1871 2*d*.; 1877 1*d*.
1851 High Tory; 1857 Conservative
Circulates North Midland counties, Belfast, Dublin, America and colonies
Advocates : 1851 High Church [1870 Conservative] principles. Political and literary journal.
organ of the High Orange [1858 Protestant] party in Ulster
Proprietor 1851 Arthur Wellington Holmes; 1857 John Holmes; 1871 William Swan

NORTHERN STAR [Belfast] (1868-72)
Tuesday, Thursday, Saturday
1*d*. and 2*d*.
Liberal
Circulates Belfast
Advocates A Liberal-Catholic journal, holding advanced views. It is an influential journal of the
party and as a political and literary journal is well-conducted.
Publisher 1869 A.J. McKenna; 1871 J. McVeagh

OMAGH NEWS (1862–72)
Saturday
3*d*. and 4*d*.
1865 Liberal; 1866 Independent
Circulates Omagh and the county
Advocates Is devoted to the policy of the Liberal party and advocates tenant right. Special atten-
tion is given to the local news of the district.
Proprietor S.D. Montgomery

THE PEOPLE [Wexford] (1845–to date)
Saturday
1857 4*d*. and 5*d*.
1857 Liberal; 1865 Independent; 1881 National
Circulates Town and district
Advocates 1857 Principles of tenant-right league and measures of the party calling itself the Irish
National Independent Party; 1864 In religion the principles and practices of the Roman Catholic
Church, and in politics the cause of Irish independence ... is also a commercial and literary journal
as well as a newspaper; 1880 National. Advocates self-government for Ireland, reform of the land
laws, commercial and manufacturing interests. Gives full reports of the proceedings of all public
bodies in the county.
Proprietor 1857 James A Johnson and William Power; 1858 William Power; 1858 Took over Wexford Guardian; 1864 M.J. Sutton and R.A. Fitzgerald; 1871 E. Walsh
Advertisement 1880 Circulates in Wexford, Carlow, Kilkenny, Waterford, Wicklow, Dublin, the
United States, Canada and Australia. Taken by nobility, gentry, clergy, mercantile classes and farmers.

PEOPLE'S ADVOCATE [Monaghan] (1876–1906)
Saturday
1*d*.

National
Circulates Monaghan, Fermanagh, Tyrone, etc.
Advocates National and Catholic questions. Fully reports all local and district news.
Publisher D. MacAleese

PORTADOWN WEEKLY NEWS/1873 PORTADOWN AND LURGAN NEWS (1859–1982)
Saturday
1864 2*d*. and 3*d*.; 1865 1*d*. and 2*d*.
Conservative; 1892 Unionist
Circulates Local and North of Ireland
Advocates Conservative principles. Essentially a family paper.
Proprietor 1864 John H. Farrell; 1877 The trustees of Mrs Farrell; 1880 Mrs Farrell; 1882 S. Farrell; 1892 John Young M.A.

PROTESTANT WATCHMAN [Lurgan] (1856) Not entered in *Newsplan*
Saturday
1*d*. and 2*d*.
Conservative
Circulates Lurgan and district
Advocates Conservative and Protestant policy. Local news of the town and neighbourhood with general news and historical notes bearing on the character of the Papacy.
Proprietor 1864 Richard J. Evans;1868 George F. Evans
Advertisement Robert Chamney of the *Kingstown Courier* is agent for their advertisements.
Not entered in *Newspaper Press Directory* after 1868

ROSCOMMON CONSTITUTIONALIST [Boyle] (1885–91)
Saturday
2*d*.
1885 Constitutionalist; 1892 Independent
Circulates Roscommon and an extensive district.
Advocates Paper is full of local and district news. All public meetings are fully reported.
Publisher 1885 C. Dell Smith; 1891 Thomas Stuart; 1892 J.C. Anderson
Advertisement Circulating extensively throughout the West of Ireland, amongst a class whom it would be of the greatest advantage to advertisers to come at. The CONSTITUTIONALIST enjoys the patronage of the clergy, gentry, merchants, shopkeepers, farmers &c. of the extensive district through which it circulates.

ROSCOMMON [1858 AND LEITRIM] GAZETTE [Boyle] (1822–82)
Saturday
3½*d*. and 4½*d*.
Conservative
Circulates Boyle and the county of Roscommon, Carrick-on-Shannon, Mayo, Sligo &c.
Advocates 1851 Conservative principles: is the friend of order and subordination; alive to the amelioration of the poorer population of Ireland. There is a column for naval and military appointments and commonly an amusing feuilleton.
Proprietor 1851 J. Bromell, general printer; 1864 E.C. Bromell, general printer; 1872 A.W. Bromell; 1877 G.C. Bromell

ROSCOMMON HERALD (1859–to date)
Saturday
4*d*. and 5*d*.
1864 Liberal; 1891 Nationalist

Circulates –
Advocates Principles of the Roman Catholic Liberal party
Proprietor 1864 George M Tully; 1866 Honoria J. Tully; 1891 Jasper Tully

ROSCOMMON JOURNAL (1828–1927)
Saturday
1851 5*d*. and 6*d*.; 1864 3*d*. and 4*d*. 1868 4*d*. and 5*d*.
1851 Liberal; 1864 Independent
Circulates Local
Advocates 1851 Political, civil and religious freedom generally, and 'Tenant Right' in a tone of
perfect independence of all religious or political parties.
Proprietor 1851 Charles Tully, Bookseller, stationer, patent medicine vendor; 1864 Mrs Anna
Tully; 1877 William Tully

ROSCOMMON REPORTER (1850–60)
Neutral
Circulates Roscommon county and Longford, Galway, Leitrim.
Advocates No particular politics in a party or sectarian sense ... general news of the week with
continuous tales.
Proprietor Landon W. Lennox.

ROSCOMMON WEEKLY MESSENGER (1848–73 revived 1892–1935)
Saturday
1857 3½*d*. and 4½*d*.; 1869 4*d*. and 5*d*.
Liberal
Circulates Local counties
Advocates Liberal principles; an alternative to the system of the tenure of land in Ireland; 1864
Liberal principles and an improved cultivation of the land
Proprietor Alexander O'Connor Eccles
[After 1892]
Saturday
3*d*.
Independent
Advocates The interests of the district. It is a good local paper.
Proprietor L.P. Hayden

SKIBBEREEN AND WEST CARBERY EAGLE/1868 WEST CORK AND CARBERY EAGLE/1891
EAGLE AND COUNTY CORK ADVERTISER [Skibbereen] (1857–1928)
Saturday
1864 2*d*. and 3*d*.; 1868 1*d*. and 2*d*.
1864 Neutral; 1878 Independent
Circulates Local throughout Cork
Advocates General newspaper with scientific and literary intelligence
Proprietor 1864 Potter Bros; 1866 F.P.E. Potter; 1871 Potter and Son; 1872 Potter and Robertson;
1873 J.W. Potter; 1882 Peel Eldon; 1886 F.P.E. Potter
Advertisement 1864 The Magnetic Telegraph Co. having taken the *Eagle* office as a station ... the
latest telegrams are supplied to the paper.

SLIGO ADVERTISER (1885–91)
Wednesday
1*d*.

National
Circulates Sligo and district
Advocates The local and district news is fully reported, and the general intelligence is epitomised.
Proprietor J. Tiernan

SLIGO CHRONICLE (1850–93)
Saturday
1851 5*d*.; 1864 4*d*. and 5*d*.; 1872 3*d*.
Conservative
Circulates Local and in Connaught
Advocates 1851 Conservative principles and protection to the industry and capital of the British Empire ... a good newspaper and the literary news, feuilleton and entertaining miscellany render it an interesting family journal.
Proprietor 1851 Charles Sedley solicitor; 1864 James W. Sedley, solicitor

SLIGO GAZETTE (1887–91)
Friday
1½*d*.
National
Circulates Throughout Sligo, Leitrim, Mayo and Roscommon
Advocates Full reports of all public proceedings, together with leading articles, paragraphs, market intelligence, &c.
Proprietor J. Stinson

SLIGO INDEPENDENT (1855–1961)
Saturday
1857 3*d*. and 4*d*.
1857 Neutral; 1858 Conservative
Circulates Local counties
Advocates General improvement of Ireland
Proprietor 1857 William Gillmor; 1858 Alexander Gillmor; 1881 Miss Jane Gillmor

SLIGO JOURNAL (1752–1866)
Friday
1851 5*d*.; 1857 4*d*. and 5*d*.
Conservative
Circulates Local
Advocates Agricultural interests, attached to the Church of England
Proprietor 1851 Anne Bolton, Bookseller, stationer and patent medicine vendor

SOUTHERN CHRONICLE/ 1872 **LIMERICK SOUTHERN CHRONICLE/** 1873 **BASSETTIS DAILY CHRONICLE/** 1884 **BASSETT'S SOUTHERN ADVERTISER/** 1888 **BASSETTIS DAILY ADVERTISER** [Limerick] (1863–85)
Wednesday and Saturday
1864 4*d*. and 5*d*.; 1865 3*d*. and 4*d*.; 1882 1*d*.
1864 Conservative; 1888 Neutral
Circulates Limerick and South of Ireland
Advocates Principles and policy of the National Conservative Party of Ireland
Proprietor 1864 G.W. Bassett; 1885 W. Guest Bassett; 1886 Bassett and Lochhead

STANDARD AND WATERFORD CONSERVATIVE GAZETTE/1884 WATERFORD STANDARD
(1863–1953)
Wednesday and Saturday
1864 3*d*.; 1865 2½*d*. and 3½*d*.
Conservative
Circulates Waterford, Dublin, Kilkenny, Wexford, Tipperary among nobility and clergy.
Advocates 1864 Principles of the great conservative party and the established Churches of England and Ireland
Proprietor 1864 Waterford Publishing Company Ltd. Publisher W. Croker; 1865 Waterford Publishing Company Ltd.; 1868 Robert Whalley (who also ran *Waterford News Letter* devoted to shipping movements)

TIPPERARY/1883 TIPPERARY LEADER [Thurles] (1882–5)
Wednesday and Saturday
3*d*.
1882 National; 1884 Neutral; 1885 National
Circulates Limerick, Waterford, Kilkenny, Queen's and King's County, Galway, Clare and Kerry and Dublin
Advocates The politics of *Tipperary* represent the National spirit which is characteristic of Tipperary, as the premier county of Ireland. It is the recognised organ of the people.
Proprietor 1881 Thomas P. Gill; 1885 W.G. Fisher

TIPPERARY ADVOCATE [Nenagh] (1857–89)
Saturday
1858 £1 p.a. 16*s*. unstamped; 1872 4*d*.
1858 Liberal; 1864 Independent; 1871 Republican
Circulates Nenagh and Roscrea
Advocates 1858 Interests of Roman Catholics and civil and religious liberty, aiming at the emancipation of the country from the effects of bad legislation ... good epitome of general intelligence;
1871 Civil and religious liberty all over the world; aims at the emancipation of the country from the effects of bad legislation and Repeal of the Union; 1883 The above journal believes in peasant proprietary as the only means of bringing to a final settlement the present pernicious land code, which has been the direct source of agrarian outrage in this unhappy ill-governed country. It is especially devoted to the principles of the Irish National League.
Proprietor P.B. Gill

TIPPERARY AND CLARE INDEPENDENT [Nenagh] (1867–69)
3½*d*. and 4½*d*.
Advocates Tenant right and in politics is impartial and independent. As a local organ all the important connected with the town and counties is fully reported.
Proprietor John O'Shea

TIPPERARY CHRONICLE [Clonmel] (1839) Not in *Newsplan*
Wednesday and Saturday
5*d*.
Conservative
Circulates Clonmel, Carrick-on-Suir, Tipperary, Thurles, Fethard
Advocates Commercial and agricultural interests of the kingdom
Proprietor Edmond Woods

TIPPERARY FREE PRESS [Clonmel] (1826–81)
1851 Wednesday and Saturday; 1864 Tuesday and Friday

1851 4*d*. and 5*d*.; 1871 3*d*.
Radical
Circulates Co. Tipperary, Waterford, Cork, Limerick and Kilkenny
Advocates 1851 The interests, and is the organ of, the Roman Catholics, the Whig [1865 Liberal] Protestants, and Dissenters of Tipperary; the advocate of the agricultural and commercial interests, of tenant right, vote by ballot, and independent parliamentary action.
Proprietor 1851 John Hackett, bookseller, stationer and patent medicine vendor, music and musical instrument warehouse; 1864 Hackett Brothers; 1877 E.C. Hackett; 1883 taken over by the *Tipperary Independent.*

TIPPERARY INDEPENDENT [Clonmel] (1881) Not in *Newsplan*
Neutral
Circulates counties of Tipperary, Limerick and Kilkenny
Proprietor 1881 J. Fisher; 1883 W.G. Fisher; 1891 H.D. Fisher
Advertisement 1883 A national and tenant farming paper; commands the confidence of all classes.

TIPPERARY NATIONALIST [Clonmel] (1889–90)
Wednesday and Saturday
Nationalist
Proprietor Nationalist Newspaper Co. Ltd

TIPPERARY NEWS [Clonmel] (1891) Not in *Newsplan*
Saturday
1*d*.
Nationalist
Circulates Clonmel, the county and district
Advocates Nationalist views, and fully reports all the local and district news.
Proprietor Resident

TIPPERARY PEOPLE [Clonmel] (1865–1921)
Saturday
3*d*. and 4*d*.
Independent
Circulates Clonmel and the county
Advocates The *People* contains all the local and district intelligence. The London gossip and Dublin intelligence are given in letters from special correspondents.
Publisher O'Connel Hacket

TIPPERARY WEEKLY NEWS [Clonmel] (1858)
Saturday
2½*d*. and 3½*d*.
Independent
Circulates Tipperary and Limerick
Proprietor Edmond Woods

TRALEE CHRONICLE (1843–81)
1851 Saturday; 1865 Tuesday and Friday
1851 6*d*.; 1857 4*d*. and 5*d*.; 1864 3*d*. and 4*d*.
1851 Neutral; 1865 Independent; 1867 Liberal
Circulates Kerry and south of Ireland
Advocates The interest of agriculture. Neutral in politics enjoys support of persons of all opinions including the landed proprietors resident gentry and numerous visitors to this highly fa-

voured locality ... gives during the season detailed reports of district sports, including red deer hunting &c. List is kept of fashionable arrivals at the various hotels in the vicinity of the lakes.
Proprietor 1851 James Raymond Eagar; 1867 John William Weekes; 1874 Mrs Blanche Weekes and J.J. Long; 1877 Mrs Blanche Weekes
Advertisement The medium by which the Catholic clergy advertise.

TUAM HERALD (1837–to date)
Saturday
1851 6*d*.; 1857 5*d*. and 6*d*.; 1858 4*d*. and 5*d*.; 1888 2*d*.
1851 Liberal; 1883 National-Independent
Circulates Local and in Mayo
Advocates Interests of agriculture, commerce and manufactures. [1858 Popular rights] Is attached to the Roman Catholic religion and is the organ of the Roman Catholics in the locality. See English and American journals on its character as an advertising medium – second to none in Ireland.
Proprietor 1851 Richard John Kelly; 1864 Jasper Kelly; 1868 Richard J. Kelly B.L.

TUAM NEWS (1871–1904)
Friday
2*d*.
Independent
Circulates Tuam and the Province
Advocates Special information concerning the Catholic church
Proprietor 1870 E. Byrne; 1877 John McPherson; 1879 John McPhilpin

TYRAWLEY HERALD/1872 BALLINA HERALD [Ballina] (1844–70)
Thursday
4*d*. and 5*d*. 1872 3*d*.; 1888 2*d*.
1851 Neutral; 1888 National; 1889 Neutral
Circulates Ballina, Castlebar, Boyle, &c.
Advocates Agriculture, commerce and the manufacturing interests.
Proprietor 1851 William Richey, bookseller, stationer and patent medicine vendor; 1864 R.W. Joynt, printer

TYRONE CONSTITUTION [Omagh] (1844–to date)
Friday
1851 5*d*.; 1857 4*d*. and 5*d*.; 1864 2*d*. and 3*d*.
Conservative
Circulates Locally, and in Londonderry and Dublin
Advocates Agricultural, commercial and manufacturing interests of the county. Not an organ of any particular sect, being opposed to political differences among Protestants.
Proprietor 1851 John Nelis printer, bookseller, stationer, perfumer, patent medicine vendor and circulating library; 1864 George W. M'Cutcheon; 1868 Nathaniel Carson

TYRONE COURIER [Dungannon] (1880–to date)
Saturday
1*d*.
1880 Liberal-Conservative; 1885 Conservative
Circulates County and province
Advocates A Liberal-Conservative [1888:Conservative] policy [1883: and Evangelical Protestantism.] Pays special attention to the staple trades of the district.
Proprietor 1880 A.J. Mathews; 1891 J.D. Crockett

ULSTER ECHO [Belfast] (1874–1916)
Daily
½*d.*
1874 Neutral; 1879 Liberal; 1889 Liberal Unionist
Circulates –
Publisher A.G. McMonagle [publisher of *Witness* a Presbyterian church newsletter.]

ULSTER EXAMINER [Belfast] (1868–82)
1869 Tuesday Thursday and Saturday; 1871 Daily
1869 1*d.* and 2*d.*; 1871 1*d.*
Liberal
Circulates Ulster
Advocates Liberal principles and in support of the cause of the Catholics, addresses itself directly to the clergy and people of the province.
Proprietor 1869 Kerr and Fitzpatrick; 1871 J. Serridge
Publisher 1872 D. MacAleese, editor; 1875 C.J. Dempsey
Advertisement 1869 only autharised exponent of Catholic principles in Ulster ... a medium for addressing ... the hierarchy, clergy and the people of the province.

ULSTER OBSERVER [Belfast] (1862–68)
Tuesday, Thursday and Saturday
1*d.* and 2*d.*
Liberal
Circulates Belfast and Ulster
Advocates Free trade, civil and religious liberty and great measures of reform
Publisher A.J. McKenna
Proprietor The Ulster Catholic Publishing Co. Ltd
Advertisement The Ulster Catholic Publishing Co. Ltd has upwards of 500 shareholders, residing in the towns and districts of Ulster and having a highly influential board of Directors, 31 in number, gives a widespread advantage in circulation.

ULSTER GAZETTE [Armagh] (1844–68)
1851 Saturday; 1870 Tuesday and Friday; 1872 Wednesday and Saturday; 1873 Saturday
1857 4*d.* and 5*d.*; 1869 2*d.* and 3*d.*; 1870 1*d.*; 1874 2*d.*; 1885 1½*d.*
1851 Neutral; 1857 Conservative
Circulates City/county of Armagh, Newry, Monaghan, Dungannon, Dundock [*sic*], Lurgan, Loughall, Moy, Markethill.
Advocates 1851 Church and conservative principles and devotes attention to sporting and veterinary affairs as well as such other matters as come under the range of a local journal; 1864 Sound Conservative principles coupled with progress. Sporting edition published Fridays; 1873 Supports the Church of Ireland.
Proprietor 1851 Matthew Small, V[eterinary] S[urgeon]; 1857 E. Darlington; 1866 J. Heatley [bankrupt]; 1874 Thomas White; 1884 McClelland and Peel [bankrupt]

ULSTERMAN (Belfast) (1852–59)
Wed and Sat.
2*d.* and 3*d.*
Liberal
Circulates Belfast and Ulster
Advocates The cause of Roman Catholics and what it considers 'the just demands of the people' extension of the franchise, vote by ballot, what the Roman Catholics denominate 'religious equality' and 'tenant right'. It is a political and literary journal.
Proprietor D. Holland

WATCHMAN [Enniscorthy] (1869–86)
Saturday
1*d*. and 2*d*.
1865 Neutral; 1881 National
Circulates Enniscorthy and Wexford county
Advocates Local news and advertisements
Proprietor George Griffiths

WATERFORD CHRONICLE AND (1868) NEW ROSS REPORTER (1866–1910)
1851 Wednesday and Saturday; 1871 Tuesday and Friday; 1873 Wednesday; 1874 Saturday
1851 6*d*.; 1857 4*d*. and 5*d*.; 1868 1½*d*. and 2½*d*.; 1877 1*d*.
1851 Liberal; 1884 Independent-Liberal
Circulates Locally and in South of Ireland
Advocates The measures and principles of the 'National' Irish party and of the Roman Catholic
religion
Proprietor 1851 H.M. Flynn; 1857 Patrick Flynn; 1858 P. Flynn and Co.; 1864 Patrick Curran;
1867 W.R. Ward and James Longmire; 1877 W.R. Ward

WATERFORD MAIL/1871 WATERFORD DAILY MAIL (1823–1908)
Wednesday and Saturday
1851 5*d*.; 1857 1½*d*. and 2½*d*. daily; 3*d*. and 4*d*. weekly 1872 1*d*.
1851 Conservative; 1882 National
Circulates Local
Advocates 1851 Freedom of commerce, Irish agricultural improvement and advancement of literature. A revision of the entire commercial system is a principle supported with much strength of
argument in this journal and it is therefore closely in agreement with the plans of the late Sir
Robert Peel. Independent of local interests, the social condition of Ireland generally forms a subject of frequent discussion. The literary portion is extremely well-conducted and the reviews are
more than ordinarily ample; 1857 The principles of progress and liberty in connection with Protestantism which it believes is based on the principles of civil and religious liberty while Popery is
the embodiment of despotism; 1865 Advocates the principles of progress and liberty
Proprietor 1851 R. Henderson; 1857 Joseph Fisher; 1883 W.G. Fisher; 1891 H.D. Fisher

WATERFORD MIRROR/1874 WATERFORD MIRROR AND TRAMORE VISITOR (1860–1910)
Wednesday
2*d*. and 3*d*.
Circulates Waterford, Tramore and district
Advocates News, markets, time-tables
Proprietor 1871 John S. Palmer; 1877 Ward Bros.

WATERFORD NEWS (1848–1958)
Friday
1851 3*d*.; 1857 3*d*. and 4*d*.; 1885 2*d*.
Liberal
Circulates Locally and in England and America
Advocates 1851 Liberal principles and Roman Catholic interests, being one of the Organisation
of that Party; 1864 Advocates Liberal principles and popular interests: is the organ of progress and
the development of the material resources of Ireland.
Proprietor 1851 Cornelius Redmond; 1857 Edward S. Kenney; 1888 C.P. Redmond

WEEKLY EXAMINER [Belfast] (1870–92)
Home Rule; 1889 National

Circulates Belfast and throughout Ulster, Has also a large circulation in Scotland.
Advocates All the news of the week, with original articles, serial tales, etc.
Proprietor 1885 Publisher G.H. Page; Proprietor E. Dwyer Gray MP; 1892 The Morning News Co. Ltd.

WESTERN NEWS [Ballinasloe] (1878–1926)
Saturday
2*d*.
Catholic and National
Circulates Ballinasloe and district
Advocates An exponent of Irish, Catholic and national feeling. It contains leading articles on political and local subjects with the general local news reports of meetings &c.
Publisher 1877 John Callanan; 1889 Michael O'Brien

WESTERN PEOPLE [Ballina] (1883–to date)
Saturday
2*d*.
National
Circulates Ballina and Co. Mayo
Advocates This paper is very popular as a local organ, and advocates sound National principles. It fully reports all meetings, and the local intelligence is well arranged.
Proprietor: 1883: P.J. Smyth; 1889: Western People Co. Ltd
Advertisement 1883 The WESTERN PEOPLE was established in July 1883 by the clergy and people of Ballina to supply a want long and deeply felt in the locality, viz. that of a paper of sound national principles ... has met with great popular support.

WESTERN STAR [Ballinasloe] (1845–1902)
Saturday
1851 5*d*.; 1857 3½*d*. and 4½*d*.; 1869 3*d*. and 4*d*.
1851 Neutral; 1857 Conservative; 1870 Liberal-Conservative; 1873 Independent
Circulates Galway, Roscommon, Mayo &c.
Advocates 1851 Without reference to political party it supports every measure calculated to promote national advancement; is friendly to the church of England but no enemy to conscientious dissent. A moderate and liberal tone prevails in the management of this publication which befriends the improvement of national resources and would strongly resist absenteeism ... all immoralities are carefully excluded; 1857: The interests of agriculture, commerce and manufactures and every measure favourable to the development of the Protestant Religion. It befriends, however, every movement really national, and is a good agricultural and commercial authority. Literature receives attention.
Proprietor 1851 Thomas French: bookseller, stationer and general printer. Proprietor, Publisher and Editor; 1857 Robert Hood Smythe; 1870 Henry McClenaghan; 1888 S.J. McClenaghan
Advertisement 1851 Extensive circulation amongst the Nobility, and Gentry of the West of Ireland, and the fact of the Great National Fair of the Empire being held in Ballinasloe gives an importance to the Journal it might otherwise not possess. [It] affords ... unusual facilities for the Advertisement of Lands, Stock, Agricultural implements and everything connected with husbandry.

WESTMEATH EXAMINER [Mullingar] (1882–to date)
Saturday
2*d*.
Independent
Circulates Westminster, Longford and Meath

Advocates The *Examiner* is entirely devoted to the local and district news.
Proprietor L.P. Hayden

WESTMEATH GUARDIAN/1877 WESTMEATH GUARDIAN & LONGFORD NEWSLETTER
[Mullingar] (1835–1928)
1851 Thursday; 1885 Friday
1851 5*d*.; 1857 4*d*. and 5*d*.; 1866 3*d*. and 4*d*. 1885 2*d*.
Conservative
Circulates Locally
Advocates 1851 Maintenance of the Established Church. Union with Great Britain, protection and employment for the labouring classes; 1875 the maintenance of the Union with Great Britain, protection to agriculture and employment for the labouring classes.
Proprietor 1851 J. Siggins; 1875 S. Wallis

WESTMEATH INDEPENDENT [Athlone] (1846–1906)
Saturday
1851 5*d*.; 1857 3*d*. and 4*d*.; 1875 2*d*.; 1889 1*d*.
1851 Independent; 1857 Conservative; 1877 Liberal; 1885 National
Circulates Athlone and adjoining counties.
Advocates The general good of the country as developed in public measures, without respect to public men – It is a good readable newspaper, containing a carefully selected mélange of news, politics, literary and miscellaneous articles, with well-written 'leaders'.
Proprietor 1851 James Martin; 1871 William N. Martin; 1873 P.S. Walsh; 1883 M. Walsh; 1885 Chapman & Co.; 1888 T. Chapman
Advertisement 1851 Advocates the general interests of the country without reference to creed or party. A commercial and family Paper. A local intelligencer. The peculiar local position of Athlone, the town standing in two counties Westmeath and Roscommon – being one of the largest garrison towns in Ireland – likely to be greatly increased by the railways now in course of formation – renders the Independent one of the First mediums for Advertising ... superseding the necessity of advertising in seven other Papers.

WEXFORD CONSTITUTION (1858–87)
1864 Saturday; 1871 Wednesday and Saturday
1864 4*d*. and 4*d*.; 1871 3*d*.
Conservative
Circulates Wexford, Wicklow, Carlow, Kilkenny and Waterford
Advocates 1864 Professes to be conducted on the principles of truth of justice of honour and loyalty. Organ of the Conservative and Protestant party in the county; 1873 The numerous shipping disasters which take place on the dangerous Wexford coast are promptly, correctly and fully recorded in its columns.
Proprietor 1864 Alexander Mackay; 1884 Isabella Mackay

WEXFORD HERALD (1787–1865)
Saturday
2*d*. and 3*d*.
Neutral
Circulates Wexford district
Advocates Local and social reforms and improvements; with the news of the week blends nouvellettes varieties &c.
Proprietor 1858 James Anglin

WEXFORD GUARDIAN (1847) Not in *Newsplan*
Saturday
1851 5*d*.; 1857 2*d*. and 3*d*.
Liberal
Circulates local
Advocates 1851 Tenant Right and was a staunch support of the repeal movement and all other measures of the liberal Roman Catholic party in Ireland. It possesses merit as a political and literary journal
Proprietor 1851 Thomas Roche; 1857 Robert Pitt
Taken over by *The People*, January 1857

WEXFORD INDEPENDENT (1830–1906)
Wednesday and Saturday
1851 5*d*.; 1864 4*d*. and 5*d*.; 1872 3*d*.
Liberal; 1891 Liberal-Unionist
Circulates Local and in south of Ireland
Advocates 1851 Strenuously eschews all religious rancour being attached to no sect whatever; 1858 Agricultural interests, which it does not consider incompatible with its advocacy of commercial and manufacturing affairs. It repudiates all religious and [omitted 1888] sectarian rancour as injurious to the best interests and welfare of the country
Proprietor 1851 John Greene, bookseller, stationer patent medicine vendor. 1858 Alderman, J.P. Ex-Mayor of Wexford; 1868 John Greene

WEXFORD RECORDER (1880) Not in *Newsplan*
Friday
2*d*.
Conservative
Circulates Wexford and district
Advocates The *Recorder* is of moderate Conservative views.
Proprietor Albert Hastings
Not entered in *Newspaper Press Directory* after 1882

WEXFORD STANDARD (1879) Not in *Newsplan*
Saturday
1*d*.
Catholic and National
Advocates Self-government for Ireland, and the establishment of a peasant proprietary by purchase of the landowners' interest.
Proprietor E. Walsh
Not entered in *Newspaper Press Directory* after 1887

WICKLOW NEWS LETTER (1858–1927)
Saturday
2*d*. and 3*d*.
Neutral
Circulates Wicklow neighbourhood
Advocates Local improvements and gives a comprehensive summary
of the news of the week with tales, varieties &c.
Proprietor William M'Phail; 1877 William M'Phail and Sons

WICKLOW PEOPLE (1882–to date)
Saturday

2*d.*
National
Circulates Wicklow, Dublin, Colne and Kildare
Advocates Home Rule for Ireland, land law reform, extension of franchise, full reports of all
public boards; legal, agricultural and commercial intelligence; reviews of books &c.
Proprietor E. Walsh

Select bibliography

NINETEENTH-CENTURY PRINTED WORKS

Andrews, A., *The History of British Journalism* 2 vols (1859)

Bagehot, W., *The English Constitution* (1878)

Becker, Bernard H., *Disturbed Ireland: being letters written during the winter of 1880–1881* (1881)

Bryce, James, *The American Commonwealth* (1889)

Carlyle, Thomas, *Reminiscences of my Irish Journey in 1849* (1882)

The Celt, A Weekly Periodical of Irish National Literature, edited by a Committee of the Celtic Union (1857)

A Conservative Journalist, 'Why is the Provincial Press Radical?' *National Review*, 7 (1886)

Dicey, A.V., *Introduction to the Study of the Law of the Constitution* (1893)

Dicey, E., 'Provincial Journalism' *St. Paul's* III (October 1868)

Duffy, C. Gavan, *Young Ireland: A Fragment of Irish History* (1896)

Forbes, John, *Memorandum made in Ireland in the Autumn of 1852* (1853)

Gladstone, W.E., *Gleanings from Past Years* (1879)

Grant, J., *Impressions of Ireland and the Irish* (1844)

Grant, James, *The Newspaper Press* 2 vols. (1871)

Greg, W.R., 'The Irish Cauldron', *Quarterly Review*, 128 (April 1870)

Head, Sir Francis, *A Fortnight in Ireland* (1852)

Hunt, Frederick, *The Fourth Estate* (1850)

King, David B., *The Irish Question* (1882)

Leadam, I.S. *Coercive Measures in Ireland* (1880)

Macaulay, J., *Ireland in 1872* (1873)

MacKnight, T.J., *Ulster As It Is* (1896)

McPhilpin, John, *The Apparitions and Miracles at Knock* (1880)

O'Connor, T.P., *The Parnell Movement* (1887)

——, 'The New Journalism', *New Review* I (October 1889)

Osborne, Sidney Godolphin, *Gleanings in the West of Ireland* (1850)

Pigott, Richard, *Personal Recollections of an Irish Nationalist Journalist* (1882)

Pope-Hennessy, J., 'What do the Irish Read?', *Nineteenth Century*, 15 (June 1884)

Reid, Arnot, 'How a Provincial Paper is Managed', *Nineteenth Century*, 20 (September 1886)

Reid, T. Wemyss, 'Our London Correspondent', *Macmillan's Magazine*, 42 (May 1880), 18–26

Salmon, Edward G., 'What the Working Classes Read', *Nineteenth Century*, 20 (July 1886)

Scott, J.A., 'The British Newspaper: the Penny Theory and its Solutions' *Dublin University Magazine*, 361 (March 1863)

Stead, W.T., 'Government by Journalism', *Contemporary Review* xlix (May 1886), 653–74

Stephen, James Fitzjames, 'On the Suppression of Boycotting'. *Nineteenth Century*, 118(December 1883)

Stephen, Leslie, 'On the Suppression of Poisonous Opinions', *Nineteenth Century*, 13 (March and April 1883)

Thackeray, William Makepeace, *The History of Pendennis* (1848–1850, Penguin edition, 1986)

Whorlow, H., *The Provincial Newspaper Society 1836–1886* (1886)

TWENTIETH-CENTURY PRINTED WORKS

Adams, J.R.R., *The Printed Word and the Common Man* (1987)
Akenson, D.R., *The Irish Education Experiment* (1970)
Alexander, William, *Popular Literature in Victorian Scotland* (1986)
Altick, R.D., *The English Common Reader* (1957)
——, *Writers, Readers and Occasions: Selected Essays on Victorian Literature and Life* (1989)
Anderson, Benedict, *Imagined Communities* (1983)
Aspinall, A., *Politics and the Press 1780–1850* (1949)
Barnes, Margaret, 'Repeal Reading Rooms', *An Leabharlann*, 23, 2 (1965)
Bew, Paul, *Land and the National Question in Ireland 1858–1882* (1978)
——, and White, Frank, 'The Agrarian Opposition in Ulster Politics, 1848-1887 1 in Clark, Samuel
    and Donnelly, James S. Jnr. (eds), *Irish Peasants: Violence and Political and Unrest 1780–
    1914* (1983)
de Blaghd, E.P., 'I was a Teenage Press Baron', *Dublin Historical Record*, 41, I (December 1987)
Bodkin, M.M'D., *Recollections of an Irish Judge: Press, Bar and Parliament* (1914)
Brake, Laurel, Jones, Aled and Madden, Lionel, (eds), *Investigating Victorian Journalism* (1990)
Walling, R.A.J., (ed.), *The Diaries of John Bright* (1930)
Brown, Lucy, *Victorian News and Newspapers* (1985)
Campbell, A., *Belfast Newspapers Past and Present* (1921)
Casteleyn, Mary, *A History of Literacy and Libraries in Ireland* (1984)
Clark, Samuel, 'The Social Composition of the Land League', *Irish Historical Studies*, 17, 68
    (1971)
——, 'Patriotism as Pastime: the appeal of Fenianism in the mid-1860s', *Irish Historical Studies*,
    22, 87 (1981)
Cullen, L.M., 'Establishing a Communications System; News, Post and Transport' in Farrell,
    Brian, (ed.), *Communications and Community in Ireland* (1984)
——, *Eason & Son: A History* (1989)
Daly, Dominic, *The Young Douglas Hyde* (1974)
Daly, Mary, 'Literacy and Language Change' in Daly, Mary and Dickson, David, (eds), *The Ori-
    gins of Popular Literacy in Ireland: Language Change and Education Development 1700–1920*
    (1991)
Feingold, William, *The Revolt of the Tenantry: the Transformation of Local Government in Ireland
    1872–1886* (1974)
Foster, R.F., 'Anglo-Irish Literature, Gaelic Nationalism and Irish Politics in the 1890s' in Bean,
    J.M.W., (ed.), *The Political Culture of Modern Britain. Studies in Memory of Stephen Koss*
    (1987)
——, *Paddy and Mr Punch: Connections in Irish and English History* (1993)
Geary, L., *The Plan of Campaign* (1986)
Gibbon, P., *The Origins of Ulster Unionism* (1975)
Matthew, H.C.G. (ed.), *The Gladstone Diaries* (14 vols, 1982–94)
Gross, John, *The Rise and Fall of the Man of Letters: English Literary Life Since 1800* (1973)
Hachey, Thomas E. and McCaffrey, Lawrence, (eds) *Perspectives on Irish Nationalism* (1989)
Bahlman, D.W.R., (ed.), *The Diary of Sir Edward Walker Hamilton* (1972)
Harrison, Brian, 'Press and Pressure Group in Modern Britain' Shattock, Joanne and Wolff, Michael
    (eds), *The Victorian Periodical Press* (1982)
Harvie, Christopher, *The Lights of Liberalism* (1976)
Healy, T.M., *Letters and Leaders of my Day* 2 vols (1929)
Hoppen, K. Theodore, *Elections, Politics, and Society in Ireland 1832–1885* (1984)
Jordan, Donald Elmer Jnr., 'John O'Connor Power, Charles Stewart Parnell and the centralisation
    of popular politics in Ireland' *Irish Historical Studies*, 25, 97 (1986)

——, *Land and Popular Politics in Ireland: County Mayo from the Plantation to the Land War* (1994)
Kearney, H.F., 'Father Mathew: Apostle of Modernisation' in Cosgrave, Art and McCartney, Donal, (ed.), *Studies in Irish History Presented to R. Dudley Edwards (1979)*
Kenealy, Mary, 'Finn's Leinster Journal', *Old Kilkenny Review* (new series) 5 (1979)
Koss, Stephen, *The Political Press in Britain* 2 vols. (1981)
Larkin, Emmet, 'The Devotional Revolution in Ireland 1850–1875' *American Historical Review*, 77 (June 1972)
——, *The Consolidation of the Roman Catholic Church in Ireland 1860–1870* (1967)
Lee, Alan J., *The Origins of the Popular Press* (1976)
Loughlin, James, 'Constructing the Political Spectacle: Parnell, the press and national leadership 1879–1886 in Boyce, D. George and O'Day, Alan, (eds), *Parnell in Perspective* (1991)
Lunny, Linda, 'Knowledge and Enlightenment: attitudes to education in early nineteenth-century East Ulster' in Daly, Mary and Dickson, David (eds), *The Origins of Popular Literacy in Ireland: Language Change and Education Development 1700–1920* (1991)
Lyons, F.S.L., *Culture and Anarchy in Ireland* (1982)
Malcolm, Elizabeth, 'Temperance and Irish Nationalism, varieties of tension' in Lyons, F.S.L. and Hawkins, R.A.I. (eds) *Ireland Under the Union* (1980)
Moody, T.W., (ed.), *The Fenian Movement* (Dublin 1968)
——, and Hawkins R.A.J., (eds), *Florence Arnold-Forster's Irish Journal* (1988)
Moran, Gerard, 'James Daly and the Land Question 1876–1879', *Retrospect* (1980)
——, *A Radical Priest in County Mayo: Fr. Patrick Lavelle the Rise and Fall of an Irish Nationalist 1825–86* (1994)
Munter, R.L., *The History of the Irish Newspaper 1685–1760* (1967)
Murphy, Maura, 'The Ballad Singer and the role of the Seditious Ballad in nineteenth-century Ireland: Dublin Castle's view', *Ulster Folklife*, 25 (1979)
Norman, E.R., *The Catholic Church and Ireland in the Age of Rebellion* (1965)
Ó Ciosáin, Niall, *Print and Popular Culture in Ireland 1759–1850* (1997)
Oram, Hugh, *The Newspaper Book 1649–1983* (1983)
Parnell, Anna, Hearne, Dana (ed.), *The Tale of a Great Sham* (1982)
Porter, Bernard, 'The *Freiheit* Prosecutions 1881–1882', *Historical Journal* 23 (1980)
Smith, K.J.M., *James Fitzjames Stephen: Portrait of a Victorian Rationalist* (1988)
Gordon, Peter, (ed.), *The Red Earl: the Papers of the Fifth Earl Spencer* (1981)
Thuente, Mary Helen, *W.B. Yeats and Irish Folklore* (Dublin 1980)
Tierney, Mark, *Croke of Cashel: the Life of Archbishop Croke of Cashel, 1823–1902* (1976)
Townshend, Charles, *Political Violence in Ireland* (1985)
Tulloch, Hugh, 'A.V. Dicey and the Irish Question 1870–1922' *Irish Jurist*, 15 (new series) (1980)
Vance, Norman 'Celts, Carthaginians and constitutions: Anglo-Irish literary relations, 1780–18201, *Irish Historical Studies*, 22, 87 (1981)
Vaughan, W.E., (ed.), *New History of Ireland*, V Ireland 1800–1870 (1989)
Vaughan, W.E., and Fitzpatrick, A.J., *Irish Historical Statistics* (1978)
Williams, Martin, 'Ancient mythology and revolutionary ideology in Ireland 1878–1916', *Historical Journal* XVI (1983)
Walker, Brian, (ed.), *Parliamentary Election Results in Ireland, 1801–1922* (1978)
——, *Ulster Politics: The Formative Years, 1868–1886* (1989)
Whyte, J.H., *The Independent Irish Party 1850–1859* (1958)

Index